DEVOTION

DEVOTION

A Memoir

Mickey Harte

with Brendan Coffey

HarperCollins*Ireland*

HarperCollins*Ireland*
1st Floor, Watermarque Building, Ringsend Road
Dublin 4, Ireland

a division of
HarperCollins*Publishers*
1 London Bridge Street
London SE1 9GF
UK

www.harpercollins.co.uk

First published by HarperCollins*Ireland* 2021

1 3 5 7 9 10 8 6 4 2

© Mickey Harte 2021

Mickey Harte asserts the moral right to
be identified as the author of this work

A catalogue record of this book is available from the British Library

ISBN 978-0-00-847303-7

Typeset in Sabon LT Std by
Palimpsest Book Production Ltd, Falkirk, Stirlingshire

Printed and Bound in the UK using 100% Renewable Electricity
at CPI Group (UK) Ltd

To my family members who have gone to their eternal reward. Please God we will meet again one day.

DAWN

Age has turned me into an early riser. I wake on the dot at six and make my way quietly out of the bedroom. Times past, I slept on as long as possible; I just relish the morning now.

Those days when I rise before the sun, a light from the corridor guides me through the house. Michaela's room looks across from ours, still much the same as it was the night before her wedding. Just down from our door, her picture rests against the wall, lit from above. She smiles down on me from that frame and I close my eyes, tripping through time. One look at Michaela takes me back to her brightest day. December 30, 2010: we paused outside the church and I could sense her glee. I like to remember her that way, the way she was on her wedding day.

Each morning, I pause here beside Michaela and pray.

Then I slip down the stairs, out and into the car. Turn left at the bottom of the drive, then right onto the main road, heading for Ballygawley. Half a mile down, turn left, to reach the church in Ballymacilroy. Three minutes, door to door.

I change the car every couple of years but always the same registration plates: M11 CMA. C for Caela, MA for McAreavey. M11 gives the year.

On Sundays, the chapel is still warm from the heat of Saturday night Mass. I set down my prayer books and fix new candles on the altar if they have run low. Next, I turn to face the tabernacle. Then, I kneel, before blessing myself, preparing to expose the Blessed Sacrament. The next hour is spent in the presence of the Lord.

Time passes quickly while I pray, always thinking of people. I read different passages from various religious books, marking pages, taking notes. My heavy Tyrone jacket, padded and quilted, provides a much-needed layer of insulation in winter. Nature is all you can hear this early, the stream behind the church, its gently flowing water.

At 7am, my stopwatch beats to signal the hour. My mind settles: I feel at peace.

These mornings are special to me. For 200 years, people have prayed in St Malachy's. I get a sense of all the believers who came before me. Every time I come here, I walk into history.

This hour of Eucharistic Adoration has become part of my daily routine these past few years.

First, I thank God. I feel grateful for being in His presence. I feel His mercy and love; those gifts coming to me from the host on the altar. The Eucharist is God, Jesus Christ, body, blood, soul and divinity. No longer do I look on my belief as a story learned in childhood. My comprehension of this reality took years, and it has changed my life. If God is not there, our faith is in vain. As the Catholic American author Flannery O'Connor once said: 'If it's just a symbol, then to hell with it.'

Why did I not devote more of my life to Adoration in the past? I probably felt too busy. On reflection, I had plenty of time. The pattern of my days has developed gradually. Initially, I went once a week. After a while, I was going twice. Lent seemed a time when I should go every day. Then I thought: 'Why not Advent as well?'

Those blocks made me realise how precious Adoration is, time spent in silence before the Lord. Now, my day is not the same without that hour.

But I am not here to make an impression; it is not a way for me to get good with God. All the years I spent without this morning retreat were my loss. Really, I am making up for lost time.

I can only be grateful, thinking on my life, the turns taken. Never have I seen myself as a victim. How can I explain these feelings? People rarely seem to get this far beyond grief. Logic cannot explain everything: many experiences in life defy reason. I think you have to go through this experience for yourself to truly understand. Yet I consider myself one of the lucky ones. Every time there has been a loss in my life, I find some new gift. And, when you weigh one side of the scales against the other, I still hold the balance. My faith has taught me to see the crosses as gifts.

Children change your life. Until the weans arrived, I

was happy to sleep on. Once they were old enough to dress themselves, I enjoyed not having to rush out of bed. Youngsters fill a house with energy. As soon as you reach them in the morning – do their feeds, talk with them – a new world opens.

Our children, as I watched them grow and develop, gave me such a thrill. I have no memory of learning to walk and talk. We take those gifts for granted but when your own family embark on those first steps, discovering life's essentials, the heart soars: they belong to you, you belong to them.

First, we had Mark, then Michael. Having a girl after two boys was another exploration of life as a parent: different toys, different clothes, different strokes. Michaela was wild talkative from a very young age. She was inquisitive by nature. You would never be idle with Michaela. She made for great company. Mattie, our youngest, took after her.

I still speak with her now. These mornings in Ballymacilroy, I sense her presence. I loved Michaela so much when she was with us, but now I can connect with her any time. I hope and pray that she is in heaven, more alive than we are. She has become a spiritual presence for me. Michaela is there for me whenever I think of her.

I visit the graves on match days, after my hour of Adoration. The graveyard lies behind the church, across the lane. From there, I can see into my original family home just below.

Whatever resilience I possess comes from my father, Peter. He took life as it came, a stoic man but far from humourless. I remember him teasing the women who looked after the church. They were meticulous about their work and the pews would be gleaming, slick with polish.

'It's that well done,' he used to say, 'I'd need a seatbelt to sit in it.'

Daddy never used bad language, which was the way for most of his generation. Naturally, he could get annoyed, but his temperament always remained fairly level.

Family was hugely important for him. Every year, on St Stephen's Day, he visited his brothers and sisters. They all lived within about a 15-mile radius, around Pomeroy and Donaghmore. Paddy, my eldest brother, used to take him. Daddy rode a motorcycle at one stage, but he never drove. There was no car about our house until Pete, the second eldest, finished university. He had a Vauxhall Cresta, I think.

Daddy worked with the local council, labouring on the roads, doing work that machinery takes care of nowadays. I look a bit like him. He was slightly taller than me and always stood very straight, especially for a photograph.

My father introduced all of us boys to football, though I never heard if he played much himself. I have no memory of my parents coming to matches. My mother, Mary, looked after the club jerseys, but she hardly ever left the house.

Daddy took great pride in his children. We could sense that warmth from him, but nobody spoke much about their feelings back then. I never told my parents how much they meant to me: speaking about those things would have only embarrassed them. Typical Irish, you might say, but sometimes I think their way was better. We can be too dramatic these days, everything over the top.

My father lived a very disciplined life: up at the same time, meals by the clock, Rosary every night. He led by example; both of my parents did. Their lives were simple, orderly. If I achieved something, I knew it would make them happy.

One time, when I was about seven, I felt these awful pains in my stomach and the doctor had to be called. Turned out my intestine was tied in a knot and I needed an operation. The thought of going to hospital petrified me. What was an operation? I thought I might fall through the sky.

I spent three weeks in hospital, six stitches running down my side, like the laces on an old football. I was so scared the day the stitches came out, I pleaded with Mummy to stay with me. That connection seems natural to me, but I know I was blessed to grow up in a loving home. Not everyone gets that lucky.

I never saw my father overcome. Some siblings died before him, but he took those losses with quiet grace, treating them as another part of life's cycle.

Two of my brothers are gone more than ten years now. As my family breaks up, faith helps me through: I can accept life as it unfolds, the same way my father did.

The walk through the graveyard first takes me past my parents. Beside them, my brother Paddy, the eldest. Beside him, Veronica, my middle sister. I never knew Veronica:

she died on January 27, 1948, the day after she was born. It took me several years to fully appreciate this precious little baby, whom I never knew, as my older sister. Why, I am not exactly sure. She was a beautiful soul, sacred, a gift to my parents. Some might ask, what is in a life? She lived for one day but that does not diminish her as a person, as a daughter or as my sister. All life is to be celebrated and cherished. So many do not get the chance these days. I am thankful that I have a saint in heaven who has been praying for her little brother all these years.

A pathway runs up the middle, taking me towards Pete. The row behind him leads to Michaela: her precious smile greets me again. The same photograph we keep in our hallway adorns her headstone.

Even now, people leave gifts. I picked up a sliotar recently, signed by a family from Wexford. These gestures still amaze me.

I stand for a short while, say a prayer and wish her well. Then I bless myself and walk back out, ready to face the day about to break.

The morning of an All Ireland Final comes quick. Blink and the day is upon you.

Our first All Ireland, 2003, we got the players to write notes, listing each other's strengths. First thing the following morning, I got Mickey Moynagh – our kit man – to leave those messages under the boys' bedroom doors. They loved it. Gavin Devlin, Stephen O'Neill and John Devine were part of that breakthrough team in '03. By 2018, they had all moved into the backroom. So we considered doing that exercise again. They were keen to repeat it, but my feeling was not as strong. Whatever you do must be unique to the group.

My son Michael, one of the team physios, suggested that I do the writing: a letter to each player.

Michael was always the quietest in our house, the total opposite of Michaela, even though they were closest in age. He was happy to let his younger sister do the talking. And Michaela was only delighted to have the floor, chatting her way through every car journey. You could be fooled into thinking Michael had tuned out. Yet he was listening intently all the time, forming his own mind. Those skills have stood to him. He often picks up important information from the treatment table, far more than I might get talking to the same player face to face.

Michael can sense what the situation demands. And he kept on at me about the letters. Eventually, I came around to his idea.

The Saturday before that Final I spent writing letters at a furious pace. The time was gone past 11:30pm when I finally put down the pen. I chose not to type the letters because each one was personal. I knew the boys would recognise my handwriting and I wanted each man to know how much I valued him. A player is more than a number in the squad and he has to feel that way.

Meanwhile, Michael had taken it upon himself to write his own letter to me. He wrote about the things our family had faced and how my actions offered hope for others. He felt that the players believed in me because I had shown them how it was possible to cope with adversity.

I got upset reading Michael's words. Emotions have that effect: you cannot resist them when they hit. Suddenly, your guard is down, the voice fades. Then your eyes glaze. Tears fall.

Emotions can be hard to handle when they surface. But those tearful moments remind me how much life means, how much football means. There was another reason why I felt overwhelmed that September morning in 2018. The week before the Final, I met Michaela's husband, John McAreavey, for lunch. I had tickets to give him for the game and, during the conversation, we got chatting about the team. I told him why the Rosary was part of our pre-match preparation. It seemed an appropriate moment to tell him, just the two of us together.

Some time ago, around 2016, an elderly woman contacted me. She told me that Michaela had appeared to her while she was in her local chapel with a message for the players: 'Tell the boys to pray the Rosary.' I was never one to take every call and story unquestioningly. People come to me and I hear them out. I thought it was a beautiful story, but not much beyond that.

Not long after that encounter, and totally unrelated to it, a priest from Longford, Fr Colman Carrigy, just happened to send Rosary beads to the house, 36 sets. At the time, there were 36 players on the panel. The beads were red and white. How could I ignore the connection? I told the players the story and left it with them. Mattie Donnelly came back to me and said: 'Let's pray the Rosary together as a group.'

A shiver went up John's back when he heard the story.

It floored him. He, too, had dreamt about Michaela just days before we met. He was lying on the sofa, watching television, when her face appeared. She spoke to him: 'Come on, let's say a few decades.'

John took it as a sign. At our lunch, he had Michaela's Rosary beads, the ones that were with her when she died. But he was worried they might be too much for me. Only when I told him about my encounters did he produce them.

Michaela kept her beads in a special case, a figurine of Our Lady on the cover, classy and distinct. She was elegant to the very end.

I put those beads in my hip pocket for the Final, a piece of Michaela safely tucked away.

Before breakfast, I opened them. All the emotion hit me again. I rarely cry but you cannot do much when the tears come. For a few seconds, I felt frozen, unable to function the way I normally do. All you can do is wait until the moment passes.

I thought about my father, his firm nature. He never wore his emotions, whereas my mother would cry if she saw a bird hurt outside. Knowing this emotional side comes from my mother gives me comfort.

You see so much in life that damages people, leaves them burdened, weighed down by the world. There is no shame in walking away from difficult situations. But facing those challenges can lead to something more than we could ever imagine. We can strive to do something great, something magical and memorable, regardless of our circumstances. At times, we must be willing to be vulnerable.

On big days at Croke Park, we can all feel exposed.

An All Ireland Final puts you on public display, everything on the line. So many people feel good or bad about their lives depending on the result of a match. But our opportunity to win a game of football gives us power, the best kind. We can elevate people.

On those days, I feel privileged to be alive.

My name is Michael. My mother only ever called me by my given name but I could only be Mickey in a small world of big families. Among the tribe we had our own codes and our callings came from above: family, faith and football, though not always in that order.

Mummy carried me downstairs in the mornings, settling me in front of the fire. I warmed my feet there before putting on socks. Out the window, two huge beech trees dominated the view. I can see them still, coming into leaf. Funny, I cannot remember the leaves falling, though they must have. I can only recall the sunny moments. Life always seemed to be that way, warm and clear, tree leaves glinting in the sunlight.

All my childhood pictures are cheerful and cosy, toast freshly buttered every morning. We got up around 8:30am, Daddy already gone to work. School started at 9am and we ran the short distance down the pad, a path across from our house. The journey took us by The Holm, a small pitch behind St Malachy's. The goalposts are still there. A river, which flows alongside, has been rerouted since the time that I first kicked ball. No longer does the water keep the sideline so tight on one side and there is less chance of finding a football partially submerged.

I can still walk that way today, my mind replaying those schooldays. Some scenes are so sharp they wash away the years. Suddenly I am seven years old again, the sun shining, our lives bright and green.

The path that led us to school ran past the local shop. I sprinted down there all the time, over and back, whenever Mummy wanted something: a pound of butter, a bag of sugar. I loved doing those jobs.

The heat from the kitchen range hit us when we came home in the evening. Most days, we ate champ, mashed spud mixed up with small slices of bacon. The champ was crispy brown underneath, the butter melted on top. Pure delicious. We had small bottles of milk with our dinner, which we took with us from school.

Much of life revolved around the chapel next door: Mass every day, Stations of the Cross during Lent, Easter ceremonies, Devotions in October. At home, we made St Brigid's Crosses for February 1. My mother set out a May altar for Our Lady.

First Mass was 8:30am on Sundays. From then until midday, a constant flow of people came through our house. Mummy made soup. And tea. Lots of tea. People walked from miles around. There were two more Masses at 10am and 11:30am. The conversations went on and on and on. People talked about everything and anything and mostly things they had talked about before.

My mother was always a central figure, though never centre of attention. Elderly neighbours called regularly. They watched her making soda bread, asking questions all the time: 'Now, Mrs Harte, how much of that do you put in?' She never measured anything – a fistful of this, a pinch of that – and yet seemed to know exactly what she was doing.

Every week, she heard the same questions. And every week she patiently answered. What to me sounded so boring she never dismissed. Mummy never judged anyone. If dinner was made for six, and two more landed in, she simply divided the pot to make sure everyone got fed. She might even go without food herself.

I would love to think that people see something of her when they look at me. Some traits are obvious, but patience was often in short supply.

I was born on October 19, 1954, the youngest of ten. Paddy was 15 years ahead of me. Then came Pete, Mary, Joe, Francis, Bridie, Veronica, Brendan (Barney to us) and Martin. I grew up in a house with six older boys. So there was plenty of rough and tumble: we settled a lot of arguments with our fists. Generally, I came off second best, being youngest and smallest. We never fell out for long. Those rows hardened me, I suppose.

Our parents stepped in when needed, but home was a good place to be. We were a very united bunch. I came from a loving family where everyone was cherished. And we all got a good education.

We played, ran up and down the road, went to Mass on Sundays. Daddy led us through the Rosary every night. Mummy was ever-present, minding us, feeding us, doing whatever she could for us. The road outside our house in Ballymacilroy was quiet: motor cars were exotic sights in our corner of the countryside. Our house was next door to St Malachy's, one of four churches in the parish of Errigal Ciarán. Everything we needed was around us.

We could even have fielded our own seven-a-side team only there were 15 years between myself and Paddy. Pete, the second eldest, played for Tyrone, which meant more to me and to him than the fact that he was the first from our house to go to university. I know how significant it was, looking back, that Pete studied Civil Engineering at Queens. The 1947 Education Act was a landmark in the North as it guaranteed free education for all children over the age of 11 and grants were introduced for university students.

The Hartes came from modest means. My parents rented from Francie McKenna, who lived in another part of the house. Francie, an elderly man, lived on his own. He had a wee shop that sold bread and cigarettes, penny sweets, that sort of thing. You could get meal for animals too. By today's standards, his place was more like a storeroom.

Not every room in our house had light, but you were seldom alone there were that many around. We relied on Tilley lamps, using oil and methylated spirits to get the mantle lit. At night, we took small oil lamps with us walking around the house. To this day, I hate the dark.

Our kitchen was the busiest room, scene of all the action. I can still see the Sacred Heart picture on the wall. Tea was made when neighbours called and the men lit pipes, speaking through the smoke. There was no end of chat.

We played marbles outside, using any wee hole in the road as a target. You scored by shooting your marble off another one. Whoever got their marble in the hole won that round. A photograph at home shows Barney, Martin and myself playing a game while Bridie watches on. That picture takes me back: my mother in the kitchen, front door open, key in the lock.

Behind the house, we played games on the river, picking out twigs to race in the water. We marked out start and finish gates. Some days the water ran slow and we prodded the sticks to set them free whenever they got stuck.

Other times, we fished for trout. My brothers knew much more than me, seeking out stones where fish lay underneath. They captured them by placing one hand either side of the stone.

Ballymacilroy was all that mattered growing up. I never thought of the town: Ballygawley seemed a distant land.

Summer days were never long. We had plenty of time for play even though there was turf and hay to be won. We cut the hay in fields near our house, heading out with rakes and pitchforks to make up the stacks. The bog was only a few miles up the road. While Daddy worked with a spade, we lifted the turf, setting it on the bank or on a flat wooden barrow. Then the sods were left out to dry for a few weeks before we came back to foot them. We gathered them in triangular shapes, building clamps, bigger piles. Finally, we bagged. Then the turf was ready for the trailer and the journey home.

Picking spuds was a community affair in autumn. We

shared the load and sometimes got a few bob for the work. I was never vital for any job, just an extra pair of hands when required.

They say first born is quickest reared and the last one gets to be a child for longer. But I think everyone got a fair deal in our house, even if I fared best.

As the youngest, I had a serious sense of security: everyone looked out for me. I learned from my siblings. My own grandchildren are the same now, following after each other. I always had somebody to call on for help. My brother Joe changes a wheel quicker than I can get out the jack. I was never the most practically minded. Through Pete, I had a short-lived career as a builder's labourer. Never ask me to put up a shelf!

Speaking and thinking – they just came easier.

Our house of ten – seven boys and three girls – was typical enough at that time. If not family then community kept you company. Most nights another neighbour would come to the house. We referred to those visits as céilís. A céilí was a social visit, one neighbour visiting another, very informal, a chat and a cup of tea. This custom kept everyone connected. We still céilí nowadays; even my children use the phrase.

The Rosary was said every night. My father decided the hour, though it varied. He led us through the decades, everyone down on their knees, family and visitors alike. Whoever was there at the chosen time joined the chorus.

I remember the night Francie McKenna died. Our neighbour knocked at our door: 'Come on quick! Come on quick! Francie's taken a turn.'

We got up from saying the Rosary and walked into Francie's. He was lying on the floor, flat on his back, mouth open. His throat made a rasping sound. I remember Mummy's words so clearly: 'That's the death rattle. Poor Francie's gone.'

He died in front of us. His mouth hung loose because he had no teeth. So they wrapped a scarf around his face, which was an unsettling sight.

Francie died on January 12, 1966. We prayed while he lay there. I was 11, just about old enough to understand. That night should have scared the life out of me but, because Mummy was there, I felt safe.

I fell in love with the world of my childhood. We were innocent youngsters. The early 1960s, before the Troubles started, life was good in the North. St Malachy's in Glencull was an integrated primary school in all but name: maybe eight local Protestant families sent their children. We were pleasant with each other. Both sides tended to stick with their own, but there was no talk of sectarianism.

Faith was hugely important to my parents. Daddy served as the sacristan in St Malachy's and was a great advocate for the Pioneers. He had seen the misery that drink can cause: my grandfather did very well as a cattle dealer but blew everything. So abstinence was ingrained in us. My father sat on the local committee of the Pioneers, always eager for others to join. I remember looking at a picture of the Ballygawley team that won a Junior Championship in 1959 and all but one wore the pin.

Football played a huge part in all our lives, linking generations. Mark, our eldest, played all three grades with Tyrone, winning All Irelands at Under-21 (2000) and Senior (2003, 2005). Davy Harte, who played in the 2005 and 2008 All Ireland Finals, is my brother Francie's boy. Peter Harte, Barney's lad, plays on the current Tyrone team.

Paddy considered the priesthood but went into the building trade. He worked on our house in Glencull, where we live today, about five minutes from my original family home. Paddy was a tasty tradesman, always taking care with his work.

Pete was the first to go to grammar school. He passed the 11 Plus and went on to the Brothers, Omagh CBS. Bridie qualified as a teacher while Mary taught typing and shorthand. Barney trained as a plumber, Joe became a mechanic and Francie worked as a welder. Like Pete, Martin went to the Brothers. He studied Engineering across the water in Bolton.

Mostly, I did enough to get by in school. I was certainly never top of my class. But I managed to pass the 11 Plus and headed for the Brothers, like Pete and Martin before me. I liked Maths and languages. And English just seemed to come to me.

On summer evenings, we organised games outside the chapel with our neighbours. Cassidys lived across the road and the Mallons' house was within the chapel yard. Between those three families, there could be 20 children. We played football all the time. Even boys from Ballygawley travelled out to play. The chapel gates served as one goal and two jumpers marked another. Because the space was so confined, we could only play soccer: street football, Ballymacilroy style, and me thinking I was George Best.

A field behind our house provided another pitch. Two poles marked the goal and a length of bailing twine formed the crossbar.

Pete set the standard for football in our house. He was big and strong and ferocious, the brick-wall type. Pete was 'The Man', loved a battle. If the game was flagging, he would bring it back to life, lifting somebody with a shoulder. He played with Tyrone in the 1960s, a County footballer at a time when they towered on the club scene. Everything revolved around him. If we were going to football, Pete brought us. The games we went to, Pete starred in. And, if we were talking about football, Pete led the conversation.

Physically, I was much lighter. Pete powered through players; with my pace, I was better off running around them.

I practised constantly at home. At the beginning, I made do with an empty tub of Fairy liquid, kicking the container across our yard. My goal was always the same: get the bottle through the front gate in as few shots as possible. Every day, I tried to beat my previous best.

Footballs were hard to come by back then. Eventually, I got my hands on a plastic ball and spent hours banging it off the gable wall. Each shot was the greatest free in the world. I got used to playing on my own and developed practice routines: left foot, right foot, left foot, right foot, volley, repeat.

I was self-taught, really, like most players. We learned

from each other. In that sense, Pete was my first coach. I watched him closely in club matches. He was class, single-minded too. He often trained on his own, running up and down the pitch in Dunmoyle or practising frees and 45s. Other times, he trained with his county colleagues Liam McGrath and Tom McKeagney.

Pete perfected the drop kick, too, which was a powerful weapon at that time, ideal when through for a goal. On a blustery day, you could fly the ball a long way against the breeze, like a low golf shot under the wind.

But club training only happened when you were going well. And going well meant getting to the Semi-Final of a Championship. Pete took us down in his car to the pitch in Dunmoyle, about four miles from Ballymacilroy. Our neighbours joined us for those sessions and there would only ever be one ball. I hovered around the main action, hoping for a break. Then I might get a kick at it before someone bigger came along.

My first official game of football was at the age of 11, an Under-16 match in Dunmoyle. I lined out at corner-forward in a pair of jeans. A minibus went around the parish to collect us. I lived for those games.

The first formal coaching came from Paddy Joe McClean. A player split his fingers one time, which could easily happen on a bad day. Paddy Joe was explaining to the poor lad that he had his fingers spread too far apart when he was attempting a catch. And, on a wet day, the ball got heavier as the game went on. Those old leather balls, swollen with water, could chip a bone.

Before my time, Frankie Donnelly had been a big name

with Tyrone. He was a prolific full forward. Apparently, he got something like 3-8 against Fermanagh one time. After his playing days, he took up refereeing. Now, he could be a gruff character. I set the ball down for a free during an underage game one day when he lit on me. I had the laces on the ball facing into the ground.

'Never do that,' he warned. 'Never do that when you're taking a free. Turn the ball and have the lace facing up in the air the right way.'

Such a simple notion. Yet his instructions stuck in my mind. I am still conscious of those details. Never be casual in the way that you go about things. Find the right way and repeat every time. Make sure the O'Neill's logo reads correctly from left to right when kicking a free from the ground. That position is natural to your eye.

Years later, I found myself in Frankie's shoes while refereeing school games. I was inclined to guide players in the same way whenever I thought it might help them.

• • •

Those early memories seem to grow more vivid over time, but then you need a certain distance to see things clearly. Football, being such a big part of my life, can be like a window into the past. From this position, I have a better view of my time with Tyrone.

The game was far less strategic when I took over the Senior job in 2002. Teams spent most of their time focused on what they were going to do – opposition analysis had yet to take off in a serious way. I think people forget just how different the game was even ten years ago. Pre-planned kickout moves seemed like revolutionary concepts in 2003 and, even then, they were fairly basic: we broke the ball and attacked the break in numbers. Our approach was really born out of necessity. You need big men to win high ball and we were dealt a different hand. This notion that football should be played in one particular way never made sense to me.

First of all, consider the players at your disposal. What have you got? What style works best for them? Those are the questions you need to answer. Then, of course, you have to match up with what the modern game demands.

Just as there are hinge moments in the lifespan of every player and every team, the sport you play takes a definite change in direction at certain points. But those junctures might only become obvious with the benefit of hindsight. I think our performance against Kerry in the 2003 All Ireland Semi-Final was one of those moments when the game itself altered course. Armagh had brought new levels of power and professionalism with their breakthrough the previous year. Our game plan was based on the concept of condensing the pitch. We dropped deep, half forwards especially, and defended in packs. My rallying cry was simple: I wanted my players to be psychos for the ball. At first, it looked like a frenzied approach, but the chaos concealed much of the blueprint. Why should a forward stand idle when his team are defending? I wanted our number 15 to think like a defender when the opposition had the ball. We played football based on that principle.

I was a bit taken aback at the criticism when we came on the scene. Pat Spillane, in particular, seemed affronted by our approach, but what did he expect us to do? We had never beaten Kerry in the Championship.

Spillane was a half forward who spent as much time inside the Kerry 45 as he did in the opposition half. I remember him regularly picking the ball up on his own 20-metre line. Yet he seemed to forget about all that stuff when he watched us.

Maybe Kerry can play a more beautiful game, which is fine. But nobody enjoys playing pretty football if they lose.

After 2003, we became the enemy. Pretty soon, it became clear that we had overstayed our welcome. I can understand why Kerry felt that way: our three major wins against them in the period from '03 to '08 upset the natural order. Only for us, that team might have won four, five, six or even seven in a row. Losing hurts, maybe more so when you expect to win. No wonder Jack O'Connor, their manager, looked on us as this 'nouveau riche' outfit. Really, Kerry's reaction was a compliment. And they changed their ways, adopting some elements of our play.

I have the greatest respect for Kerry. They come back, year after year, which is no accident. They are always there and always will be there so long as football is played. Lots of counties come and go. The Kingdom are constant, the measure for everyone else. Dublin, dominant for so long, are perhaps the greatest team of all time.

Yet Kerry are still pushing them all the way and they came within a whisker of denying Dublin five in a row.

Football during the 2010s became a back-to-front game, akin to basketball. Donegal beating Dublin in 2014 was the hinge moment of the last decade. Jim Gavin won an All Ireland playing his preferred way in 2013: flamboyant football with an emphasis on attack at every opportunity. Their style of play gained lots of admirers but there were obvious risks too. That gung-ho attitude was not for me. And Donegal were the ones who exposed Dublin during that famous Semi-Final win. Jim McGuinness took advantage of the space behind midfield and sent his charges flying through an unprotected defence. McGuinness pulled off a tactical masterstroke. That day in Croke Park, we saw just how much the game had progressed in terms of analysis. Where Dublin won an All Ireland in 2013 with attacking blitzes, Donegal took down the champions by decoding their opponents. They hit on a virus that corrupted Dublin's system.

But Dublin's loss that year was ultimately their gain. Gavin saw, in the most painful way, how his team could be exposed. Their flamboyance, a supposed strength, had been turned against them and he needed a fix. The five All Irelands that followed for Gavin tells its own story. Dublin changed, in a fundamental way, after that loss. And the game changed fundamentally as a result. We have been playing in the era of strategic football ever since, which has had consequences for all of us trying to compete with Dublin.

Tyrone in 2014 were at a low ebb, certainly the lowest

point in my time as manager. We went out of the Championship early, losing a fractious game against Armagh in the second round of the Qualifiers. Monaghan had already beaten us by a point in the Ulster Quarter-Finals. Our only wins of the Championship came against Down, after a replay, and Louth. The loss to Armagh was a real sickener, the nature of it, the way they got at us. That season was easily my worst.

Six years on from our last All Ireland, there was a growing impatience within the county. The game had moved on and plenty of people felt it was time for me to move on as well. That period, in football terms, was the most challenging of my career. But I never lost faith in our ability to come back and compete with the best. The day I lose hope is the day that I stop managing football teams.

Ultimately, management really boils down to one thing: how you engage with people. I never got a sense from the players that they had lost faith in me. And their view is always paramount. Player power might be seen as a negative thing, especially when a manager is forced out, but the players have to be central. The setup is doomed anyway if the squad is at odds with the manager. Had the players looked for change at the time, or at any time, then I would have walked.

Managerial decisions are not always a matter of simple majority, but you have to read the room. 2004, the players were getting restless. The year before, Bart McEnroe had worked with me in the lead up to the All Ireland Final. I met Bart through the business world. He had a coach's outlook and challenged my thinking in a way that I found productive. I really valued his input and thought the players could benefit too. He took a session with the squad during the Championship. But I could sense the boys were unhappy. You could see it in their body language. The vibes were not good.

Bart is intense and some people struggle with that approach. The situation came to a head for us before we played Mayo in the Quarter-Finals. We had to thrash it out, players and management. Obviously, I wanted to keep Bart on board, but the players come first. That said, the whole thing left me in a difficult position: I was caught in the middle. Now, I still have a good relationship with Bart and we speak on the phone regularly. But, on that occasion, there was only one way to go.

We all get knockbacks at some stage. Sport is like romance that way, forever tugging at the heartstrings. I got my kicks playing football but my teenage dreams were no different than the rest.

Before I left the Brothers, I had a girlfriend for six months. I only went with a girl if it was serious. So my relationships tended to last. My first year at college, I was with a different girl for nine months. She finished with me, my first heartbreak. I felt that sense of rejection – 'she doesn't want me anymore' – and it was a real hit.

Approaching girls was a daunting experience back then. At the dances, the boys stood one side and you walked a gauntlet in search of a willing partner.

April time, 1975, my brother Francie was heading over to the dance in Carrickmore. It was a Sunday night but he had a job persuading me to come for some reason. Eventually I relented.

I was only there a short while when my eyes lit up. Off I went, across the open floor. First, we danced. And in those days the next step was just as innocent: 'What about going for a mineral?'

We talked for a long time. Marian Donnelly was new to me, even though Beragh, her home place, is just beyond our parish. The two of us meeting in Carrickmore was a chance encounter. Like me, she travelled reluctantly.

After the dance, we dropped her home: Francie driving, Marian and me chatting away in the back.

She brought me in for a cup of tea when we got to her house. All was grand until Marian produced these sandwiches dressed with salad cream. At that stage, salad cream was like poison to me.

I said: 'Lookit, they're lovely sandwiches but I really don't like them.'

She changed them for me, which was probably a good omen, looking back. Chat over, we had a kiss or two, and I headed off.

We began to meet regularly in Belfast, then, where Marian was working with the bank. That time was lovely, the two of us just enjoying each other's company. Simple, sweet happy days.

And we had lots in common. The things that mattered, mattered to both of us. Marian was a Pioneer as well and committed to her faith. She was also close with one of her aunts. Mary Elizabeth, or Velva as the family called her, had MS and Marian used to help her a lot, writing letters and doing other little jobs.

Marian was good with people, affable and sociable. She always wore this really bright smile, pretty as a picture. I knew she was the one when I met her.

As it turned out, we were confirmed on the same day in Ballymacilroy. Marian went to school in Altamuskin, which is in our parish. Years later, we found a picture with the two of us standing close to each other in a group photograph outside the church.

December 1977, I proposed. Marian thought it might have been a bit soon because I was in my last year of college. But there was no mad rush in those days to start planning a wedding; we had time on our side.

Barney (always Brendan to Joan!) got engaged around the same time. And, as it turned out, we picked the same month to get married: July '78. For whatever reason, we never consulted about the dates beforehand. Nearly everyone got married on a Saturday back then. There were fewer weddings and weekends were easy to come by. We went for July 8 and booked Malta for our honeymoon but Barney's wedding was due to take place while we were away. So he ended up moving his date. I think our generation were more relaxed about getting married. We breezed into it.

Now, we still had to get some money together. I remember saving like mad from the time we got engaged. We put away something like 200 pounds a month between us, which was fair going. My first salary was only £152 per month.

1980 was the closest I came to winning an Ulster Championship with Tyrone. Our expectations were so low at the time, we had booked our summer break for the first two weeks of July. I spent the fortnight before the Final on a camping holiday in France.

Holidays meant a lot to Marian back then because that was all the leave she got during the year. And football took precedence the rest of the year. My brother Barney and his wife, Joan, travelled with us. I trained as much as possible, stopping off to go running whenever I came across a rugby pitch. Was it the worst way to prepare, being away from the hype? Art McCrory, Tyrone manager at the time, had no need to worry about me drinking or staying out late. I minded myself. The only hiccup was the journey back.

We took the ferry over – Rosslare to Cherbourg – but our boat home, scheduled for the Friday before the Final, was cancelled. We drove three hours north to Dieppe instead. From there, we reached Holyhead on the Saturday. Barney then drove to London so that I could fly home in time for the match. Some preparation for my only Ulster Final! We lost to Armagh, 4-10 to 4-7.

That stage of my life was hectic. Marian and I were married in July of 1978. We bought our first house the same year. The following June, Mark arrived. Life moved a lot quicker back then. Three years earlier, I was a carefree student.

A bunch of us from the Brothers moved to Belfast at the same time. 1974, the city was turning into a war zone, but we went there without much apprehension. We had our own readymade bubble going into this new environment. Living in that world, we almost became oblivious to the rising temperature. You know the parable about the frog in warm water? He never thinks to jump out in time.

We had no real awareness of this abnormal world becoming normalised. Anyone dropped into it would say: 'This is mad.'

But, for us, things just evolved that way. Tensions escalated. You might get stopped five times going on a six-mile journey. We just went with it. What else could you do? People adapt; you make allowances almost unconsciously. And you get on.

Whether it was lack of bravery or something else, fighting for the cause seemed futile to me. I worried about the dangers and the implications for my family. And politics seemed pointless as well; I was never tempted. But we were all conscious of the need for change: it was beyond time us Catholics got a level playing field. We felt we always had to fight for our rights.

Everybody had their own take on things and I played football with plenty of boys who held views far more extreme than mine. Some, inevitably, were drawn into violence. But we left our troubles at the gate while the matches were being played. That period, when I look back on it, taught me to treat each person as an individual. I learned to look beyond groups and see the various personalities within them. My mother's patience and understanding worked for me when I found myself in complicated situations. Empathy guided me through those places and beyond.

We were students living through revolutionary times. Our world was shaped by a unique set of circumstances and we tried to keep step. Same time, we were just ordinary young lads from the country, coming of age, out on the town. College took us to Belfast but we were chasing life and all it had to offer: girls in dancehalls, nights in the pub.

Some people find it hard to credit but I look back on my student days in Belfast with mostly fond memories. I moved there in 1974 to study at St Joseph's Teacher Training College – The Ranch as everyone knew it. Tony Donnelly, my best friend to this day, trained there too.

Tony comes from Augher, about five miles from Ballygawley. We first met at the CBS in Omagh, 1972. Like me, Tony took a minimal approach when it came to study. Our paths never crossed in the library. Avoiding authority was our game then and Tony always wanted to skip off so he could smoke a cigarette. I never smoked but I knew the best places to go without getting caught.

One day, we made our escape on the back of a furniture truck. There was a knock at the door of the classroom. The school piano was to be sent away for retuning and the removal men needed assistance.

'We want two bodies for help with moving a piano.'

Our hands shot up.

There was a half door, like a stable door, on the back of the removals truck. We pushed in the piano and closed ourselves in. As the driver took off across the front of the school, we waved back at everybody looking out. Who knew where we were going!

To keep us entertained, Tony picked up a guitar and started singing. Next thing we know, the driver jams on the brakes. Some boy on the street watched as we went flying up the truck. We jumped out and headed on up Omagh town.

Tony stuck it out for a year in the Brothers. He moved to South West College – the Tech – but we continued meeting down the town. We shared the same passion for football, though Tony never regarded himself much as a player. He described himself as a 'working-class Tony Cascarino', the ball bouncing off him at full forward for others to pick up the pieces. He never fails to make me laugh.

Teaching was my suggestion, though you could hardly describe us as career driven. We discussed our future in the dole queue one day. That time, you could sign on for the summer.

'Donnelly,' I said, 'dead handy number for us.'

Tony jumped at the chance when he heard the details: 'And you get a grant! Show me the form.'

We sent in our application and were called for interview. Two fellas who spent all their time trying to get out of class were set to become teachers. The Ranch was a glorified version of school. Each lecture ran for 45 minutes and the bell rang at the end. Five minutes later, the bell rang again to signal the start of the next lecture. You had to sign in each time. And you needed 70 per cent attendance. For Tony, it got to the stage that if he did go to class, it was pointless signing the sheet. His real signature looked too unlike the fakes that others had been signing for him.

The college grant was worth £300 per term, a valuable sum. We shared digs on the Whiterock Road, just off The Falls, and headed home at the weekends, working to supplement our income for those student weeks in Belfast.

Tony joined the darts club. For him, darts was an obvious calling: fitness was never an issue and it went with a pint. I tagged along for matches, following Tony from pub to pub. One night, we came home late and were stopped by a British Army patrol, a regular occurrence near Whiterock. For some reason, I had Tony's darts in my breast pocket.

'Give me those,' the solider demanded. 'You're carrying a dangerous weapon.'

'They're only darts,' I protested.

Tony spotted his opening: 'Obviously you've seen him play.'

Maybe humour is what we needed to get through those days. Student life in Belfast during the 1970s was more fun than people could have imagined.

On nights out, I drank Club Orange while Tony and the boys had their pints. Then we might head for a takeaway in Andersonstown, careful to get home safe and sound. There was an element of the Wild West about it all. You can normalise almost anything when you find yourself in that kind of world, which is the really scary thing.

The most serious issue we talked about was football. And girls, occasionally. We had no career aspirations. If you needed 40 per cent to pass, that was our target. But, with football, we wanted full marks.

We spent more time together at The Ranch than we did studying. We were country people with similar backgrounds. Tony had six brothers and one sister. I was comfortable calling to the Donnellys and Tony felt at home coming to mine. If you were a friend of anybody in our house, you were a friend of everyone: all welcome, no appointments necessary. And it was the same with the Donnellys.

Whiterock was one of the hottest places in town. We were oblivious to the dangers without being blasé about them. Some days, you could see smoke from a car bomb in the distance. We were regularly searched, spread-eagled on the ground. Par for the course. We rarely discussed it.

Silence greeted you walking into the Whiterock bar. Then you heard a few murmurs – 'them boys are up at The Ranch' – and the volume returned.

Because we were on The Falls, among our own, we felt nothing bad would happen. Really, it was the most dangerous place to be. The likes of the Shankill Butchers targeted that area, always trying to kidnap and murder people.

A student we knew, another first year, was caught on his own, late one night. More than likely, he got a taxi to drop him within walking distance to save on the fare, which was common practice. We never walked alone. Luckily, he got away: his attackers were disturbed.

I never thought of leaving: I could see there was a future for a teacher in the North. But our parents must have gone through hell. I would hate for my children to have to live in that environment.

One summer on a building site dispelled any lingering

doubts about teaching. Cold mornings outside mixing cement held no appeal. I remember Tony worked Fridays and Saturdays when he was at school.

We talked about football all the time, analysing players and teams. On odd weekends, I headed over to McKenna's pub in Augher to throw darts or else Tony called to Kelly's in Garvaghey, where we played pool. Augher and Ballygawley were rivals, the Celtic and Rangers of South Tyrone. And we were stalwarts in our clubs. People wondered how we could be friends.

Tony has a rare gift for making people laugh. I know nobody else like him. I remember calling him with the news the time Mark was born: 'Donnelly, will you come down here for a night to celebrate?'

I took him to the hospital first. Afterwards, we popped into a bar. I ordered the drinks: my usual orange and a pint for Tony.

'Alright, lads, something to celebrate tonight?' the barman asked.

'Aye,' Tony replied, 'the birth of a baby son.'

The barman, when he saw me handing the pint to Tony, took him to be father. Not that Tony minded: he got a free drink and a fine cigar.

Tony moved back home after we finished college while I stayed in Belfast. He went labouring for a few months before taking a job on a Youth Training Scheme in Dungannon. I had gone straight into teaching at a Catholic Boys Home run by the De La Salle Brothers. Kircubbin was an isolated place, about 50 minutes from Belfast, out on the Ards Peninsula.

I taught PE primarily but covered English and Maths and RE as well. The curriculum was broad because the boys had mixed levels of education. Most of the students in Kircubbin came from difficult backgrounds. They had grown up in deprived areas or broken homes, which was a catch-all phrase at that time. They were about as far removed from my upbringing as you could imagine and nothing about their lives was conventional.

The biggest class might have had 16 students but I was working in challenging circumstances. A lot of boys came from Belfast, city kids shipped out from hard environments. Some came from Derry and an odd boy from the country. The regular school system was probably a bad fit for them: they were dealing with stuff in their lives that most children, thankfully, never have to contemplate.

Kircubbin was a shock to my system. I knew nothing of their worlds: it took time to get a handle on things. Some lads were determinedly defiant and if the teacher lost the class he might as well go home. At college, we covered Youth and Community Studies. So at least I was familiar with the idea of more informal education. But I stumbled my way through those early years. Experience, really, is the only way you learn how to cope with the practicalities of running a classroom.

From a PE point of view, the facilities were great. We had an all-weather pitch and a big indoor hall. For the boys, sport was a great way to let off steam. Inevitably, there were rows. Posturing, mostly. 'See when I get you' was the big statement and then the response would be: 'Well, I'm here.'

And you had to be up early to get ahead of them. Some boy might go down after a clash, writhing about on the ground, pretending his leg was broken. Then you go running over and he gets up, laughing at the good of it. You learned to assess situations before rushing in.

Convention was out the window: in class, you had to allow a wider berth for all sorts of things. A 'blind ear' was needed much of the time. The boys could fight with each other very quickly and then make up just as fast. To connect with the boys in Kircubbin required patience and compassion. I learned nearly as much. My time there opened my eyes because I came to understand how hard growing up could be.

The school used to enter a team in GAA Scór events – dancing, singing, recitation, all the traditional Irish past times. About 12 boys came down to Emyvale in County Monaghan one time for an Ulster competition. On the way back, I got them to call in to Ballymacilroy. Mummy made them a big feed, sausages and beans and toast. They ate all around them. I thought it would be good for them to see what my home looked like. I felt it might help them in some way.

Becoming a teacher also made me a better coach, although that education began much earlier.

The club reached the Championship Semi-Finals in 1963. St Kieran's, as we were then known, rarely went that far. I remember preparations for the game. The team trained two nights a week in Dunmoyle and, because Pete was playing, I got going. And I had full access. I was in the dressing room, watching the players get ready, listening to the team talks, a child in the company of these big, strong football men.

Sean Canavan tore the laces out of someone's boot one day. He was livid because the laces were rotting away. They needed waxing to stop the rain from ruining them. Your boots were no good if the laces ripped during a match. Keeping your gear right was a basic.

Years later, when I started reading John Wooden – the revered American basketball coach – Sean came to mind. Wooden valued the same kind of attention to detail. For him, it was important how you put on socks and tied laces. What if you had to stop during a game because your laces came undone?

I picked up some early tactical lessons in those dressing rooms. The manager, Paddy Joe McClean, commandeered a blackboard one time, chalking out various Xs and Os to show the forwards what he wanted in attack. His plan seemed straightforward: the corner forward was to make a diagonal run towards midfield whenever we got possession.

'You go out and demand the ball,' Paddy Joe told him. Meanwhile the full forward was making his move into space that had been vacated. With our decoy in place, our midfielder was primed to play the ball into the corner, seeking out the full forward. Unfortunately that tactic came to nought when he drilled his pass out over the endline.

Even then, that tactic was limited. The forward still had a lot to do when he got the ball. Nowadays, the defence would force you to recycle possession. What you really want is a player making his run from the corner, moving towards the centre. That way, he picks up the pass heading for goal.

Ballygawley were hammered in that '63 Semi-Final. Even during my time playing with the club, we never got beyond the Semis. 1974 was the closest we came to making a County Final. I had an option to go to America that summer but decided to stay after we won Division 2 of the League. We were knocked out by Carrickmore, a goal that we felt should have been disallowed. As a club, we needed to make the breakthrough at that time.

The scene in Tyrone was hard and uncompromising back then. And brutal at times. Some teams, if the game was slipping, would start a row and force the referee to abandon it. They fancied their chances in a replay.

Luckily, I suffered no major injuries, but football cost me a few teeth over the years. 1972, I was full forward with the County Minors. We played Donegal in Ballyshannon. At one stage during the game, I turned to walk in towards the goal. Bang! My marker hit me flush in the face. I was seeing double for the rest of that game.

Physically, that period was unforgiving. You hit first and made sure you hit last. The Donegal incident happened off the ball but there was no word about it: everyone carried on. The law of the jungle prevailed.

Teams from the Loughshore, any of those clubs from around Lough Neagh, had the reputation of majoring on the physical side of the game. They rarely disappointed. I was fast and nippy, which invariably made me prime for attention.

I lost more teeth in Moortown, even when I was wearing a gum shield. I passed the ball over an opponent's head to one of our boys coming through and the defender came straight into me with his fist, not even looking at the ball. I got a prize for that punch: a plate in my mouth.

I had to stand up for myself, maybe throw an odd dig or call on my older brothers. More often than not, they arrived before I sought them out. If somebody hit me, I was never afraid to strike back. I never did anything I regretted but often regretted not striking out.

The thing about football, whatever your era, you feel it cannot get any better. But I know our game has improved beyond all recognition. Just look at the skillsets, the physiques: every player is an athlete. I would relish the chance to play nowadays because the game has become faster, more fluid. There is more room for the kind of player I was. I burned defenders for pace and scored goals for fun in club matches. One day, I bagged 3-5. And I loved seven-a-side. We won an adult tournament in Clogher when I was only 15.

I never liked the phrase 'win your own ball'. That concept made no sense to me. If you are in possession, why the need to win the ball again? Your teammate should always have a distinct advantage when the pass comes in.

Forwards fought for every possession because, generally, the ball was hoofed in. Teams needed big men in the full forward line to win those long aimless deliveries. Those players might not score to save their lives. Football, at least the version we were playing in Tyrone, was not much of a thinking man's game.

Tyrone did not win Championship matches when we were young. We got battered everywhere. We supported Down in the 1960s because they were the first team to bring Sam Maguire across the border. Those Down players were our idols; they came to Tyrone clubs to make medal presentations.

Sean O'Neill, their legendary full forward, was my hero. I loved the way that he would present himself for a ball and then give the pass to the player running by him. I still say to players: 'You cannot run in the air.' If a player has to jump to catch the ball then he has to run from a standing start. Much better to give the ball to somebody running past because you gain so much more yardage on your opponent. So many goals are scored by the man coming off the shoulder.

I can still picture Sean O'Neill against Kerry in the 1968 All Ireland Final. We watched that game in a neighbour's house on a black and white television. At a key stage in the game, the ball came back off the Kerry upright. Everybody was waiting to see what would happen when O'Neill fired the rebound past Johnny Culloty. Anticipation got him that goal.

I make the same point with every team: expect the unexpected. Awareness, especially around the goal, creates opportunities for defenders and for forwards. Players closest to the goal should chase every shot: the wind might alter its flight, it might drop short and ricochet. Forwards profit from being alert; defenders can avert a score.

In time, I got to see the big games up close. My

brother Pete was always generous with tickets for All Irelands. Several of us brothers would travel down to Croke Park and link up with the McAleers. I knew Colm from school and his brother Gerard had been in the same year as Martin. Gerard was teaching as a Christian Brother in Dublin at the time. We would analyse the games together, trying to figure out each team. Like me, he was fascinated by the Dubs and the way they were doing things.

After games, we called to my sister in Castleknock. Mary and her husband Lee always put on a big spread for us, dinner and dessert, the works. And she would have the match recorded. Before the food was out, we were sat in to watch the Final again. We dissected the whole thing like pundits. Looking back over those All Irelands, I used to think: 'Why not Tyrone?'

We were busy admiring players from other counties when we could have been watching our own.

My GAA club meant the world to me.

Ballygawley St Kieran's played a central part in the life of my family: the Hartes were deeply embedded in the history of the club. My mother looked after the jerseys and us boys played all the way up. My brothers represented St Kieran's on Tyrone teams when not many from the club made it to County level.

I served as chairman while I was in college, only 20 or 21 at the time. We ran a world record attempt as a fundraiser, playing indoor soccer for 72 hours. I remember being interviewed on Radio Ulster, which seemed like no big deal at the time. Even then, I felt comfortable being out front. Who knows where that instinct came from? I was a talker, certainly. I could be single-minded. And public speaking held no fears for me. To influence others, I think you need to be articulate.

So how did we manage to fall out?

The GAA was much different when I grew up. Our club, like so many others, was a far smaller outfit. Most players came from a handful of houses. If you played football, more than likely your father played. The game was an inheritance, rarely spreading beyond those born into it. Basically, there were footballing families and the rest.

Within the club, we identified with our parish areas. So the Hartes were Glencull people first and foremost. The same held true for families from Ballygawley and Garvaghey and Dunmoyle. Most of the time, there was no obvious friction. But, given the parochial nature of a country GAA club, there could be tension from time to time.

And people often passed remarks about the situation at the time. They used to say: 'There's no such thing as a Ballygawley man.' There was this impression among other clubs that we had no sense of collective identity. Nowadays, our club is all-encompassing: any household could be represented. The explosion at underage level and the growth of ladies football has widened the net. There are more ties to bind us.

Go back to the 1980s and you find fewer roots. Any kind of a fallout had the potential to be spectacular.

September of 1982, Marian and I were living in Dungannon, having moved back from Belfast. That year, we decided to revive the parish league. I was the 16th man for Glencull when we last played, about 13 years previously, which told its own story. Needless to say, there had been a history of rows.

Fairness, or the lack of it, was at the heart of the '82 dispute. At this remove, it might seem a minor issue. From my point of view, there was a principle at stake. Glencull, our end of the parish, felt I had been unduly punished by the club for my part in a fight that broke out during our first game against Dunmoyle.

Marian was in hospital that day, having given birth to Michael, our second child. Meanwhile, I was stood on the sideline for Glencull, nursing a twinge in my knee. The hits were going in hard and we were one point behind. I was getting twitchy. On I went, hoping to turn the tide.

One moment turned our football world upside down. I went for a ball in the air with Brendan McCann: we both tried to punch it but Brendan's jaw blocked my fist, an accidental hit. Instinctively, I suppose, he took a swipe at me but missed. My strike was unintentional, though that fact was lost in the chaos. Other players traded blows as the melee developed. Brendan and I were sent off.

By the time I visited Marian that evening, the news had already reached her hospital bed. Next day, the club called a meeting to deal with the fallout. I got the feeling Glencull were being fingered as the main culprits and my punishment confirmed that suspicion: a two-game ban.

Meanwhile, Brendan McCann played a handball match for St Kieran's. The same night that I was suspended from our internal league, Brendan represented the club in an official competition. There was a complete lack of fairness, number one, and the decision to bar me from the sideline as well made no sense. I could live with a playing ban, but the club were making it almost impossible to manage the team. Naturally, I protested. My appeal fell on deaf ears.

From there, the row escalated. We held a meeting in Glencull and put our complaints in writing. By then, we were prepared to withdraw from all club activities. But our letter was met with indifference. The parish league finished without us. We met again in Glencull and decided to go one step further: it was time to form our own club.

As my boys will tell you, I love a cause. But nobody could have foreseen what lay ahead. The whole thing took on a life of its own. What began as a fairly minor issue, one that should have been resolved quickly, turned into this eight-year odyssey.

The decision to break away from St Kieran's was a massive wrench for me given my history and my family's history with the club. My suspension from the parish league, the way things were handled, it hurt.

Same time, setting out with Glencull seemed like a great opportunity to revive our end of the parish. But nothing came easy. We thought that forming a new club would be straightforward, a simple matter of signing forms. The county board rejected our first application in 1983. Four years earlier, Aughabrack had been in the same position. Like us, their original request was turned down. So they went seeking support from the Ulster

Council instead. Once they got provincial council approval, the county board relented. A precedent had been set: we figured the same thinking would apply with us.

For whatever reason, the board refused to budge when it came to Glencull. An endorsement from Ulster Council was no good in our case. To further complicate matters, we had no right of appeal, which left us in an impossible position. A higher body, in those circumstances, could not overrule the board's decision. Even the GAA rulebook was against us.

The county board continued to stymie Glencull in subsequent years. As far as we could see, they had no good reason. True, some officials were sympathetic but there was never enough support to get us ratified. Even after I made an impassioned speech at the county convention in 1984, nothing changed. We were cut adrift. Other clubs were warned not to play in our annual nine-a-side tournament at The Holm, our local pitch. Our status, or lack of, meant we had no insurance cover for those matches.

Yet we made the best of things. Sundays, we ran underage training sessions and then played our own games. Any willing club, we travelled for a match. And our tournament went off each year: visiting teams paid no heed to the county board.

There was a great spirit around the place during that time: we developed a serious sense of community. We held blitzes and bazaars, organised all kinds of events. We were forever selling tickets. The children learned Irish in a prefab at the back of the church, which served as a kind of clubhouse. Mark had his first lessons there. And we raised our own funds too. One raffle brought in £40,000. We were a club in all but name.

Around the parish, there was an odd stirring, attempts to heal the rift. For me, the row was purely a football issue. Others found it hard to make that distinction. Over time, people become entrenched. The longer it went on, the more complicated things seemed.

At the time of the split, I had plenty of good playing years left. I turned 28 in 1982 and still had the potential to make Tyrone teams. Leaving the club effectively ended my County career. Tyrone won Ulster in 1984 and made the All Ireland Final two years later. I can only wonder about those years.

Would I do anything different if I had that time over? No, for a few reasons.

A lot of the traits that I developed during that period stood to me later in life. I was determined by nature but I definitely became more resilient. And I learned how to organise, how to bring people together. I turned out a different manager for that experience. I broadened my thinking; I had to. I needed to make myself more valuable to the community. What we did, in time, benefitted the whole parish.

The situation with the club was everything at that stage. Some people may not have been as committed as I was but they were still happy to back Glencull. Given all that we knew at the time, it was the right way to go. You cannot live your life in reverse.

Football, ultimately, brought us back together. Too

many talented players were in limbo. Steven and Pascal Canavan, Sean's sons, had emerged. And then came Peter, one of the all-time greats.

Take Peter out of the equation and the rift takes longer to heal. Some players are so good, they change the people around them. By rights, he was ineligible for the Tyrone Minors when they came calling. Peter played all his underage football with Glencull and we were an unofficial outfit. To play for the county, he had to be registered with a club. For Tyrone, the stakes were bigger this time and too big to end in stalemate. The solution came from an unlikely source: Killyclogher Hurling Club. Peter, having never hurled in his life, represented Killyclogher playing for Tyrone in the 1988 All Ireland Minor Semi-Final.

The following year, Ballygawley were beaten in the County Final. They played without the Canavans.

The time was ripe for reconciliation. Fr Sean Hegarty, our new curate, acted as go-between, slowly untying the knots. Finally, in 1990, we relaunched as Errigal Ciarán. Had we tried before then, maybe Errigal would have subsided. But we were successful almost immediately, which cemented the whole thing. Within three years, Errigal were County Champions. And we went on from there, adding the Ulster title, the first Tyrone club to make that mark. Those heady days were also healing days.

I was still fit to play, second-team football mostly. Mark actually replaced me in a Reserve league game for Errigal once, but we never got playing on the pitch together. He was about 17 at that time.

Coaching kept me busy. I threw myself into the new club, taking charge of the Under-12s and the Under-16s. We won the top division of the League with the 16s that first year, 1990. Eoin Gormley, who went on to play for Tyrone and Ulster, came through from that group. The 12s grew into a Championship-winning team at Under-21 level. Those early years with Errigal Ciarán were the richest period the parish had ever seen. Between 1993 and 2002, by which stage I was over the Senior team, we had five County titles. Few rated us before then. Suddenly we were the power in Tyrone football.

When I think back on my own time playing with the club, the images are fairly raw: two feet off the ground trying to burst the net with every shot.

I played by instinct, fast and direct. I always took on my man: I had enough pace to skin a defender in one burst. And I wanted goals. Kicking points almost bored me. Our Mark reckons I played like Hotshot Hamish, a character from one of his childhood comics. Hamish would hit these penalties that put ball and keeper in the goal. I used to stand about 12 paces back, running a straight line towards the penalty spot. Finesse was never a concern.

My brother Martin played in goals for the club and we figured out our own set play. Defenders marked you from behind that time. So, the space was always in front of the forward. I made runs out to the half forward line, knowing Martin would aim his kickout down my wing. Man-to-man marking made life simple for a forward with speed. And a footrace always favoured someone like me.

Training was sporadic for the County team in the 1970s. During the winter, we ran up and down a field in the dark. There were no floodlights in places like Dungannon. All that training seemed like such a waste, not just the time spent running but the travel to get to those sessions. I envied soccer players who could play under lights. Even when I managed the Minors in the 1990s, training only really got going once the days started to stretch.

1972 was my last year playing Minor. Frank McGuigan, whose sons Frank, Brian, Tommy and Shay went on to play for Tyrone, ran the show at midfield. I made the team at full forward. We beat Cavan to win Ulster. Frank and I scored a goal each against Meath in the Semi-Finals. Only Cork stood between us and the ultimate prize then.

I went shopping in Portadown for a new pair of boots before the Final and my brother Joe came with me. I had picked out the regular Adidas pair but the shop assistant wanted me to try something different, the Predators of their time. Boy, were they class! And, at 12 pounds, they were double the price.

I had no notion of buying them but then Joe stepped in. I was gobsmacked. His gesture means even more now because I can better appreciate its significance. To think that he gladly paid 12 pounds just so I would have the best boots for the Final still amazes me. I suppose his gesture showed how much pride my family felt about the fact that I would be playing an All Ireland at Croke Park.

Those boots got me a goal in the Final. Michael Quinn scored another and Frank kicked four points, but we finished three shy of Cork. My opposite number bagged 2-1. Unfortunately, we ran into Cork when Jimmy Barry Murphy was still a Minor.

I played rugby for a brief spell with the Omagh Academicals club that winter. At that stage, I was finished with school and getting ready for college. Omagh played me on the wing to take advantage of my pace. I enjoyed those games but football was everything for me. Who knows what I might have achieved in another sport, but our opportunities were limited. And I cannot imagine my life without GAA.

The following year, Tyrone went all the way. I learned early on in my career the gulf between winners and losers. People still talk about that '73 team. They celebrated their silver jubilee in 1998. By then, I had bigger things on my mind.

● ● ●

As a younger man, I struggled to control my temper. I was fiery. I took strong views and was quick to express them. On the pitch, I rarely held back either.

The Hartes, the boys at least, were known to be tough in a quiet way. We were steely, I think, and Pete epitomised that trait. But where Pete had size and strength, I had to be quick and clever. The forwards of my era took a lot more punishment. Defenders had licence to deal with you how they saw fit – you crossed them at your peril.

We all played on the edge. Once, I came to blows with a full back in a club game. Joe refereed that day. He grabbed the ball and ran into us, shouting his orders: 'Either the two of ye go off or this game's finished.' So I have the rare distinction of being sent off by my own brother.

Football was a more primitive game back then. I never went out to hit anyone but you got that many clips that you often had to give one back. I ran at defenders when I got possession. Inevitably, that led to conflict: I was carrying the ball at pace into people who were going to nail me.

My early years managing the Tyrone Minors, I was all go on the line, reacting to everything that happened. I was too wrapped up in the games, far too animated.

Paul Doris, a former county board official, pulled me aside one day. 'Just settle down,' he said. 'Don't be as agitated.'

I credit him for changing my approach. His advice was something I needed to hear at that time, and it made me a calmer person. Managing younger players is a serious responsibility: boys are more impressionable at that age.

Funny, Paul served on the selection committee when I was first appointed manager of the County Minors. I remember his words: 'This is one of the most difficult jobs you'll do in sport.'

At Minor level, the players are just passing through. You have a quick turnover. If the man in charge is behaving like a madman, what chance have the players to develop good habits?

Again, I looked to John Wooden. Wooden stressed the importance of the coach's demeanour because of its impact on the players. Me getting all worked up on the line would hinder rather than help them.

Not that things clicked overnight. I had been a barking dog for so long that it took time for me to change. Watch me now on a sideline and this guarded man in glasses keeps track of the game. Behind that picture, an awful lot goes on. You have to stay calm in order to make good decisions and, at this stage, I know how to keep my composure. But I was much different in the early days.

I squared up to players numerous times. We never came to blows but there was always plenty of mouthing going on. My son Mattie, when he started coming to games, used to be worried that I might get hit. I was regularly booked. And every referee was biased: in my eyes, they were all out to get us.

But I still emphasise the value of raw emotion: 'Boys, we are not going to take a step back. It's not an option. Look at the boy beside you and say: "I'm not going to lose. Are you going to lose?" If you want to win, you have to want it. How big is your why? How much do you want to win?'

Even if some of it sounds like cliche, I speak with total conviction. I believe every word.

1991, my first year, was bittersweet. We reached the Ulster Final and I can still remember the excitement. Travelling on the team bus was a novelty for the children. Mark loved being around the players. I gave him small jobs to do: collect a lock of cones, put out biscuits, gather footballs. Everyone likes to feel like they can contribute. Seán Teague was captain and Mark would mind his gloves. He would sneak them on and kick the ball around, pretending to be Seán. Those little things meant the world to him: he got to emulate his heroes on the same pitch where they trained.

Donegal beat us in the Final that year and Seán spoke in the dressing room afterwards. He was a huge figure, a real aggressive full back, passionate, no nonsense. He started apologising, fighting back the tears.

That defeat was an awful disappointment. A few things went against us. Donegal were playing in the Senior Final as well that day and you could sense they had the pull of the crowd. Then they got a soft penalty, which clinched it for them. We missed a chance to equalise and lost by one.

After the game, a wise owl approached me from the crowd as we headed out to the team bus. These people always come out of the woodwork when you lose. He had all these bright ideas about how the Final would have run for us if we had used a player from his own club. He reckoned his one move, in a one-point game, would have made all the difference. I let him say his piece and walked on.

● ● ●

I had firm views about football back then. My thinking ran along rigid lines: 'I know how this game should be played and I know what I want to see.'

I was hungry for the Minor job when it came around in 1990: I wanted to go all the way, to win that All

Ireland we missed out on in '72. A defeat or a setback always made me more determined. I took that job with a clear target in mind.

And, when you got me as manager, the family came too. I was babysitting on the job. From Marian's point of view, this management business was a good thing because she got some time to herself. We can all be selfish about sport. No sooner had I finished playing than I started out in management. Marian saw that if the children liked being involved then it could be a good thing.

Only the boys came with me to training at first. They could kick around together and collect footballs behind the goal. Michaela plagued me before I allowed her to come. The boys used to say to her: 'What are you going to do at training?'

But she loved being there, watching all the action from the stand. In time, she took charge of sharing out milk and biscuits after the sessions. That way, she got to know everyone. For an extrovert like Michaela, it was the dream job.

She had a soft spot for certain players. Of the '93 Minors, she was very fond of Barry O'Hare or Hair Bear as everybody knew him. I think his nickname endeared him all the more. Ironically, she was later to become a teaching colleague and close friend of Barry's wife, Aileen. Naturally, she had great affection for the '97 Minors because that was Mark's team. To her, they were 'the boys', and she loved them like they were brothers. She had a great affinity for Kevin Hughes, in particular. Hub was the life and soul of every team he played on. He showed incredible courage all through his career and I think we all felt a deep connection to Hub watching how he coped with so many losses so young in his life. His brother Paul died in a car crash during the summer of '97 and Hub's performance against Kerry in that year's All Ireland Semi-Final replay still ranks as one of the greatest individual displays that I have ever seen.

Tyrone football became an extension of our family. I know Michaela saw it that way. She was tuned into everything: compiling CDs with everybody's song on it; writing out the national anthem, 'Amhrán na bhFiann', phonetically for the players; always keen to know who made the team. She felt part of the scene. In her eyes, Tyrone defined us. The County team represented who we were and what we were about. At home, Marian washed the jerseys and then we got them ready for the next match. The whole thing made total sense to Michaela.

The day of her First Holy Communion, she went straight to a Minor game. Out of the dress and into a tracksuit: that was the way with her.

1993 was our breakthrough year with the Minors. That team were significant for me in the overall scheme of things. Our Ulster title really set me on my way as a manager.

Not much was expected from that group. Only a couple of players were still eligible from the previous year. To win Ulster with a whole new squad was a real coup. The players presented me with a team photograph, which they all signed, and I put it in the sitting room beside the television. And I am a bit of a hoarder: when something goes up in our house, it tends not to move. That frame still takes pride of place.

Playing in Croke Park for the first time was a bonus. But we got wiped out by a super Meath team. I realised then how much work was required to reach the next level.

Three years later, we went out in the first round to Fermanagh. From the outside, it looked like we were going backwards. I am forever grateful to the county board officials who stuck with me then. They were willing to look beyond the results because they appreciated the value of our approach. For them, it was about the process. I knew that we were creating better people and better footballers. And we had more to offer: decent players were coming through.

Mark made the cut in 1997. For Michaela, it was an even bigger deal. She kept scrapbooks that season whereas Mark was all business, keeping his football head on. He wanted to play; he wanted to win things.

Michaela looked up to Mark and '97 cemented their relationship. She was fiercely loyal to family and Mark being in the team made her feel even closer to that group. I think she saw herself as being part of the team. The players embraced her that way. And she was intelligent enough to know when to stay out of the way. Sometimes, especially around family, you have to keep to yourself. But, if someone in the stand had a pop at one of us during a Tyrone match, as inevitably happens, she would have to challenge them and challenge them right away. She had my temperament in that sense: 0 to 100 in no time and cool down just as quick. Michael was similar but Mark and Mattie were calmer. They were harder to wind up.

Mattie, our youngest, was also a regular at training come '97. While the older boys were busy with their own football by then, Mattie was caught up in the excitement of being around the team. Mattie and Michaela became a double act. Michaela took him under her wing, something she relished. For a young lad, Mattie always amazed me the way he took his lead from Michaela. Her word was Gospel.

And he was sharp. Naturally, as Michaela got closer in age to the players, some boys showed more than a passing interest. They saw that Mattie could be their ticket to Michaela. But he had them clocked.

'Do you think I'm stupid?' he said one day.

'Wha'?' this boy replied.

Mattie says: 'I know exactly why you're over here.'

'No. No. Wise up. Wise up.'

One of the other players came over to him then.

'You're not so slow,' he said.

Mattie might have been four years younger than Michaela but he was already tuned into the bigger picture. And his sister played a huge part in that regard.

At home, they were often in cahoots. Mark and Michael, being older than her, were out of reach for Michaela. I guess she saw that Mattie could be put to good use at times! They were fierce close. And because of that relationship, Mattie was not your typical young fella. He became, in his own words, her guinea pig. But she taught him lots of valuable things, the kind of things you can only learn from an older sister. As Mattie often says now to young fellas he teaches: 'If you have an older sister, make use of her. She's a great resource.'

Michaela guided him when he started going out with girls. She used to draft text messages for him to send and then interpret the responses for him. And Michaela was well fit to advise. She might tell him: 'Here's what she's trying to say. Here's what you're trying to say back.'

Inevitably, there was a price to pay for that kind of insight. Mattie got lumbered with all sorts of jobs. If Michaela was getting ready for a night, Mattie would have to help tan her back and straighten her hair. She even had him doing French tips for her fingernails. But what he gained from her was invaluable. Michaela instilled in him the kind of values any parent would want for their children.

Respect was a huge thing for Michaela. She warned Mattie: 'Just because your friends are doing things, don't you do it. And don't kiss two girls in the one night. That's not cool. It doesn't reflect well on you.'

She had this phrase: 'Value your kisses.' Michaela believed that you should only kiss someone you really like. She used to say to Mattie: 'Don't give your kisses away for nothing. If you like somebody, like them. Don't be chasing after somebody else. What if they find out and then you lose them?'

• • •

As a player, winning was everything to me. Always, victory was the driving force, all my efforts focused in one direction. I never deviated in terms of ambition. And

I carried that mentality into management. If anything, I became even more competitive. My mindset hardened. I took the view: 'If I'm one of the boys on the team, I want to win.'

I was motivated to win for others as much as for myself. Being manager intensified my attitude because I had more at stake. Entertaining people is important but not at the expense of results. I never wanted to be like Kevin Keegan when he was Newcastle United manager: play attractive football to please the crowd and let Manchester United win the League.

Progress is fine but you need something tangible. The world at large gives little credit to those who make things better. People remember titles and trophies affirm progress. How else do we recognise success? Each trophy has inherent value.

Coaching was an obvious progression for me, especially when I started teaching. I thought about the game all the time, talked about it constantly. All those conversations in the kitchen with my brothers informed my outlook. I thought deeply about football and developed clear views on how it should be played. My own playing experience was a factor as well: I struggled to progress at inter-county level because football favoured bigger and stronger men. Few people talked about tactics. And a lot of the training that teams did was quite basic as a result.

I saw coaching as an extension of teaching. I liked helping students develop, in every sense. As footballers, I wanted them to recognise their talent, realise their potential. Sport is about creating a sense of community and a sense of cooperation. Together, then, we become interdependent.

I count myself lucky to have had Jim McKeever as one of my lecturers. He was a big name in the GAA world from his exploits with Derry in the 1950s. And he had a lovely way about him. He managed our college team. Jim made you a better player: he was big into developing your skillset. Effectively, he was coaching us how to coach others. And I quickly discovered how much I loved helping others improve.

Like him, I wanted footballers first and foremost: players who could use both sides of their body. From the get-go, I had my own vision for the game. Mastering basic skills was essential. The players heard the same mantras from me all the time at training: 'Attack the ball'; 'First touch'; 'Get the ball moving'.

My first teaching post in Kircubbin, much of my time was spent in the classroom. But my circumstances changed when I moved to St Ciaran's, Ballygawley in 1982. Half my time was taken up running a youth club. PE took up the rest of my working week. At that stage, I was 28 and still playing at the top level. Moving to St Ciaran's gave me another outlet. I took charge of the school teams there, which was the first serious coaching that I did.

Everything had to be done with purpose. We spent less time on the pitch but every session was intense. As much as possible, I wanted our training to resemble matches: high tempo, playing under pressure. Back then, you regularly heard of teams training for two and three hours at a time. I could never understand that approach. If you play for 60 or 70 minutes then you should train for that length of time.

Most of all, I wanted to get away from the traditional style of football. My own playing experiences showed me how limited catch and kick was. You were expected to fight for possession in the air every time. My idea was different: I preferred to see sympathetic ball played into spaces where forwards could exploit defenders with their speed. I had seen how effective that approach could be when I played for the club: my teammates realised that if they put in a decent supply, I would win it ahead of the full back. Then I could get scores or set up chances for other players running off my shoulder.

Drills we ran with those early underage teams I no longer use, but my fundamental belief has not changed. Our game is played with a ball on a football field. So, most of your time should be spent working in that environment. Running through forests or hiking up hills never held much appeal. I might take a team to the sand dunes on occasion but those sessions serve a different purpose: they help to build mental toughness.

To me, positions were not the most important thing. You needed a certain amount of flexibility, an ability to defend and to attack. The team ethic was another key component: play for each other, not for yourself. Everyone had to take responsibility for winning back the ball. We defended and attacked together.

I think innocent is the best word to describe football in the late '80s and early '90s. The opposition allowed you to play how you wanted. There was no talk of systems; the game was more fluid. Teams were less inclined to try and stifle their opponents.

Even then, in my early years as a coach, I used video. St Ciaran's had a camera and I did a short course on how to film, learning the basics: how to frame shots, where to position the camera, best use of light. I filmed lots of shows and presentations in the school over the years. But the camera was far more valuable to me when it came to football. To get any football on film was a gift when I started coaching. I remember using two cassette players to copy and record matches.

I videoed matches and training sessions, then pored over the footage. Even a well-trained eye can only see so much in real time. You learn a multitude watching back.

Coaches have often asked me for advice over the years. Invariably they would ask: 'Can you give me one tip I could take away with me on my coaching journey?'

My answer is always the same: 'Video your games. No way you can spot and fix if you aren't videoing your games. That's your way of learning.'

Video remains integral to the way that I coach today. The process is much easier now: I can do it all on my laptop after a match. Given the way that the modern game has gone, with intense focus on strategic play, this kind of analysis is more important than ever.

Nowadays, quality footage is essential. Tripod cameras that you often see behind the goal provide the best shots. The broadcasters, especially TG4, are good at making tapes available and Brian Carthy was always a great help in that regard. This work was made easier thanks to the expertise of Eamon McGirr and Pete Quinlivan. Sometimes, you have to rely on other teams, especially for Qualifier games against sides from lower divisions and different provinces. The work can be frustrating: some people should never be let behind a camera.

Every day, the week of a Championship game, I spend most of Monday reviewing our last performance. No doubt some managers delegate this work but I like doing it. Given the level of analysis in the current game, I imagine Dublin gain an edge because they have the resources to monitor more teams. And they probably get through their analysis work quicker as a result.

To review one half of football can take a few hours. You need to be clear-sighted about it, take a forensic approach. The work is mentally draining. After an hour, I need a break to clear my head. You lose focus if you do too much all at once. At home, I camp out in the sitting room, a pillow on my knee to cushion the laptop.

Each game, broken down, becomes a series of plays. First you have the throw in. Then the first attack, the first shot. On it goes in this manner, a new play each time possession changes hands or the game restarts. During the review, I create clips that I want to show to the players. I tag those clips using keywords that become unique terms for the team. We create our own language within the group. So a term like 'structured attack' describes a formation that our players know instinctively. The tags are like an index. That way, all the kickouts can be grouped together or subdivided into short, medium or long.

I make notes as I work through the film. Every game that we play, there must be something to learn afterwards. I want the players to see what they did well and compliment them accordingly. If they can see the link between what we practise and how we perform, then our message becomes more powerful. Video has greater impact because the footage speaks for itself.

The most valuable view of the game comes from behind the goal. That angle allows us to see how the play developed: what move, what vision made it happen; who worked hard; who won the ball back. Patch together as many good passages as you can.

I want to find the pieces of play that shape the move. Then I can explain to the players why it happened: 'because you put in that tackle; you had somebody supporting; you played with your head up; you made the right run; you delivered the ball correctly.'

Because, because, because...

Then we look at a move that broke down. Without that camera behind the goal, we might not know the reason why. There are two ways of approaching this kind of work with the players. I can show them the play in real time, tease out the situation, ask them what happened: 'Where do you think that goal started?'

Sometimes the players see things I fail to pick up. In that way, it becomes an interactive process. Together we develop solutions.

But I can be direct as well.

To go through one passage of play might take five minutes. First, we look at it in slow motion. I stop the recording at certain stages to show the setting on the field: 'That's why your man got that room. You're watching the play. He's looking for an opportunity. You switched off.'

Reviewing games is an endless process. Something comes up every minute. Watch 20 minutes and you could easily find 20 things to discuss. The most difficult part of this process is deciding what to leave out. Everything seems important. So you have to group them and pick the best passages. That way you can show trends in the play. Condensing the game takes a lot of time. I suppose you could compare it to teaching. The work is tedious but I want to bring back something to the players to let them know that I have watched the game closely. You keep them on their toes that way.

The best clips I can show reinforce what we have been doing on the training field. The players need to see that their training relates to what is happening in games.

But you can overload the players with information. I definitely did too much analysis at times in the past. I do very little work on the morning of a match nowadays, just two or three clips. Most of the work is done the day before to let the players reflect on it overnight. Then we can just talk it through before the game. You learn as you go.

Communication is another fundamental aspect. Our WhatsApp group makes it a lot easier. Years ago, I had to make 30 phone calls if our training plans changed. I rang house numbers not knowing if anyone was home. Nowadays, I can deliver a message instantly.

I sometimes send around quotations, valuable sayings that I come across: 'You may fool the whole world down the pathway of years / And get pats on the back as you pass / But your final reward will be heartache and tears / If you've cheated the man in the glass.'

Meetings are tightly run affairs, just like training. They last no more than 45 minutes. Players make huge commitments and I want to show my appreciation by making the most of their time. I am conscious not to keep people too long.

If training starts at 7.30pm, the players are finished at 8.45pm. Every minute counts. I believe you should train for the same amount of time that you play, somewhere between 75 and 85 minutes. As long as everything is done in a quickfire fashion, the training is enjoyable because the session seems to be over in a flash.

The players arrive from 6.45pm, in plenty of time. Training should not feel like an imposition. To say that players are slaves to a system is untrue.

My basic philosophy is simple: when we lose possession, everybody has responsibility for winning it back. Why stand idle? That was how I first set out with the County Minors.

The sweeper was the other major element I worked on. My thinking stemmed from watching Dublin's Bobby Doyle play as a third midfielder in the 1970s. Doyle dropped out from corner forward, which left his marker with a dilemma: stay in the corner or follow Doyle? Generally the forward was more comfortable venturing out. So that move was a win–win for Dublin.

Coaches had to figure out what to do with the spare defender. A sweeper could play in front of the full back line, cutting out ball into the two inside forwards. That was the beginning of strategic play in football.

Perhaps the biggest challenge for any coach is finding a new way to say the same thing. First principles will always govern the game. But, no matter how many times you mention them, you have to remind players. They forget.

I was never really inclined to roar and shout in a dressing room: that approach gets old very quickly. But I always spoke with total conviction. Every game, we were going to war.

Energy was a massive thing for me. If someone has a bad attitude, they can be a drain on the group. I worked hard on building a sense of togetherness, everyone loyal to the cause. Always, I focused on what each player could bring to the game. That way, you build energy. And you could sense it in the dressing room before games. Winning, then, becomes a natural by-product. With every win, the players grow closer, the group become stronger.

Of all the great days I enjoyed coaching those school teams in St Ciaran's, one game stands out. We were playing St Paul's of Bessbrook, an Ulster Under-14 clash. At full time, we were level. Then they blitzed us in the first period of extra time, scoring 2-1 without reply. What do you say at that point? However bad things are you have to give the players something useful. Frame the situation in a way that makes them feel like they have some control. As the manager, I need to be calm in those moments: think clearly, speak rationally.

I could see a way back for us. And I laid it out for the players in the simplest terms possible: 'If they can get 2-1 in 10 minutes, nothing to stop us scoring 2-2.'

We won by a point. That result still gives me huge satisfaction. I felt my input, at that crucial stage, made a difference. Years later, I enjoyed a similar feeling, only the stakes were much bigger. 2005, we went the long way round with Tyrone. We met Dublin in the Quarter-Finals at Croke Park.

The Dubs got off to a flyer. For most of the first half, we managed to stay on to their coattails. Then Tomás Quinn got a goal to put them five ahead, 1-9 to 0-7.

Tony Donnelly, who was a selector that day, said to me: 'Best thing that could have happened. Now the boys are going to have to listen.'

If we went in 9-7 behind, the boys might not have fully understood the urgency of the situation. We made that many switches at half time, Tony decided to call out the new team, from one to 15. I remember Ricey, Ryan McMenamin, went out to the half-back line and we brought on Joe McMahon to curb Ciarán Whelan at midfield.

'Six balls Whelan has won,' Tony reminded them. 'He's feeding that crowd. This is the time the oxygen stops. No more big snatches.'

We heard afterwards that Philly Jordan thought he had been replaced. Sean Cavanagh corrected him: 'No, you're corner back.'

Then Philly said: 'I don't know which is worse.'

We turned the game. Our decisions at half time were key. From a management point of view, I felt we influenced the result that day. That was satisfying. On any given day, you want to feel you made a difference.

An odd day, I resort to the hairdryer. Take 2020, my final year with Tyrone. Galway hammered us in the League, 2-25 to 0-12, the worst result of my career.

The Galway result came from nowhere. Really, it was an accumulation of events that went against us. Kieran McGeary was sent off, a harsh decision I thought. We got the deficit back from seven to three and then Cathal McShane went down in agony, a shocking injury and a huge psychological blow. The game suddenly seemed immaterial. Still, our collapse was hard to watch. Our performance was lethargic. Some bemoaned our warm up, as if that was a factor. I found that one hard to credit.

But no two games are the same. You have to sense what the situation demands. And timing is everything. My first League campaign in 2003, we played Donegal in the fourth game. Our first-half performance was dreadful. Even the supporters were fed up. One boy had a pop before the start of the second half: 'You know, Mickey Harte, I think that's the worst Tyrone performance that I've ever seen.'

I could only agree.

'You're probably right,' I said to him. Little did he know that I went berserk in the dressing room at half time.

The players had never seen that side of me before. But I felt I had no choice. Another defeat at that stage – we had already lost two – would have put us out of the running for the League. We rallied in the second half, winning comfortably (1-14 to 0-10), and won our next five, including the Semi-Final and Final, to retain the Division 1 title. Would Sam Maguire have come our way without that success? I have my doubts.

When I reflect on my time in football, I know that management gives me the biggest kick, way more than anything I did as a player. I love seeing players blossom, doing things nobody expected. No particular element makes a County player and I would never dismiss someone because he lacks one thing or another. You need a certain set of basic skills, but each player possesses a different skillset. You have to look behind the player, imagine what he might become.

People within Tyrone doubted Colm Cavanagh for a long time, but I felt there were certain aspects of his game that could make him very effective. He was a no-frills kind of player, big and strong and mobile. We created a role for him and he added value to his game, becoming far more than a ball winner. Colm grew in confidence playing as our sweeper to the point where he was among the best in the game two years running. Individual awards are always dependent on a team effort, but there is something special about a player who wins an All Star in a year that his team are not All Ireland champions. To see Tyrone players make that mark in recent years has given me great satisfaction. Stephen O'Neill (2009), Philip Jordan (2010) and Seán Cavanagh (2013) were multiple winners. Then came Mattie Donnelly in 2015, our first new All Star since we last won Sam Maguire in 2008. Petey Harte made the team alongside

Mattie the following year. Colm Cavanagh got his due in 2017. He was rightly honoured again in 2018 along with Pádraig Hampsey.

Ronan McNamee and Cathal McShane making the All Stars in 2019 was another thrill. Ronan made his debut against Kerry in 2012, the Galatasaray game as we called it. I was chancing my arm putting him on Paul Galvin that day in Killarney. Ronan had a rough baptism: Galvin was too cute for him. But there he was, seven years later, the best full back in Ireland. And he came through really tough personal circumstances to reach that level. He might easily have slipped away from football.

Cathal, at Minor level, struggled to hold down his place. Even with the Under-21s, when they won the All Ireland in 2015, he had to prove himself. We had to be patient when he came into the Senior setup: it took time for him to develop as a full forward at that level. Mistakes never got to him, which was the thing that always stood out with Cathal. For any player, that kind of temperament is a major asset. Ronan and Cathal are two guys who fought their way to the top, something I always admire in people.

• • •

One win leads to the next. So you play to win every game: nothing less will do. People often wondered why I stayed clear of challenge matches: I never felt the team got enough out of them. Remove that competitive element and you risk losing an edge.

Simply put, preparation for an All Ireland starts the first

day of the McKenna Cup. You build from there, taking each game as it comes. With that approach, the jump from one stage to the next never seems insurmountable.

How many boys dominate at underage level but struggle as they get older? Too many coaches neglect those players. At 14, you might be able to overpower other lads because they have yet to develop physically. But, when they catch up, your shortcomings get exposed. And, at 18, it might be too late to develop the skills that you really need.

I was always conscious to strive to make every player better, regardless of his initial ability. Cormac McAnallen is a great example of someone who came from a relatively low base. I remember coaching at an Easter camp in Eglish, Cormac's club. They had a decent Under-16 team at the time. Cormac was a strong, determined fella but far from the lean athlete he became. Of those Under-16s, there would have been four or five players ahead of him. I always marvelled at the fact that he came through the ranks and passed them all. He was 17 when I next saw him at a trial for the Minors. By that stage, he was good enough to make the starting 15. The following year, he played midfield and captained the team. Even then, he had a thirst for knowledge. I could tell from the way he listened, from his body language too. He was grasping for information.

Cormac embodied everything I wanted in a footballer. Really, he was the dream player for any manager. He drove boys on the pitch. His actions said everything, though his words were important too. One year, playing in the Hastings Cup – an Under-21 pre-season tournament – he took the players to task. We were poor in the first half and he let rip during the break.

'Are we champs or chumps?' he said. Calling the players to order was a manly thing to do. And typical of Cormac.

Like many others, he came of age with the '98 Minors. Everything came together that season and yet I almost walked away the previous year.

1997 was a huge year for all of us. Mark made the cut, which added to the buzz about the Minors in our house. I think a lot of people in the county could see the potential within that group to do something special. We had serious talent all over the field: Ciaran Gourley and Cormac McAnallen in defence, Kevin Hughes at midfield, Brian McGuigan up front. Stephen O'Neill was just beginning to blossom. After the disappointment of 1996, that loss to Fermanagh in the first round, it felt like things were coming together.

While results had been so-so prior to that season, I knew we were moving in the right direction. Our setup was improving all the time. And there was more to come.

We beat Down in Clones at the start of that campaign. For Mark, just to get playing in Clones was a kind of dream come true. To win, even bigger again. Then he had his first Championship game in Omagh, another landmark. Each match, at that age, is the biggest match of all time. And here he was playing for Tyrone in Healy Park, an Ulster Quarter-Final against Armagh, his first time into that cauldron: no back door and everything at stake.

That day, June 15, was a seminal moment in all our lives. So much has happened since, it can be hard to convey just how much our world changed from that point on. Everybody's experience of grief is different and you can never know how it will impact on someone. Death is part of the life cycle and, in the normal course of events, you get a chance to come to terms with it beforehand. We grow up thinking that death is what happens at the end of a life. Even then, your perspective changes. But a sudden death, especially one that seems to cut against nature, alters everything. And it can take years for you to process that kind of grief. A young person is less equipped to deal with the trauma.

We went out to play a game of football and came home without one of our players. Even now, I find it hard to contemplate. The scenes from that day will always be vivid.

I can still see the ball going into the corner. Richie Thornton had possession and played it across the middle. Paul McGirr came in to meet the pass, diving at the ball and punching it home, a vital score. But he got an accidental bang in the process, the full force of the Armagh goalkeeper. I went out to him: he must have been down for five minutes. You could see the pain in his face as we stretchered him off.

At the time, I thought he might have broken his ribs. The bigger concern was how long it would take him to recover. I was saying to myself: 'We'll not have him for the next round.'

Obviously, I knew his condition was more serious when

the medics took him to the hospital but we still had a game to win. And, as it turned out, we held on by four points. Paul's goal was pivotal.

I figured we would hear the full story on Paul later in the evening. So we stayed on for the Senior game. Afterwards, we went for food in Molly Sweeney's, not far from Healy Park.

Because we were playing at home, there was no team bus. And this was in the day when very few people had mobile phones. Francie Goulding, who drove the players from North Tyrone, met me when I went around to the hospital. I think the words he said were: 'Paul's gone.'

I went numb.

Next thing, I was walking upstairs and into the room where Paul had been laid out. His parents, Francis and Rita, were there by his bedside. Paul was still wearing his Tyrone gear, a boy in his favourite football jersey. The shock of that scene was too much to take in. I was hardly able to speak. What do you even say?

The rest of that evening is blurry. We were sitting around at home – Marian, myself and the children – not knowing what to do. We watched *The Sunday Game*. Meath and Dublin in the Leinster Championship was the big game and the Dubs had been beaten. Paul Bealin missed a penalty for Dublin and the panel were reflecting on the outcome. Whoever was analysing made the comment: 'This may have been a big loss but it's nothing compared to what happened in Tyrone today.'

Then the programme closed with a photograph of Paul on the screen. And, in that moment, you realise just how fragile life can be. What should have been one of the happiest days of Paul's young life turned out to be his last.

We set out that day on a mission to beat Armagh, to win an Ulster Championship match. Football, this game that bound us together, suddenly seemed irrelevant. What did it matter, what did anything matter if a young man could be taken away from us in such a cruel manner?

We all lose sight of the most important things from time to time. Football was our great escape in Tyrone: a hobby, a passion, an obsession. You strive and strive and strive, driven every step of the way by the thought of success. Along that journey, everything else fades from view. We become so focused on one thing that we almost have no space leftover for any other thing in our lives. How could we even begin to make sense of what happened? How could we recalibrate our senses?

However shocking Paul's death was for me, the players suffered an even greater blow. Teenagers, especially boys, have that feeling of invincibility. But, for that group, it was gone in a heartbeat. What happened to Paul shattered their view of life. To this day, I think those boys have been affected in ways that they still might not fully appreciate.

Coming to terms with what happened was complicated for me. We needed to figure out a way forward for the team. And, as their manager, I had responsibility for the players. But I also experienced that day as a father: my son played in that game. Paul played in the half-forward line, wearing 12. Mark lined out in the number 13 jersey. He could have been the one diving for that ball.

Mark had a good relationship with Paul. They knew each other from the club at home; they were friends growing up. The McGirrs lived in Garvaghey originally and Paul played with Errigal up to Under-12 when the family moved to Dromore.

Himself and Mark clicked. Paul was instantly likeable, a wee glint in the eye, always up for the craic. They were different on the pitch: Paul was bigger and stronger, a good ball winner and well able to cover ground. Mark was more of a finisher.

Mark was close to the action when the goal went in against Armagh. He heard Paul struggling on the ground. Paul kept saying: 'I can't breathe.'

But, like the rest of us, Mark had no idea the situation was so serious. He thought Paul might have been winded. Most young players experience that sensation at some stage, a bang that takes your breath.

Naturally, everyone was in good form after the game. The boys arranged to meet in Cookstown that night to celebrate the win. While the Dromore lads called around to the hospital to check on Paul, everyone else headed off. Mark had driven to the game with Stephen Donnelly and Cormac McGinley. He was dropping them home when they met Johnny McGirr, a big football man from Errigal.

Mark pulled up and let down his window: 'Well, Johnny, what about the match today?'

'It's wild about Paul,' he replied. Normally Johnny is all positive about football.

Mark said: 'Aye, I know. He seemed in a lot of pain.'

Then Johnny broke the news: 'Paul's dead.'

The boys just sat and looked at each other.

Mark managed to drive as far as Stevie's house. Cuthbert, his father, was a major figure in Tyrone GAA. They assumed that he would know for sure. Mary, his wife, answered the door. She had heard the news. Then Cuthbert landed home with the full story. He brought the boys down to Omagh Hospital. Most of the players were outside, crying in their cars.

I was already inside when the boys came up to the room. Mickey, Paul's brother, was standing there, his hand against the wall. I remember Mark staring at me in disbelief. And then he looked at Paul laid out on the bed, still wearing his jersey, shorts and socks.

No teenager can prepare himself for that scene. Mark's only previous experience of death was within the family. Mummy died in 1996, the same year we lost Marian's aunt Velva. And there was Daddy's funeral in 1990. My father walked to his death. He was coming from the shop, carrying a box of groceries, when he took ill at the side of the road. At that time, 79 looked like a big age. And he was perfectly well before he died. While his loss shocked us at the time, on reflection it was a kind way to go. Daddy breathed his last walking back home.

Paul was only getting started in life. His death made the world seem fickle: the players saw that a life could be extinguished in a heartbeat. You grow up quickly after that kind of experience. I think the hardest thing for most people, in the aftermath of tragedy, is the knowledge that the rest of the world goes on.

And, for us, football went on. The team had to pick up the pieces for the next game against Monaghan. The support of the McGirr family was crucial for us during that period. From them, the players came to understand the need to carry on. Football could never be the same afterwards but nobody lost sight of its significance either. The game brought us together in the first place. Now it could help us to move forward because we had created something bigger than ourselves.

As a coach, I am always conscious of what lies behind the player: the life he leads, the family he comes from. You need an idea of someone's background to really know what makes him tick. Because we are all unique. Those things that set us apart can be harnessed for the benefit of all. Creating teams, then, is about learning to appreciate the difference in people.

Life is about celebrating that difference, building relationships, developing lasting connections. Paul's death was another reminder that the journey is more important than the destination. Whatever way you travel with people, you want them to have good memories. A team, something bigger than yourself, is a wonderful place to be.

● ● ●

The death of Paul McGirr cast a long shadow. I felt his loss more acutely because Mark played with him in '97.

How the players responded was remarkable. Something came over that team in the aftermath: they bonded really quickly in a very intense way. The bond that they developed with each other could only have come about because of what happened. Suddenly these young men began to fully appreciate each other. And it seemed to happen organically.

The game following Paul's death, against Monaghan, the boys agreed among themselves that they would walk out on to the pitch, their way of paying respect. Our captain, Declan McCrossan, took the lead with the rest of the team following behind in single file, all wearing black armbands. I thought they showed remarkable maturity for lads that age, making such a dignified tribute. The significance of their gesture was unmistakable.

We had already decided to retire Paul's jersey for the year but, that day, the players took charge, a quality inherent in all good sides. There are moments in the lifespan of every team when the players do something exceptional, something that sets them apart. Our season took on a life of its own after that game.

We met Antrim in the Ulster Final and I told each player to bring his club jersey. We tied all the jerseys together using the sleeves, creating this circular shape.

'This is what we're about,' I said. 'This is you: your place, your club, your family. This is the collective. We're in this together.'

1997 was a huge year for all of us because it was about so much more than football. We tend to let sport become a life and death issue. You never want to diminish someone's passion for the game because, at certain moments, it is the biggest thing in their life. But there are more important things. Paul McGirr's death might have been the first time that fact was brought home to many of us.

There were larger forces at play throughout that Championship. Still, you have to be careful with emotions. Yes, we had a cause, but it can become too much if you lean too heavily on that cause. Nobody knows what lies ahead.

Kerry stood between us and an All Ireland Final, a mountain in every sense. We were pushed to the limit just to stay with them in the first game. Mark kicked the leveller with time almost up. Maybe there was a growing sense of destiny at that stage but we had no time for those thoughts. Six days later, Kevin Hughes suffered a devastating blow. His brother Paul was killed in a car crash travelling to watch a game in Eglish.

At home, a magnet on our fridge door reads: 'Life is fragile, handle with prayer.'

That saying comes to mind whenever I think back on those moments. Those teenage summers playing football should be your brightest days, everything fresh and exciting and vibrant. Yet Kevin spent those months coming to terms with tragedy. He watched a teammate lose his life on the pitch and then buried his brother just days before an All Ireland Semi-Final.

Football hardly mattered at that point. Then again, what is life without the things we love? Instinct is often our best guide in difficult times and the game became a focus for Kevin through that period. But it was always his decision whether to play. We paired him with Cormac at midfield and he produced one of the finest displays ever seen, given the circumstances. Again, the match went to extra time but we managed to slip ahead. Fittingly, Kevin emerged with the ball when Kerry launched their final attack. We won with two points to spare, 0-23 to 0-21. Our name was on the Tom Markham Cup, it seemed.

But life, as we knew by then, does not always turn into expectation. Laois, reigning champions, completed a double and our All Ireland quest, which had become this epic journey, ended on a downbeat note.

I thought that was it for me with the Minors. 25 years after playing and losing an All Ireland Final, I had managed and lost. We went through so much in '97, I felt my time was up. Usually, defeats strengthen my resolve. But that season was like nothing I had been through before.

The players encouraged me to carry on. A lot of them were still eligible the following year and, when you come so close, all you want is another chance. Michaela played her part as well. She was convinced that we would go all in the way in '98, so much so that she wrote out this list of predictions:

1. WE WILL: *Win the All-Ireland Final in 1998 (minors)*
2. WE WILL: *Win the All-Ireland Final in 2000 (U21s)*
3. WE WILL: *Win the All-Ireland Final in 2003 (seniors)*
2&3 with special 1997 team

Their encouragement lifted my spirits. I was never short on resilience but the manager, no more than any player, needs to bring a lot of energy. And I needed to be sure that I had enough energy to go again. Within a couple of days, I found myself looking ahead.

NOON

I love the spontaneity of my life now, how the days unfold. Beyond my hour in the chapel each morning, I have no set routine. The day could take me anywhere: a match, a visit, a talk.

My world is still full of the things that have meaning for me but I feel like I have more time to appreciate everything now. Contentment is my overriding feeling. To me, pleasure is something that you consume. And it ends. Contentment is a state of being, nothing to do with material gain, something that lasts. I think of it as a form of constant happiness, a peace the world cannot give, the kind of feeling I had with Michaela.

Michaela and me were great buds: we hated to be on bad terms with each other. Only something trivial ever caused us to fall out. And we were always quick to make up.

The boys often gave me stick because Michaela could do no wrong in my eyes. And I cannot pretend otherwise. She definitely got away with more. Mattie reckons she was a Daddy fan more than a Tyrone fan. I think every father–daughter relationship is special; Michaela being the only girl pushed us closer. We had similar personalities and were thick as thieves in many ways. I can understand when Mattie says he felt jealous at times when he was younger.

Michaela spent so much of her time around boys – at home and at football – that she felt comfortable around them. She was probably far happier with a gang of lads. Rivalries can develop among girls and then you get fallouts. Now, Michaela was well fit to get stuck in when there was some giving out to be done. But she preferred to keep things simple and direct.

I always considered her a charming person. She was very respectful, especially towards older people. That side of her personality stood out from a young age. She adored her grandparents, loved their wisdom.

And her level of self-awareness was always apparent. You could see how younger cousins loved being around her. They looked up to her. Of course, she would be all over them, making a big fuss.

My first image of Michaela still brings a smile to my face. People are naturally attracted to wee ones and here she was, our very own beautiful girl: brown eyed, black haired.

Becoming a parent requires you to be selfless. Life is not all about yourself anymore: your children become your world. For someone like me, who was used to doing his own thing, adapting to fatherhood was hard at times. I was a serious sleeper before the children arrived. Marian had to climb over me to switch off the alarm.

A baby decides when it needs to be fed. For mothers, the maternal instinct kicks in but the father has the same duty. Children are a gift and a responsibility. To be fair, we were good at sharing the load: I did their feeds, changed nappies. I might have felt tired in the mornings but children radiate energy. Once I picked them up, I was into a new world. You feel invigorated; you find new resolve. And we would always have a bit of fun. Children make you feel young again.

I think family life is harder nowadays: the pressures on parents have grown bigger. And I think you become fearful of pushing children away then. So you tend to appease them most of the time. Children need to be treated with respect but you must also demand that they do the right thing. We should be brave enough to challenge them. The most important thing is to work from the right place, a loving place.

I was a young dad by today's standards, still in my early 20s, still playing football. So, I was fit for games with the children, kicking ball with the boys in the garden. Michaela wanted to be part of the action when she saw the boys playing, though she had a short-lived career. She broke her finger at a school game one day and that ended all interest. Okay, in her eyes, to play for fun, but not at the expense of getting hurt.

Michaela was more like Mark. They both enjoyed older company and were great talkers. Michael was always the quiet one, though it would have been hard to get a word in anyway. Just over a year separated him and Michaela: he was born in October 1982, three years after

Mark, and Michaela arrived in December '83. Mattie – like me, the baby – came along five years later.

Mark, being the first born, spent a lot of time around adults: he was constantly picking up new words. And he knew every hit in the charts. I always had the radio on going to school. Before the second beat, he could name each song. Before long, he had me copped as well. I was like a demon if we got stuck behind a bus or a lorry. Slow drivers drove me spare. The children regularly heard me giving out: 'You'd be better off walking a dog than driving that car.'

Things got so bad, Mark started mocking me. He could preempt what I was going to say: 'Let me guess, another Sunday afternoon driver.'

Marian often kept me in check too. She reckons I suffered from road rage before they invented the term. Now, at least, I can laugh at myself.

With Michaela in the car, there was never an idle moment. She loved conversation; she wanted to engage with everyone she met. Michael, only two years older, was different: quiet and reserved. You could easily forget he was there.

And yet they were alike, very much their own people. The fact that they were close in age made for plenty of conflict. Michael wanted his own space, particularly at school, and at times he felt cramped. Michaela was in the year behind him at St Malachy's, which meant that they were usually in the same classroom. So, Michaela knew everything – not that Michael was ever in trouble, just the normal stuff that boys get up to, wrecking about in a classroom. Naturally he wanted that information to stay in school but Michaela would often spill the beans. And, if his friends were in the house, there was always a chance that Michaela might land in on top of them. She was on his coattails the whole time. And Michael was at an age where he would have gotten annoyed if she became friendly with his friends.

Marian and I were out one night when the two of them nearly came to blows. Michael's GCSE Maths exam was scheduled for the following day but Michaela had gotten hold of the text book. Michaela was adamant that she needed it to study for a class test. Michael went spare, as you might expect. Then she locked herself inside her room. Next thing, he put his foot through the door. At that stage, there was only one solution that he could see. No doubt I would have been tempted to do the same thing!

Mattie reckons she got a kick from those things. I suppose we all know the right buttons to press with our siblings and, for teenagers, that kind of stuff is far from unusual.

Generally, girls develop quicker than boys. Even allowing for nature, Michaela was razor sharp. She was ultra-organised, diligent about everything, nearly always a step ahead.

She went to a music festival one year and, however she managed it, herself and a friend booked a bed and breakfast beside the venue. Everybody else camped, slogging through muddy fields for the weekend. Not Michaela. She came in for the concert and then went back to the B&B for a shower and a hot meal. Back in, then, the next morning.

Marian's car was a constant source of dispute once the children were old enough to drive. Of course, Michaela would have the car booked weeks in advance but she might not say it to the boys. She knew how to scupper their plans, which I think is funny, looking back.

Those were trivial things, really. What mattered most to Michaela was the kind of person she wanted to be. Even as a teenager, she was not prepared to compromise her principles. I know popularity is important for youngsters: you want to be liked by your peers. To hold fervent beliefs is difficult for a teenager. Along the way, she would have picked up a few enemies because of her strong-minded nature. She was fit to report on other girls if they got involved in the drinking culture. At school, she touted on girls who brought vodka into class one time. Michaela had no time for that type of behaviour; she would have been disgusted.

Some girls felt that Michaela was not one of the gang. And that atmosphere can lead to problems. We were aware of some bullying behaviour directed at her, taunts and gestures, but nothing extreme. Mostly, those incidents just irritated her. And I think it was good for her that she felt able to talk to us at home. Those episodes could have been destructive otherwise. Her experiences certainly opened our eyes to the dangers that lurk for young people.

Michaela had her insecurities too, good days and bad. We all do. But life never got on top of her. She was happy in her own skin and there were no major dramas. I was never worried about Michaela's wellbeing. We were lucky that way.

At home, Michaela's personality was reflected in her friends. For her, friendship was about trust. So, the friends she kept were tried and tested. They were fiercely loyal and she reciprocated that loyalty: the same faces always appeared around the house.

Michaela had this infectious energy about her no matter where she went. She stood out. And she was comfortable being on stage. People within the GAA knew her from going to matches and then she was exposed to the wider public through the Rose of Tralee in 2004. Michaela was the Ulster Rose that year, so we all enjoyed a brilliant trip to Kerry for the annual festival.

Of course, Michaela had shortcomings: I would never make her out to be a saint. Like me, she was opinionated and could lose her temper. Some people she could never warm to – usually the same people I could never warm to. She took serious pride in her appearance and could be selfish at times. But anybody who says that they were never selfish in their time is probably not telling the truth.

The story of Mark's 25th birthday is a classic. She was going to miss the day because of college. So, before Mark ever set eyes on his cake, she had Marian cut out a square for her. That year, Mark ended up with this L-shaped cake.

• • •

Those early years with the children were busy and brilliant and precious. Only now, looking back, do I realise how much was going on. And football remained an essential part of our world, the training, the games, my tribulations with the club.

Who knows where life would have led had we resolved that dispute sooner? You could say that I missed out on some of the best years of my football career but look at the things that came our way afterwards. Errigal Ciarán won the Senior Championship in 1993 and went on to take the Ulster title as well.

And I had set sail with the County Minors. After all my travails with the county board, they appointed me manager in 1991. I had been a thorn in their side for the best part of a decade. Now they were putting their faith in me – 'a fox in charge of the hen house' as Tony Donnelly described it. Perhaps it was a peace offering on their part but I like to think that my show of resolve convinced others how much I had to offer.

That move into inter-county management was the beginning of an unbelievable voyage for myself and my family. For Michaela, it probably felt like destiny when the Senior job came my way. By 2002, two of her predictions had come true. But I gave no real thought to the role until that opportunity came up.

The timing was right. After those Minor and Under-21 titles, it was an obvious move. Again, I went in with one clear ambition: to win the All Ireland. Yet, for all the success that came our way, I rarely look back on those glory years. My recollections are hazy. Even the detail of certain games I struggle to remember. Ask me about an All Ireland Final from the 1960s and my memory is razor sharp. Maybe, as manager, you have to process too much information at the time to remember the specifics.

Others have to remind me about particular incidents. Some players believe that the biggest moment in 2003 came after the Quarter-Final win against Fermanagh at Croke Park. We played on the Sunday of the August Bank Holiday weekend and stayed over in Dublin. Kerry played Roscommon on the Monday and beat them convincingly. The game was over after 15 minutes but Kerry conceded a bag of scores. If Roscommon could get three goals, I felt we could prosper too.

The players were up to high doh after the Fermanagh game and then watched Kerry devastate Roscommon. Suddenly the prospect of meeting them in the Semi-Final seemed daunting.

Some players, faced with Kerry's flamboyance, begin to fear them. My job is to look at the opposition from a different perspective. I saw a vulnerability. The following night, my antidote was ready.

I set out exactly how we were going to beat them. I showed clips of all their previous goals and how they loved to litter the D. They did very little running with the ball. I told our defenders: 'This is your food and drink. They will have to find a different avenue. Can they find that avenue? We'll be hunting in packs. When they're heavy legged, we'll take them. These boys will not see this coming.'

After that session, I got the sense that the boys believed they were going to beat Kerry. We were on the same page from that night on.

Nobody envisaged what we did that day. Our

performance has been a major reference point ever since. Those first-half scenes of Kerry All Stars being ambushed by frenzied Tyrone men is an abiding image for most GAA people.

Tony Donnelly analysed our games from the stand that season. Nowadays, when we look back on that famous game, he frames our win against an image from the past.

1973, Tyrone beat Down to win Ulster and set up an All Ireland Semi against Cork. Reality hit hard when we reached Croke Park. The scoreboard, down at the Nally Stand, read: Corcaigh 0-07 Tir Eoghain 0-00.

'Would there ever be a team that hasn't scored in the first half of a match at Croke Park in an All Ireland Semi-Final?' Michael O'Hehir wondered on commentary.

We looked down at that scoreboard again, 40 years later, approaching half time: Tir Eoghain 0-06 Ciarrai 0-00.

Whatever was said against us, I found ways to use it in our favour. 2003, when we made that breakthrough, the media became another source of motivation. I would tell the players: 'They're only knocking us because we're winning matches.'

You can only push those buttons at certain times. For a player like Ryan McMenamim, spiky and aggressive, that kind of thing really fired him up. For underdogs, negative press is a powerful spur but you need something substantial to really stir the players. My approach to that first All Ireland against Armagh was straightforward: 'If you're good enough to be in a Final then you're good enough to win it.'

Armagh were renowned for size and strength. They had powerful men all over the field, a team who forced their opponents into submission. Before that game, I calculated the combined weight of each team. The difference came to four pounds per man. So, I got four pounds of sugar and passed them around among the players.

'That's how much more powerful and stronger they are than us,' I said. 'Would that scare you? Could you handle that? Would this prevent you from winning an All Ireland?'

I used all sorts of ways to motivate players. 'Losing is not an option' became one of our mantras. I wrote out the quotation and stuck it underneath each jersey. After the jerseys were handed out, I asked the players to lift them up. Then they would all read the mantra together.

Gavin Devlin could get very emotional, on the verge of tears. At times, I had to calm him down. Gavin had everything as a player apart from pace. We were on the same page in terms of how we thought about football. If something was going wrong, he would jog over to me during the game.

And he knew when to pick his moments. We had a team meeting the morning of the 2005 Final against Kerry. We went through everybody's role. Conor Gormley was detailed to mark Eoin Brosnan, to live with him.

Gavin came to me after the meeting. 'Mickey,' he said, 'that's not correct. That's exactly what they want.'

Gavin was spot on. Gormley staying with his man would have created gaps for Brosnan to run into behind him. Kerry could then exploit that space by playing ball over the top. Gormley holding his position meant that Brosnan met a rock whenever he reached the 45.

The annoying thing about that Final was Tony

Donnelly's suspension. Some officials love to find fault. Basically, if Tony spent too long talking to me on the sideline, he fell foul of the regulations. He got a one-match ban after the first Dublin game and missed the replay. He got another ban after the Semi-Final and, because it was a second offence, his suspension was doubled.

Tony's input was vital. Everybody can see the roasting but not many can see the solution. 'Do something, Harte' is what you usually hear from the crowd.

Tony and I are constantly talking during the game. We think out loud, talking through various scenarios, a constant dialogue. The easy option is to take a player off when things are not going well for him. That may not necessarily be the right move.

As long as you can, delay introducing new personnel. If you are good enough to make the first 15, you deserve the benefit of the doubt. Always worth trying a player in another position. Brian Dooher would have been the first man substituted in the 2008 Final if we were making changes based on errors in the early stages of the game. He must have fumbled four balls but you knew that there was more to come from him and that that was something he could overcome. A younger lad might lose his nerve in those circumstances.

We were two down against Armagh in the 2005 Semi-Final when they took off Kieran McGeeney. Their move allowed us to do something: we pushed Sean Cavanagh to wing forward because we needed more drive in attack. Positional switches are often more effective than substitutions.

Tony's personality was great for the group as well. Hub – Kevin Hughes – used to say to him: 'Tony, I always listened to your team talks because I knew there was going to be a joke somewhere and I didn't want to miss it.'

Tony said things that only he could get away with. Brian McGuigan suffered a serious eye injury in 2007. He could have lost his sight in one eye. His first night back at training, Brian was jogging onto the pitch when Tony started waving at him.

'Brian, Brian,' he shouted. 'We're over here.'

2008, we played Dublin in a monsoon at Croke Park. Tony gave Brian Dooher the final instructions: 'If you win the toss, play with the tide.' Tony could sense any tension. So he knew when to lighten the mood.

Ultimately, we share the same philosophy: add value to the players you have. Every player has a contribution to make. In the noughties, the Mickey McGees had as big a contribution to make as the Sean Cavanaghs and they had to feel that way. Football is a team game played by individuals and each individual needs to feel valued. And he must feel prepared. No player should ever think his manager is asking him to do something he is not capable of doing.

Most of the manager's work is done before throw in. So nerves were never a factor for me coming into those games. An All Ireland Final is a massive occasion but, to me, it was just the next hurdle. Every session and every match forms part of your preparation. By the time an All Ireland looms, no longer should it seem like a major leap.

Publicly, I played up certain elements. If others thought of us as the dogs of war, far be it from me to deter them.

We were much more than that perception. Our work rate set us apart but you have to keep the scoreboard ticking over. Some people were blinded to that side of our play by the sheer ferocity they witnessed. The negative public reaction worked to our advantage in that sense.

Within the camp, everyone knew their role. No job was unimportant. There was a time when our kit man, Mickey Moynagh, would have been the subject of practical jokes. I put a stop to that stuff because he deserved the same level of respect as everyone else. Small things mattered, which is why we always took such care with the jerseys: each one neatly folded and placed back in the bag. I insisted on good manners. If you played for Tyrone then you knew to say please and thank you.

A healthy environment, a culture in which people thrive, requires that kind of attention to detail. But these things seem less important when your best player is a major doubt for the biggest game of the year. Peter Canavan's fitness occupied most Tyrone minds in September of 2003. I met Tony Donnelly a few days before the Final to discuss our dilemma. 'Canavan on a quarter leg is better than most on two,' I told him.

We met in his house and it took him a few minutes to process my plan. Having Peter on the pitch for the start of the game was crucial for the rest of the players, psychologically as much as anything else. A lesser player might have been thrown by the thought of coming back on. But I knew that Peter had the mental strength to handle the situation. My biggest concern was keeping him warm during his time off the pitch.

So much of what happened at that time passed in a blur. Truth to tell, I find it hard to distinguish between our All Ireland wins. I might mistakenly associate an incident from 2005 with 2008 and vice versa.

Each individual perspective is different. Gavin Devlin fell into conversation with Michaela at a social event in The Moy, about a week after our first win in 2003.

'This is only the start of the journey,' she told him.

'What are you on about?' he asked her.

'Daddy's going to win five.'

'What?' says Gavin.

'Daddy's going to win five Sams.'

Gavin thought to himself: 'Come on, let me enjoy this.'

Michaela knew better than anyone how my mind worked.

Success only ever gave me contentment to a degree: I was happy because we had achieved a great thing. And I savoured those special nights. Football, like life, is really about how you make people feel. I saw what winning Sam Maguire did for the people of Tyrone. Everybody, from the age of 5 to 95, shares in it.

What saddens me most, when I think about that time, is the thought of what would have become of Cormac McAnallen. He was a pivotal player on those All Ireland winning teams at Minor, Under-21 and Senior level. Yet, for all that success, he was only getting started. At 24, so much lay ahead of him. His premature death in March 2004 means we can only imagine how he would have grown. Cormac stood out, even among an exceptional group. With Cormac, the players would have been even more focused. I made him captain at 23 for that very reason. He set standards and kept others in check. I firmly believed he would become the first player to captain his county to All Ireland success at Minor, Under-21 and Senior level.

There are no words to describe the impact of his death. All of us were left in a state of shock, unable to make sense of what had happened. How could someone so young, so fit and so healthy, go to sleep and never wake up?

And while the circumstances were different, it was impossible not to think of Paul McGirr when I got the news. We were going on seven years since losing Paul to a freak accident in an Ulster Minor Championship match. How? Why? Nothing makes sense in those moments. All you know is that the world will never be the same again.

For the players, it was a scary time. If Cormac could lose his life so suddenly then it could happen to any of them. 'Who's next?' was the general feeling around the place.

We were grieving while trying to carry on. As their manager, I felt a duty to take the lead. You have to bottle some of your own emotions in that situation. I still had a job to do. And there were some practical things that we could do. Each player was given a heart screening and we brought in a doctor to explain things, which eased their fears.

But life without Cormac could not be the same. He was more than a footballer. We lost someone of serious stature that day.

Could we have won five All Irelands? All I know is that we would have had a stronger chance. Cormac was only going to get better. At the time, I did think we would retain our title. We still made the Quarter-Finals in 2004 and that game against Mayo was ours for the taking. Only afterwards, we realised we were running on empty.

Maybe we were destined to win in 2005 but I had my doubts after losing the League Semi-Final to Wexford. That defeat was horrible, an awful slap. People were talking about the need for root and branch change. The players faced a tough decision: were they going to settle for what they had or push on?

I decided to take them to Greenmount before the Championship for a boot camp. We spent three days there, nobody else in the place. The work was intense, nose to the grindstone. No luxuries either: the players stayed in dorms. We trained in the morning, came in for a bite to eat and went out again at 1pm, everything structured and strictly timetabled. We worked on tactics and kickouts, then team bonding in the evening, games and quizzes and the like. I tried to account for every detail. Owen Mulligan, Mugsy, managed to break out. There was always something going on with him. I take people as I find them and that was part of the deal with Mugsy. I just accepted him the way he was.

People often said to me: 'Why wasn't Mugsy treated the same as everybody else?'

But he only had a career because we treated him differently! Mugsy got away with things no other player in Ireland got away with. As long as he was prepared to play football, Mugsy had a place on the panel. He just had to accept his behaviour would keep him out of the team at times.

Mugsy, in fairness to him, was not to blame for every incident. If he stood at a bar to get a drink, he would attract girls. Usually, the girls had men. So he attracted them too. At the same time, he put himself in places where trouble was likely.

One day, a car flew past me on the main road near Ballygawley. Some fella was mooning me out the passenger side. Mugsy, of course, with Raymie Mulgrew driving. I just laughed it off. Those things were par for the course.

A lot of people fail to realise that management is learning how to work with different personalities. And you never know it all. To get the best out of Mugsy, I had to bend the rules. One size fits too few.

My boys look back on those golden years from different perspectives. Mark was in the squad from 2003 to 2005. Mattie watched the games with Michaela and they were always first in for the celebrations. Michael did his own thing, going to games with friends, away from all the fanfare. He preferred to watch from afar, another supporter in the crowd. Even for the All Ireland Final in 2003, he wanted Cusack tickets because he had watched all the games there. The red carpet treatment is not for him. Like Marian, he hates any fuss.

At the end of the 2003 Final, you see me hugging Mattie and Michaela. I had made a deal with Michaela that I would speak to her first if we won. For a long time, people would hardly have known that Michael existed. He was in college by the time I took over as manager. So he was more distant from the setup. Mark had his place in terms of the team. Michaela revelled in the whole thing, always our number one fan. Mattie, still a teenager at that stage, was young enough to get caught up in it. Being in the dressing room made him feel part of the group. Everybody's experience of that time was slightly different. By 2008, when we won Sam for the third time, they were moving on in their own lives.

Mark and Sinéad were married in March 2007. Michael was qualified as a physiotherapist and working in Omagh Hospital. Himself and Josephine had been going out since they were teenagers and they went travelling for eight months around that time. Mattie was at college. I know he missed being around the team but, at that stage, he was older than some of the players, no longer a youngster.

Michaela, too, had drifted from the scene. Like Mark, she went into secondary teaching and was working in Dungannon at St Patrick's Academy. Then Michaela surprised almost everyone with the news that she was seeing someone.

Michael used to tease her because she was so picky: 'You're going to be a nun. No one's ever going to be good enough for you.'

We knew her relationship was getting serious when Michaela stopped travelling on the team bus to matches. Obviously, she had better company!

John McAreavey arriving on the scene was a new experience for me, too. We were used to the boys having girlfriends; a boyfriend coming to the house was a first.

They first met in 2005 on a college night out. Michaela was in third year at St Mary's; John just finishing his second year at Queen's. But they went their separate ways for the summer: John played football in New York while Michaela followed Tyrone. By the time they got back to Belfast for the new term, we had a second All Ireland.

You could see there was a spark between them: they just seemed right for each other. The first time I met John, himself and Michaela were babysitting her younger cousins. Myself and Marian popped in but then I got caught on a call. John told me afterwards that one of Michaela's cousins put him on the spot.

'What are your intentions with Michaela?' she said to him. Her mother, Michaela's aunt Catherine Strain, put her up to it.

I suppose myself and John were bound to hit it off because he was big into football as well. Sure, we could chat all day about it. And his uncle being a bishop did him no harm either!

John has a lovely way about him, gentle and completely sincere. But he knows how to have a laugh as well. For a wind-up, he told his mates in Belfast that I had quizzed him that first night we met. As far as they knew, I was the one asking about his intentions.

John let the story run. Apparently word got back to the Tyrone camp and the boys were talking about it in training one night. I guess it was an easy one to believe, Daddy's little daughter and all that. But nothing could be further from the truth.

Anyway, I knew Michaela was in safe hands. John made

her happy: you could see it in her demeanour. She often called him her 'knight in shining armour'.

As close as I was with Michaela, the time comes when everyone has to follow their own path. For all our children, marriage was a natural extension of where they wanted to go in life. John and Michaela shared the same values, the same hopes and dreams.

John went with tradition and asked for my permission before he proposed to her. I appreciated that courtesy, though I still wonder how he managed to keep his proposal a secret from Michaela. We could never pull the wool over her eyes.

She thought they were going to Cork for the weekend. Only when they reached the airport did he tell her that they were flying to Paris. He pulled off a masterstroke.

2010 and the lead-up to her big day was a whirlwind, one of the busiest years in our house. First, we had Michael's wedding. He married Josephine on October 9. They spent their honeymoon abroad and were only gone a short while when we got the sad news that my brother Pete had died. Michael found it hard being away from home for the funeral.

But it was good that we had Michaela's wedding to look forward to. For the most part, that period was a brilliant time in our lives. I think we all felt kind of giddy: we fed off Michaela's excitement. She loved an occasion and this one was the biggest occasion imaginable.

Over the years, I felt envious watching other fathers. I thought it must have been such a thrill to hold your daughter's hand and walk her down the aisle.

And every bride is resplendent. I felt Michaela would be resplendent, too, because she looked that way to me every day.

I remember we had bad weather beforehand. The snow got so bad that Michaela was afraid to take the car. So I drove her to the dressmaker, Lily Anthony, who did all the adjustments. We had great craic in the car, just the two of us, yapping away about anything and everything. Her excitement was always palpable on those journeys.

Days before the wedding, we had a power cut. A disaster, I thought. Imagine no light and heat that close to the big day! I was expecting pandemonium. But Michaela barely broke a sweat. She simply relocated. So the preparations continued in her aunt's house. Catherine Strain, Marian's sister, taught with Michaela in Dungannon. I marvelled at the way Michaela coped with the disruption. Nothing got to her. For a girl who liked everything just so, I found it remarkable, refreshing almost.

To me, Michaela sailed into her wedding day. The stress of preparing for a wedding can take away from the occasion but she was completely at ease. She was *the* happiest bride you could imagine, determined not to let anything stop it from being the best experience of her life. Before Mattie married Catherine, he made sure to tell her all about Michaela's wedding preparation. He gave her the same advice, which worked a treat. Catherine never got to meet Michaela in person but always felt so close to her through Mattie.

December 30, the day before Michaela's birthday, was a Thursday. She loved the fact that she was 26 when she got married. Lily came over that morning to do a final check on the dress. Michaela got ready in our room, stealing looks out the window to see the latest caller. She kept singing: 'Goin' to the chapel and we're / Gonna get married.'

While Michaela prepared, I waited at the bottom of the stairs. I wanted to see her only when she was fully set. And then she appeared. My, what a vision.

I kept busy with the camera while everybody admired her coming down. Granda Pat had arrived by then. So they had their picture taken together, Michaela towering over him in her high heels. Gradually, everyone else drifted away, heading on to the church. Eventually just the two of us were left in the house.

Our good room was left unfinished when we moved to Glencull in '86. So we finally did it up in 2010. We were waiting in that room before we left for the chapel. I took a picture of Michaela while she was checking herself in the mirror. Somehow I managed to capture both Michaela and her reflection, an unusual shot. Your eye is drawn by its uniqueness: no other image portrays Michaela in the same way. I love that picture, a reminder of the time we spent together on that day, special moments only we shared.

Some people never get that opportunity. We could not have been closer during our time together before the wedding; present for each other in a way that only you can be for someone you really love. No words needed. I thought: 'What a great place to be.'

We travelled down to the church in a limousine. I remember some people were coming in the side gate as we parked. Lily had told her to put down the veil before she walked into the chapel – traditionally the veil is only taken up when the bride reaches the altar – but Lily's instructions were forgotten amid all the excitement. Beaming, Michaela walked straight in. There was no hiding her glee.

She turned towards John when we reached him. They smiled at each other and I could see the joy in their faces. Michaela was glowing, childlike almost, laughing with happiness. She had what she wanted. And she savoured every second.

We had the reception in the Slieve Russell Hotel in County Cavan. Michaela's wedding is largely forgotten about now but I still think about that day and how happy we all were.

I used to tell Michaela: 'One day, I'll be gone. And you have to accept that day when it comes.'

She hated hearing those words. And she gave out to me when I said them: 'Don't talk like that.'

But, in the normal course of events, life pans out that way. At times, I worried about how she would cope without me. I mentioned that fear in my speech, which might have sounded strange to some people. Those sentiments reflected how I felt at the time. That day never came, which is a terrible irony.

Michaela's birthday fell on New Year's Eve. So we stayed over a second night to celebrate. I remember looking up at the fireworks. There were people singing and dancing to mark the New Year, all happy, the music upbeat. I still recognise the songs, though Mark has to tell me the names. Katy Perry's 'Firework' was pretty big at the time. Even when I hear it on the radio now, that one takes me back. Mark remembers being outside, dancing around a tree at one stage. I know Mattie was thinking about going home because he had other plans that night. Thankfully, Mark persuaded him to stay. He thought it would be nice for us all to be together. Those occasions get rarer as you get older.

Even Michael had to be convinced about staying a second night. His wedding was a quieter affair, less fuss. Centre of attention was never a place he felt comfortable. So his attitude was very different to Michaela's: have the craic, by all means, but everyone home at some stage. And Michael always appreciated his own space.

His response when he heard we were staying over on the 31st was classic Michael: 'Is that not taking the piss?'

He thought one night was more than enough. I suppose part of him instinctively wanted to butt heads with Michaela. But he had a great time. Throughout that period, I think Michael saw a different side to Michaela. Before the wedding, he wrote her a letter about how much he was looking forward to the next chapter of their lives. They were setting sail on similar journeys at the same time. So that New Year's Eve celebration to mark Michaela's birthday seemed like a fresh start to him, a time for them to start developing an adult relationship with each other.

The next morning, January 1, I had breakfast with Michaela. Marian was still in bed. So it was just the two of us again, chatting about the celebrations, reliving the night before.

I had my laptop with me and we looked at all the

photographs that I took on the day of the wedding. There were hundreds of shots; we went through them all. I get some comfort from the fact that she got to see those pictures.

Nothing really stands out about our conversation. We were two happy people, in happy company.

Then Michaela came up to our room to say goodbye. They had arranged for John's parents to collect them from the Slieve Russell. Some people thought that I left them to the airport. We saw them off from the hotel, never thinking this could be such a significant parting.

There were big hugs all round, naturally. Mattie was sitting down, somewhere in the lobby, and they shared a really long embrace. When we speak about that moment now, he says it felt like the longest hug in the world, prophetic almost. She wrote Mattie a wee note as well, thanking him for all that he had done for her in the lead-up to the wedding.

The next we heard from her, they had landed in Dubai. They stayed there for the first week of their honeymoon. Michaela had been there before with us on a Tyrone team holiday. She loved the flamboyance and the extravagance, and the fact that it was sunny all the time.

She sent plenty of texts, keeping us updated on everything. I remember a message she sent when they finally set eyes on Mauritius.

'It's out of this world,' she wrote.

I thought she was going to have another great week.

I put down the phone in the kitchen and walked across the hall.

'God bless you, Michaela.' As I looked out the window

of our living room, those were the words that came to me. The news had just come through.

I cannot say what I was thinking at that stage. I felt despair and yet I saw some light. I could not explain things then. I cannot explain them now.

Brendan McAreavey, John's father, had called the house just before midday. I was on my own.

'Ring John,' he told me. 'Something has happened to Michaela.'

The tenor of his voice told me that something was seriously wrong. I got the number for their hotel in Mauritius. Somebody put me through to John. From the background noise, I could tell that the lobby was busy.

'John, is there something happened there?'

'Aye, aye … Michaela's died. Michaela's dead.' He handed the phone to a member of the hotel staff.

'Is she dead?' I asked.

'I'm afraid that's the case.'

John was hardly fit to speak. I could hear the distress in his voice. The distress is what I remember most; the details were almost too much to take in. I can only picture fragments of that day.

JOHN McAREAVEY

'It was even hard to try and utter those words to Mickey. I remember him saying to me: "What are you telling me here, John?" And then I think I dropped the phone. I don't know where I was at, really. There were people running about trying to calm me. I was trying to get them to do CPR, anything. All futile, obviously.

At times, I wish my memory was more of a blur. Seeing Michaela in the bath, the water overflowing, her body floating ... My mind, at that point, wasn't willing to accept that she was dead.

We were having lunch at a poolside restaurant maybe 20 metres from our room. Michaela wanted to have a bit of chocolate with her cup of tea after the lunch. And she kept it in the fridge because it was so hot over there.

I said I would go but she wouldn't hear of it. The previous night, we were in the lounge in the main part of the hotel and I had gone to get the chocolate. Michaela didn't want me to be running about after her everywhere.

After a while, I thought: "Where is she?"

I went over to the room and knocked but couldn't hear anything. Then I realised I didn't have my key. So I went back to the pool but couldn't find my bloody key.

I had to walk the whole way to reception. And, by that stage, I was getting nervous. She was gone more than 15 minutes. I could sense something wasn't quite right.

The hotel had sent a bellboy down with me to open the room. He was stood outside the door but came in when he heard me screaming for help.

It's strange where your head goes. Michaela had been suffering from a bit of back pain because it was her time of the month. The pain could be really intense for her. One time, she fainted in my family home because of it. So, when I found her, I thought she was after running a bath and had fainted again. I went over and grabbed her. She was cold when I took her out. And then it was evident from the marks on her neck that it wasn't what I thought.

I must have had my mobile on me. I rang Dad. He was on holiday in Thailand with my mum and a couple of friends. I think I woke him up, whatever the time was over there. It was just sheer panic.'

The news was breaking me, but the story of Michaela's death was now mine to tell. I had to carry the news to Marian and the boys. Whatever kicked in at that point, I found a way to keep my emotions in check. One thought dominated my mind: 'I have to stay strong.'

Some instinct was guiding me, telling me I had to show everyone that we could handle this ordeal. Maybe it was the strength of my relationship with Michaela sustaining me. But I was powerless to help Michaela at that stage; I needed to get to Marian.

She was at work in Dungannon but out of the office when I got there. I eventually caught up with her on the street. Her usual bright smile greeted me. Then I said: 'I've something to tell you but I can't tell you now. It's not good.'

We walked back to the office. Then I told her and she collapsed, unconscious in my arms.

The shock hit me again but I still had to get to the boys. Once Marian came around, we drove to Mark. He was teaching in Armagh and I wanted to tell him face to face. On the way over, I rang his mobile, told him I wanted to meet. He kept asking why. I tried to fob him off with vague answers. But he was insistent.

'Tell me what happened,' he demanded.

'Wait till I get there.'

'No. Tell me now. Tell me now.'

So I had to break the news over the phone.

MARK HARTE

'Dad called me at 12.20pm. It was just the start of my lunch and I missed the call. I went over to the window to ring him back. I don't know what I said initially. He just said: "I'm coming to meet you." At that stage, Daddy's brother Paddy was very ill but I knew it wasn't bad news about Paddy.

There was always a conviction in Daddy's voice but he spoke with a quiver I had never heard before. I knew there was more to it. He was on about coming over to meet me and I said: "No. I'm on my own here now and I want to know. I can take it."

I didn't know what I was going to hear but I knew I needed to hear it. He told me bad news had come back about Michaela. I said: "Is she injured or sick?"

"No. It's much worse, Mark. Much worse."

"Please tell me, Daddy."

And then he told me. I think I remember shouting and saying something like: "Please tell me this isn't true."

And then he said: "It's worse again because it doesn't sound like it was an accident."

I thought of Cormac McAnallen, actually, because Michaela didn't drink, didn't smoke, didn't take drugs. I presumed it was natural causes. To hear the next level of it was a bit much to take. Cathaoir Corr, who worked in Martin Shortt's estate agents with Mummy, drove them over to meet me in Armagh. I remember going to the canteen, which was mental on a Monday with boys queuing for lunch. I walked up to my vice principal: "Frankie, I don't believe the words I'm going to tell you here but I've just been told that Michaela's dead. I need to go, right now."

I just walked out. My school is right beside Armagh Cathedral. I thought that was as good a place as any. I walked up to the front pew and began to pray. There were tourists taking photos, smiling and laughing. I remember it struck me how different worlds can be just three feet apart. I thought: "I'd love to swap places with you."

Then I heard the back door open. I looked behind and saw Daddy coming into the cathedral. I was still thinking: "This is not happening." We got into the car then. I can't remember the journey back home. After that, we went to St Ciaran's to lift Mattie. I went into the foyer and asked for him to come down. He was insisting on knowing. I just said: "Please, Mattie, come to the car." He kept asking why.'

MATTIE HARTE

'*I was on teaching practice that day. The school office rang to say Mark had come to see me. I thought he was there to tell me that uncle Paddy, Daddy's eldest brother, had died. Paddy had been sick with cancer. The day of Michaela's wedding, he struggled to walk up the church.*

"Poor Paddy," I thought, on the way down to reception.

Mark took me to the car. Daddy was in the front. I sat down in the back. When he told me the news, I went into a daze. My head was gone. We went up to Mark's house then. Mark's wife, Sinéad, had stayed with Mummy. She was sitting there, in complete shock.

I went with Daddy and Mark to tell Michael. He was at work in Omagh. Mark went in to get him but he was reluctant to come out. He knew something was up.

Michael got really angry. He started hitting the car window and gritting his teeth. He was looking up into the air and cursing, giving out to God. I didn't feel the same way as Michael but I couldn't blame him for feeling like that. What's the right reaction?

Later, I went to get my car from St Ciaran's. I remember thinking that Michaela's death would prob- ably be big news the following day because her wedding had made the front page of The Irish News. *But I had no concept of the media frenzy that was to come.*

I drove home to Glencull. People had started to gather. Everybody was crying and hugging. The atmosphere was so surreal. Then someone from The Mirror *rang the house and asked for me.*

"Is Matthew there?"

I took the phone.

"Hello there. How are you doing? I'm from The Mirror. *I just want to know what's happened?"*

I remember asking Daddy what to say. He told me to tell them that Michaela had died and we were still trying to figure out the details. They quoted me in the paper the following day. I found out from one of my mates. That made me sick. It was a really cheap trick to ask for me. I had no experience with the media and didn't realise this was one of their tactics.

Most of the time, we were oblivious to what was going on outside the house. There were television cameras on our lane. There was live reporting from the school. Aunties and uncles chased the paparazzi off the end of our road. The locals set up a cordon then. Our home became like a wakehouse. But it felt hollow because Michaela wasn't home. When the McAreaveys arrived, they were in bits. At that stage, I hadn't thought about John.

I remember thinking: "Michaela's dead. What are you crying about John for?" I was still a bit confused. I had no idea what had happened to John.'

MARK HARTE

'We had to go to Omagh to collect Michael. He was with patients but I didn't want to tell his boss what had happened. I still didn't believe it. When he came out, I said to him: "Please, you have to come with me. Something's happened."

Michael is no-nonsense: "What has happened? You

need to tell me right now or I'm going nowhere."

I pleaded with him. But he was insistent: "I'm not coming a step further."

He agreed to come as far as the foyer. We went out and I told him.'

MICHAEL HARTE

'I was treating somebody I knew from school. There was a knock on the door. Martin, who owned the clinic, told me to get my stuff. Mark had come to get me. Me, with the thick head, said to Mark: "I am not moving until you tell me what is going on."

We went downstairs and I remember seeing my dad's car outside. I just exploded: it was like an eruption of anger and hurt. I sometimes think: "There were businesses around there. Would they not have heard what came out of my mouth?"

I got into the car and Mattie was in floods of tears beside me. Dad and Mark were trying to be strong. They would be the same character that way. I was punching doors and windows. I think I got out of the car again. I wanted to go somewhere to get away. Anyone looking out of an office window would have seen some state.

We drove to Mark's house. Sinéad was there with Mum. When I saw her, instinct took over. I wanted to be strong for Mum because I didn't want her to see how upset I was. I remember thinking: "I have to tell my wife."

I tried to park my own feelings at that stage.

Josephine is an occupational therapist and she was at work. Sinéad's mum, Sue, took me down to Enniskillen Hospital. Poor Sue was trying to comfort me on the way down. I walked into the hospital when we got to Enniskillen.

Telling Josephine was hard. We were just married at that stage. We spent seven and a half weeks in South America for our honeymoon. My uncle Pete died while we were away, which was difficult. Then we got back: new house, new life. Michaela's wedding came at us very quickly. Selfish as it sounds, we never had a proper start, really. Our marriage was only beginning.

Josephine reacted with despair when I told her. She had a funny relationship with Michaela. As much as I always thought me and Michaela never really got on, she would have been particular about who I associated with. Even though we had been going out for a long time, Josephine may have felt, subconsciously, that she had to pass Michaela's test. But they had become really close around that time. I cannot remember an awful lot after that. I must have driven Josephine home in her car.'

• • •

Mark was shocked when I told him, sad but not bitter. Michael went into a rage. He was mad with God, a real anger in his voice.

'There's no point in being angry,' I said to him. 'You've got to accept where we're at.'

Why I said that I will never know. He had every right to feel that way. The rest of us were stunned but I never got angry. Marian was simply numb the whole time.

Gerry Cunningham, a friend from my college days, came out to say hello when we collected Mattie at St Ciaran's. He was bright and breezy, full of chat.

'Gerry, Michaela's died.'

He froze. His face turned white.

My mind was chaotic but I must have been on auto-pilot. Whole blocks of time are missing from my memory. I know we went to Mark's house. Mostly, we sat in silence. I made a few calls. I phoned my brother Joe and told him to contact the rest of the family. I rang some close friends: Fr Gerard McAleer, Brian Carthy, Tony Donnelly. Next thing, the news broke on television.

Suddenly we became part of this huge public event. The world was mayhem around us and we became the centre of the storm. We could only pray for it to pass. There seemed to be no escape.

TONY DONNELLY

'Mickey rang round five in the afternoon. I was at my office in Dungannon. My brother works there too. Martin answered the phone: "Mickey! Happy New Year."

Mickey told me straightaway when I came on the line: "Michaela's gone. I want to let you know before it's in the news."

I had no words but it was a short conversation. The shock of it was unbelievable. My legs went. I felt it in the pit of my stomach. When I put the phone down, Martin looked at me. I said: "Michaela's dead."

Then my phone started hopping. "Is it true?"

Part of me thought: "How am I going to face Mickey and Marian?"

You have to be bigger than that. I went to the house that night with Fergal McCann, who was Tyrone coach at the time. The house was crowded. Róisín, Fergal's wife, made a big pot of food. We stayed until Mickey went to bed, about two in the morning. There was no real chat about what had happened.'

MARK HARTE

'About an hour after we got back to the house, there was a knock at the front door. I went out and it was Ricky Meyler, the musician who played at Michaela's wedding. She had left an envelope to pay him.

"Ricky," I said, "we'll get this sorted some day."

Then I had to tell him what had happened. He was gutted. He drove off. I went back inside.

Next thing I remember, John rang, and we went up to my old room: Daddy, Michael, Mattie and me. The line was crackly. John was emotional. He gave us key bits of information: there were intruders in the room and Michaela had marks on her neck. We were saying: "We'll get you home. Just look after yourself."

Next thing, the McAreaveys landed. We knew that somebody had to go to Mauritius. I decided to go with John's brother, Brian. My mind went to a different place then. I had a job to do. So I parked a lot of emotion. I felt useful at that stage.

We booked flights and were driven to the airport. We were fast-tracked through security. Then it was get over and get Michaela home. And John. We had to do that so we could get on with the grieving process. We were driven to the hotel in Mauritius. Brendan, John's father, had already arrived. Initially, it was very emotional. There were different practicalities to consider once we settled ourselves: paperwork, packing cases, picking clothes. Brian and I went to their room. John was staying on the far side of the hotel at that stage. Other holidaymakers were going about the hotel while I tried to process why I was there.

Michaela had to be officially identified and that wasn't a job for John. Barry McElduff, a local politician, had travelled with us. He's witty by nature and was a breath of fresh air in that environment. He can read situations and we had some lighthearted moments together. Barry took me down to the mortuary. It was not the kind of clinical environment you would get in Ireland. The mortuary in Mauritius was just a small room, really. My heart was thumping: I was still hoping to see someone other than Michaela. Barry came as far as the door. Only when I entered the room did it fully hit home what had happened.

On the way back from the mortuary, I spoke to various officials about releasing her body. I met the head of government and the ambassador as well as a tourism official. I explained about the whole process of wakes and their importance in Ireland. All the time, I'm thinking: "I was teaching Irish in a school 48 hours earlier."

I signed off on everything and then it was a case of looking after John and getting him onto a plane. I thought of everyone back home. They were helpless. At least I was doing something practical. As tough as I knew it would be, I was relieved to pull up in the street outside our house. There was comfort in having Michaela home. You couldn't thank people enough for the way they rallied around us. The wake was a total blur because of the sheer volume of callers. A million things happened without us having to think about them.'

JOHN McAREAVEY

'When the police came to the hotel, they put me in handcuffs. I was put in the back of a car with two other policemen. They took me to this shack in the middle of nowhere – they even stopped for food on the way – and I thought: "These boys are going to try and rough me up, get me to confess."

They took my top off and they put the cuffs back on, probably trying to see if there were any marks on my body, any sign of a struggle. They took my mobile off me and it was just sitting on the table. And, as news was filtering through, the phone was hopping. They were picking it up all nonchalant and looking through it. I was there for hours, late into the night, no food or water.

I guess, on reflection, it was very difficult but, at that time, I didn't really care. It didn't matter to me what they were doing or saying because I was devastated. It didn't really make a difference. I just wanted to know what was happening to Michaela.

I know that in these situations, it's often the husband who's responsible. I'm not excusing the police behaviour. They should have been a lot more sensitive. But I can understand why they needed to take me away and question me. But to just drive me off and nobody knowing where I was ... I don't know. The lack of professionalism and the lack of sensitivity was completely inappropriate. It was the start of a sense of the type of people that I would have to deal a lot with over the next ten years.

I was able to go back to the hotel that night and a policeman stayed with me, guarding the door. I was taken to a different room.

My brother Brian and Mark flew out on the Wednesday and we came home on the Thursday night. So it was actually quite quick getting home. It was good for Mark and Brian to be with me. I still remember them coming through the door.

I can remember Mark being very calm out there. His attitude was: "Let's get home and then be whatever way we need to be."

I wasn't aware of this massive story that was formulating and the media frenzy that was going on. Only when I got back I started to get a sense of the enormity of it all. Just a crazy, crazy time.'

MICHAEL HARTE

'I tried to put myself in John's shoes: "As a newly married man, what would I have done?"

That was in my psyche. My mind flashed back to some of the places Josephine and I had visited in South America. We were in Bolivia, La Paz, which is not a safe place. There were times I left Josephine on her own in the hotel. I was more sympathetic to John because I could imagine being in his position.

The wake lasted for an age. People were calling to the house and there was nothing going on. That was a weird time. Days rolled into each other. We were just willing for the official wake to start so that it could be over. You knew that it had to happen. I found it very tiring. Mum was badly fatigued. We were relieved and sort of delighted when eventually Michaela came home. I felt she was safe. We could look after her. And it was on our terms.

Carrying the coffin up to Michaela's room was an ordeal. The corners are so tight going up our stairs, we couldn't get any leverage. For years, I'd been climbing those stairs. None of the other boys would have done it. From the bottom of our banister, you can climb to the top of the landing. Only for that, a trick I had been using all my life, messing about, I don't know how we would have managed. I remember jumping on to the banister and climbing over the stairs to pull the coffin up.

I rarely left Michaela's room during the wake. I

felt close to her. I felt safe there. And I wanted to meet everybody who went out of their way to come. I wanted to meet them all. At one stage, I walked across the hall to my parents' room and looked out their window. Just seeing the sheer number of people outside astounded me. People waited for hours. I had queued at wakes for 45 minutes and thought it was a long time.

I remember Paul Galvin, the Kerry footballer, coming in. Another time, Mattie was flabbergasted. He kept saying: "Nelson McCausland [of the DUP] is in our house saying prayers."

And I thought: "Who's Nelson McCausland?" At that stage, I was not political at all. Mattie was just flabbergasted.

The GAA club were really good in terms of what they were doing with buses and food. Our neighbours in Glencull were incredible. They were really good to us in an unspoken way. They made our lives easier without taking over: they knew instinctively what to do.

Any time there is a wake in our parish now, I make an effort to help out. I want to be useful. I go out of my way to attend them. My friends slag me: "Why do you go to wakes?"

I go because I've been on the other side. I know what people are going through during that acute phase of grief. I'm not offering them anything. I'm just showing support. I go to most wakes with my dad. You can see the effect that he has on people: it shows in their face. Whenever he walks into a room, people get power from it. I cannot explain it, but they do. With grief comes a sense of desperation. You will grasp any wee bit of light or hope.'

MATTIE HARTE

'Mark went to Mauritius the day after Michaela died and the following day Daddy faced the media at the end of our lane. Michael and I flanked him. He spoke off the cuff. I still don't know how he did it. Daddy led us through that time. He is so measured and so balanced. We took our lead from him.

When Tony Donnelly came to the house, Daddy broke down: "Tony, what are we going to do?"

I remember him crying his heart out but those moments were few and far between. He was so strong. He taught me so much about what it means to be a father and how to lead your family through tough times.

I remember we lifted John from the airport when he got home. On the way up to the airport, we could already see the photographers and the long lenses on the bridge. Obviously it had been arranged with the paparazzi that they were going to get a shot of John. I couldn't understand why John was being exposed like that – his car stopped for what seemed like an age as the vultures took their pound of flesh.

There was a massive train of cars the whole way when we drove back from the funeral home in Portadown. Thousands of people came out. They were on the top of bridges waving Tyrone flags as we passed. A huge crowd gathered at the roundabout outside Ballygawley.

Mummy probably found it harder. She clung to Daddy. That was how she coped. "Don't worry about me," she would say. We were making sure she was okay. She was making sure we were okay. We carried Michaela from the road up our lane, which is a steep climb. Again, there were huge crowds at the house watching us bring her home. Inside the house, we had to negotiate the stairs, which was awkward because it's such a narrow angle. I remember Mummy standing outside watching, being helped by her sisters. She started retching. No tears. No wailing. Just the sound of Mummy almost being sick. Once we got Michaela into her room, the wake began.

The wake restored my faith in people. They estimated that 20,000 came. So many of them were genuinely cut up. They were distraught. I remember Fr Gerard told me that Donna Traynor from the BBC broke down in his arms after she interviewed him. Maurice Fitzgerald landed up with Brian Carthy. That was a big deal, to be chatting with him in my own house. I had his picture on my bedroom wall. He was my football icon growing up. Tyrone lost the All Ireland Minor Final in 1997 and I was inconsolable. We stayed for the Senior Final, Kerry against Mayo, and through my tears I watched Maurice Fitzgerald, mesmerised by what he could do. We were all in awe of him. I remember Davy, my cousin, was raging that he missed him. And Davy won two All Irelands with Tyrone!

Lots of other Kerry boys came to the house. Jack O'Connor landed up. So too the three Ó Sé brothers. Paul Galvin knew Michaela and was very fond of her. He wrote us a letter, which was a lovely thing for him to do. We still had a strong rivalry with Kerry at that point but it shows that, however deep those feelings run, people will rise above tribal warfare. Those guys are all legends of the game, who we respected. The fact that they gave up their time meant a lot. I'd say every county was represented. Many wore their club colours and pioneer pins. That gave me a great lift because we are all pioneers. Michaela's pin was on her wedding dress in the coffin.

My hand went raw from all the handshakes. At one stage, whoever was organising the practicalities tried to speed things up by asking us just to nod at people instead of shaking their hands. But you can't do that when someone has been waiting in the cold for a couple of hours. John McAreavey's brother Brian is a bodybuilder. When he stood at the door, people thought he was a security guard. That definitely sped things up for a while! Somebody else stood at the door with a hand sanitiser but the Protestant people coming through thought it was holy water and wouldn't take it. There were funny moments amid the grief and sadness.

I remember Winkie Rea, the former Loyalist

paramilitary, introducing himself. He said he had come on behalf of the Shankill Northern Ireland Football Supporters Club. Martin McGuinness might have been with him. I had studied Politics and was passionate about it. I will never forget seeing the DUP come through: Peter Robinson, who was First Minister at the time, along with Arlene Foster, Nelson McCausland and Maurice Marrow. I met them in the corridor outside the wake room and burst out crying. I buried my head in Davy Harte's shoulder. Suddenly it hit me how big the whole thing was. Michaela's death touched people on both sides of the community. The IFA held a minute's silence at all soccer league games. Stuff like that that was unheard of in the North.

A wake brings people together in sad circumstances but it's an incredibly cathartic experience. At times, we had good craic. It was cool to have those people in our house. I cannot understand why people don't hold wakes. You get that sense of saying goodbye.

At night, I spent time on my own with Michaela, talking to her. Time stands still after a death. But the thing that got me was how the rest of the world continues. Everyone else goes back to what they were doing. Life goes on for them in exactly the same way. The change, for us, is permanent.'

TONY DONNELLY

'The whole family showed amazing strength. Mickey talked about the power that Michaela had given him to deal with it. He said how grateful he was to have

had her for 27 years. He felt his power and the strength came from God. You would think he would be in pieces but he spoke to everyone. Obviously he was completely shaken and bereaved beyond bereavement. It was a nightmare in every sense.

I knew Michaela from the time she was a baby. She had a lovely way about her. I would phone the house and Michaela would answer: "Oh! Hello, Tony."

Then I'd hear her say: "Daddy, best bud on the phone." Just a lovely, lovely girl.

Marian was dazed. Who can say how you should deal with it. She leant so heavily on Mickey and has done since. Mickey is a rock, totally. Marian wouldn't want to be speaking about Michaela. Mickey can. And they both accept the different way they have of coping with their grief.'

MATTIE HARTE

The funeral was an incredible experience. We walked Michaela down to the Church and it was a beautiful day! Clear blue and sunny skies in early January. I remember making a point of remembering this walk, our last journey with Michaela. We took turns carrying her. The time not carrying, we were wrapped in each other's arms. There was a huge media presence when we got to the end of the road. Again, whoever was liaising with the media had arranged that they would get a shot of us carrying Michaela. There was a massive media tower with countless cameras and press. I didn't realise at the time but the police had actually closed that section of the A5 road, one of the busiest in Ireland. Thousands of people lined the road, following behind, waiting for us to come ahead. All you could hear was our footsteps and cameras clicking.

When we got to the church, we paused to let the rest of the family in ahead of us. We splayed our hands on the coffin and prayed, trying to feel close to Michaela. There was a massive crowd inside and out. Another sign of the magnitude of what had happened was the presence of the President of Ireland. There were other dignitaries too and churchmen from different denominations. Huge screens relayed the funeral to people outside and we prayed our way through it, hardly believing what we were doing.

We carried Michaela the short walk to the graveyard after. Frank McGirr had done a beautiful job with the grave. It was decorated with palm at the bottom and up the sides, overflowing onto the rest of the burial plot. John kissed a rose and threw it down onto the coffin. I remember wee Joseph Harte – Joe's son, our youngest cousin – who was only maybe five at the time, stepping away from his parents to peer down into the grave. I wondered what he made of it all and would he remember that look down to Michaela's coffin. There were songs and we shook more hands. Only for an announcement on the loud speaker telling people who had seen the family at the wake to go on, I have no idea how long we would have been there greeting people.

Whatever you think of the Catholic Church, it does death extremely well. The whole process of those days - the wake, the nightly rosary, the liturgy, the burial rites - is full of comfort, consolation and, ultimately, hope. Our faith is the cause of our hope, hope for this person's soul that they are in, or on their way, to a better place. I have no idea what people do without it.

JOHN McAREAVEY

'I took the view that Michaela was with God. That was really painful for me because I wanted her to be with me on Earth but it gave me a degree of contentment to think that Michaela wasn't on her own. I think that was very important for me because Michaela had this really rich faith and such a strong belief in God's plan.

That really secured me in those difficult moments. I had to get used to the fact that my relationship with Michaela had changed: it was now going to be a spiritual relationship. I think that softened the blow compared to somebody who has no faith.

If faith is all you have, then you have to use it the best you can. I think it's a lovely thing that I can do that. I believe that God is in every one of us. So, if you want to talk to God, talk to him through people.

There was a time when I felt angry with God. I had this sort of intense feeling that I wanted to have it out with Him, have an argument, eff and blind, like you would having an argument with a friend. I knew in my heart that I never would be able to fully understand the reasons for what happened. But I very much believe that God gave us free will. And that means there will always be questions unanswered.

The really difficult thing for me was the fact that I wasn't there to protect Michaela. That's something that I struggle with today and I have to try to manage that. I know the reasons why I don't need to feel any guilt over that but there you go: you feel how you feel and that has always stayed with me.

I felt that I let Mickey down. It's something that's always going to be with me. It's probably a driver for me as well that I continue to fight for justice for Michaela. It's not going to bring her back but it's my way of trying to fight back, in a way. I'm sure Mickey doesn't consider anything like that. At the end of the day, she's still his little girl.

I've attended counselling to deal with these thoughts but they're still there. And you have to be careful you don't go too far back with this because you end up re-traumatising yourself.

For years, I had visions of going into the bath. But I was eventually able to live with them. I could allow them in, process them, and then say: "Okay, I'm done with them for today."

I find a place for them in my head that I can manage. I can live my life without being consumed by these things anymore.'

• • •

The night of Michaela's death, I kept twisting and turning in the bed. No chance of sleep. But I got through the next day and slept every night from then on. Every morning, I woke on the button at 7am.

All I could do was get up. Everybody else stayed in bed. So I had nearly three hours to myself. Maybe this whole idea of early morning solitude originated from that time. Those moments, in a strange kind of way, were preparing me for where I am now.

Letters and cards came through the post within a day or two. They arrived in bucketloads. The postman left a box outside the door. For three weeks, we got anything up to 200 per day. I went through them all, reading each one. Even though those messages left me sad and emotional, I felt proud that people thought so much of our daughter they would sit down and write. Those messages became a form of therapy.

So many people made connections with Michaela. They had seen her at matches, met some place, watched the Rose of Tralee. People felt they knew her. Their memories of Michaela gave me a lift.

I cried my eyes out reading those notes. But I felt Michaela's presence as a comfort at the same time. Despite the shock and horror, I had this sense of peace. I cannot explain it in human terms. That kind of peace only comes from a higher plane.

There were so many unsung heroes the week of her death, so many kind acts. Eamon and Briege Tierney, who live at the end of our road, offered us a room. That gave Marian and me some time to ourselves, a chance to get away from the frenzy in our house. We needed an escape from that environment at times.

As a family, we closed ranks. We leaned on each other. In those moments, you appreciate how precious family is. Then reality starts to set in: what will life be like without Michaela? How are we going to manage?

Imagine the joy we had, not two weeks before, when Michaela got married. Now we were at the opposite end of the spectrum, another extreme. Your head is throbbing with all these competing thoughts but you cannot process them quick enough.

I cannot remember the journey back to our own house the day of her death or what went on the rest of that night. The days until Michaela came home were excruciating.

The day after she died, we started to get some more detail. I got very little time to speak with John and I felt so much for him. What he went through on his own, that far from home, was unimaginable. Marian and I went to Malta after we got married. I thought back on our honeymoon. Would I have been able to cope?

What John suffered is incomprehensible. The future he dreamed about was destroyed, instantly. To stay sane in that situation took extraordinary strength.

John's family are resourceful people. Amid the chaos, they realised there was a job to be done. They had flights organised in no time. Mark volunteered to go on our behalf, which I greatly appreciated. The state that Marian was in, no way could I leave.

Mark did an incredible thing for our family. To go out there and see his sister, then deal with all the bureaucracy, was beyond brave. I desperately wanted to get Michaela home. I kept thinking: 'She's out there and we're not.'

You presume it should be straightforward yet all sorts of hurdles had to be cleared. I felt that officials were deliberately putting obstacles in our way. Certain things could only happen at certain times. So many documents had to be signed; different people had to sign them. Everything moved at a snail's pace. Just when you think things are sorted, another issue crops up. Numerous times we thought she was about to come home. Then another delay. You start the next day feeling more annoyed. I struggled to control my temper: 'Why can't it just be sorted?' The frustration compounded our grief. We wanted her with us.

Seamus Horisk, a neighbour who sadly has since died, called to the house during this to and fro. His son had been killed in a road accident not long before Michaela. And Seamus had been the one to officially identify his son's body.

'This will be a hard part,' he warned. 'Just be ready for what you have to see.'

Hearing those words prepared me for the worst of what was to come when we went to the mortuary in Portadown. But looking at her was not as bad as I had feared. I felt better, if only because Michaela had come that far: we were glad to have her with us.

We spoke to her. We prayed with her. And I tried to make some sense of the situation. I thought: 'She has the ability to love everybody now.'

Michaela looked well, reminiscent of her wedding day. And yet, here she was, laid out.

Paudge Quinn, our local undertaker and a member of the club, was invaluable. Through him, we finalised arrangements for the funeral. And he guided us when it came to choosing Michaela's coffin, tasks you never envisage.

Paudge suggested a particularly good-quality one, something other than the standard version.

'Aye, that'll be it,' I said straightaway.

If something had a bit of class, even in a coffin, then I knew it would be the one for Michaela. Those details might seem trivial but Michaela was a lady of class. She would have loved the notion that, even in death, we did right by her. A lot of thought went into her headstone for the same reason.

Throughout that time, I felt Michaela helping me, as if she was saying: 'We can work through this.'

The funeral really brought home to me the value of community. There is something special about an Irish country community, the way people rally to support you at the most difficult times in your life. They carried us.

AFTERNOON

I view my life in two parts: the life that I knew with Michaela and the one that I have known without her. The world will always be that way for me.

Through the days and weeks that followed, we lived in a cocoon. All of us seemed to be together in one room all the time, moving from the kitchen table to the living room and back again. We were with each other constantly, not knowing what to say or do. I suppose there was some strength in numbers.

JOHN McAREAVEY:
'At that time, I really just wanted to ensure that I felt every emotion, and I didn't want to block out anything. I never wanted to be ten years down the line and not having dealt with the reality of my grief. I wanted to own my grief. It gave me the idea of a degree of control over grief as opposed to it being able to control me. The first couple of years, it had a strong hold and it was overbearing at times but I was able to cry it out.

After Michaela died, I spent about six weeks living with Mickey and the Hartes. It's funny now, we're in this period of isolation during a pandemic, and we're all indoors and it was almost like that in a way back then. We were all comforting each other in our own grief.

Myself and Mickey are early risers. So we had breakfast together lots of mornings, Mickey making me porridge, with fruit and everything, it was great. Maybe that's what was getting me up in the morning!

I think Mickey found that because I wasn't a son he was able to be vulnerable with me maybe more so than with the rest of his boys. Nothing intentional, just that's nature and I appreciate that more so since I had my own boy, James.

Mickey had this intense closeness with me. Maybe I was the closest thing to Michaela for him at that time. And we were just able to be vulnerable with each other and do that in a very safe place. Me and the lads get on really well, have great craic. We could sort of hide away from the world. I suppose there was a degree of sheltering ourselves. We were able to draw breath and try to understand what we were dealing with. I think that set the tone for our recovery. We had that time together to grieve. It was very, very comfortable for me being there in the family home at that time. That's where I felt closest to Michaela. And I felt ready, then, when I moved back home.

I moved back to my home house originally, which was the natural thing to do. But I really wanted to have my own space to be sad. I felt the time was right for me to have my own space. Myself and Michaela had bought our own place in Laurencetown and it was sitting empty, five minutes down the road from home. My parents were going through intense pain too and I didn't want them to be worrying about me as well. Living in Laurencetown, I didn't have to worry about anyone else. And I could still scoot up the road to get my dinner. That time formed the basis for me to slowly rebuild and pick up the pieces of what a new life would be like.

There was no manual, no guidelines, especially given the nature of how Michaela died. I was 26 at the time. There wasn't a whole lot of information out there that could help me. It was a baby-step approach. On a practical level, I kept myself fit, did a lot of exercise. I went to the gym regularly anyway.

I didn't have to forcibly pull myself out of bed. I was never afraid of the day ahead. For me, it felt natural to have some structure to my day and then repeat, repeat, repeat until the next day becomes a little bit easier than the day before.

It took about nine months and then I got back into work. We were busy forming the idea of a memorial organisation and I was able to throw myself into that, more building blocks for being able to cope. But it wasn't a conscious process. I can say, looking back, there was a lot of things that I did well there that definitely served me.'

● ● ●

For months, the same thought dominated my mind.

At home, in the chapel, walking to the grave, I kept asking myself: 'What the hell is going on?'

Nothing made sense. I was living in this strange place and figuring out how to survive in it at the same time. Ordinary experiences, like listening to the radio on a Saturday morning, seemed so different. I would imagine Michaela coming home from school, the smell of food drawing her to the kitchen. She would steal a few onions while you were frying them on the pan.

Just putting that key in the front door was unsettling: 'I'm going into the house and she's not here.' There was an emptiness in my life; the colour had drained from each day.

Those same thoughts resurfaced on the way home from training. Michaela was like a prism: her presence revealed the hidden beauty in my world. And her absence took away from the thrill of what I was looking at. A dark cloud hovered everywhere I went and I could only see so much. Everything had turned dull.

All of us were merely existing and yet that period was a kind of release. I look back on that time now and see how good it was because we were together. We comforted each other. We were safe. John moved in and stayed for a long time. He slept in Michaela's bed. We fell into routine. After breakfast, we watched television for a while. Then we walked down to the graveyard. Afterwards, we stopped in at my family home before heading back up to Glencull. We chatted as we went. Those walks were cathartic.

For months after the funeral, people kept coming to the house. Some we knew, most we had never met before. The number of callers amazed me; I found it surreal that so many people wanted to meet us and get their picture taken. Our house became like a pilgrimage site. Some days you were glad of the visit. Other times, you felt like hiding behind the sofa. For the boys especially, it was hard to face that kind of thing.

Prayer sustained me through that period, not just my own. I knew people were praying for us and that gave me comfort as well.

I thought back on Michaela's wake. There was a constant flow of people through the house. We had a network of neighbours and friends supplying food and tea, making sure everything ran smoothly. They even put up a tent in our street. All those things just happened. The way people looked after us brought home to me the value of community, particularly the GAA community.

That period, thinking back, never leaves me feeling down. Some of the letters we received were powerful. I picked out a few for Mattie to read as I worked through them. One man, a gambling addict, wrote about the effect Michaela's death had on him. He wanted us to know how much we had inspired him. He was so open. When he heard the news about Michaela, he thought Tyrone would be a good bet for the All Ireland. His head went to that place. And he was apologising for it.

There were lots of messages from women as well. Their honesty took me by surprise. I suppose Michaela seemed out of place to them, especially when she came on team holidays. Some of the wives and girlfriends of other players mistrusted her. Here was this beautiful girl hanging around with their fellas all the time. So they became suspicious. They were like: 'These are our guys. What are you doing here? What's your agenda?'

After Michaela died, we received letters and Facebook messages from some of those girls. They said that they felt jealous of Michaela and now they were sorry for feeling that way. It was no big deal, really, just human nature, but I appreciated their sincerity all the same.

Michaela's physical absence is the hardest thing for me. I miss her smile; I miss her energy; I miss not being able to give her a hug. And I will never get to see her children grow up. But I had a ball with Michaela. If we had one more conversation, I would tell her how much I enjoyed our time together. And I bet she is having a great time in heaven with Granny Harte and Granny Donnelly and all the other family members she knew and loved who went before her. I can picture her with them, not a worry in the world, happy out.

I can still identify with her spiritually. I keep returning to that scene of Michaela at the top of our stairs on the day of her wedding. Every time I see that image, we reconnect. People talk about having to die to go to a better place. But we can experience that place here on Earth if we acknowledge it. Every moment is precious. So much of our life we spend killing time. Why kill time when you can live it?

Since Michaela's death, the boys always hug us. That physical connection is vital.

My life has altered in less obvious ways. I could be

watching television at home, paying little heed, but then the news comes on – another tragic death. Straightaway, I think of that person's family: 'God help those people.'

I feel their pain to a degree: I know the darkness of that moment when you find out. Everybody else reads the paper and thinks: 'Isn't that shocking?' And then they move on to the next story. Beyond the impact of those grim headlines, most remain unaffected.

Life-changing incidents happen every day. In May 1965, two neighbours were killed in a car crash near home. They were young, 19 and 21. I was only ten at the time. You never know when your hour will come. I may not live to see tomorrow. A tragedy makes you more conscious of just how precious each existence is. So I try to make the best of every moment because life is a gift from God.

Prayer has been critical to how I have been able to deal with Michaela's death. I know it might not work for everyone. Prayer is not a prescription but it is an option for anyone dealing with grief.

Watching football on television was another way to pass the time. To spend 90 minutes sweating about Manchester United gave us a welcome escape. Michael and John often went to the gym together. Each of us had to find our own way to get through those days.

Inevitably, there comes a point when you have to get back to some sort of normality.

For Michael, the thought of returning to work was too much. A job in a public hospital was not the place for him at that time: he needed a quieter space, nobody fussing over him. So he left his position in Omagh.

He preferred a low profile anyway. Attention always bothered him and he hated the fact that someone would treat you differently just because they knew who you were. Michael refused to wear his name badge at work. He found that he could be speaking to someone as a professional physiotherapist and, the minute they clicked who he was, they suddenly become a nicer person. Michael had no time for that kind of thing.

Mattie was the first to rediscover some kind of routine. He went back to college in March, about two months after the funeral. At the time of Michaela's death, he was in the middle of the PGCE, his teaching qualification. Mattie resented going back but he was better off. Otherwise, the year would have counted for nothing academically.

Being on your own exacerbates grief. Michael found out the hard way when Josephine returned to work. Suddenly, he was alone in the house all day. They were the toughest weeks for him. Michael realised he was worse off being at home. So he started doing a couple of days per week in a private clinic and built from there.

One thing really angered me during that period. About three months after Michaela died, a journalist from *The Mirror* contacted me. She had compiled various emails and said they would make a nice memento for us. So she travelled down from Bangor to present this book to me.

I invited her in for a cup of tea when she called. Considering all her efforts, I felt that was the courteous thing to do. The next day, our conversation appeared in the paper under the headline: 'Mickey Harte talks exclusively to *The Mirror*.'

I thought I was speaking in confidence. She called to the house on the basis of bringing goodwill messages. What we discussed was not fit for public consumption, things I had yet to talk about within the family. I spoke about my hopes for John's future and my wish that he might meet somebody else. That journalist took advantage of me by exposing my private thoughts in that way.

And they caused a lot of pain for the boys. Michael was livid. Seeing a big spread in the paper brought back all his anger. Mattie was annoyed with me at first. He felt I had been very naïve. I could understand his reaction because the things that came out in the paper were deeply personal. And then I got upset seeing how hurt he was by what happened.

Sadly, Michaela's murder exposed us to an ugly side of the media.

JOHN McAREAVEY

'I haven't gathered too many new friends since that time. I probably learned a few hard lessons. My nature is to be pretty frank and pretty open with people. I would have been trying to publicise the work of the Michaela Foundation but the media always wanted to talk about what had happened. The Foundation was all about positivity and I wanted to separate the two things. I probably should have been a bit more selective with the media that I spoke to.

Mickey literally wants to live a quiet life and he's not really interested in much adulation. He's very open about the fact that his faith means the world to him. People think there must be something dark going on there and they want to find out what that is. People just don't want to accept that someone is how they appear.

People will read this book and they will have their own spin on things. They'll choose to believe things or not but there's only ever one truth. Am I going to bother myself with what people believe? I can't control it.

When your world is shattered, you never think that you could love again. We did the Match for Michaela at Casement Park in 2012, November time. I put an enormous amount of energy into that. There was a particular point where we organised these Chinese lanterns to go off into the sky. I didn't notice it at the time but someone told me to watch it back afterwards. The camera went up into the sky and the lanterns had formed into the shape of an M. Amazing. I read the situation as if Michaela was saying: 'I'm fine here, John. You need to move forward.'

We had the event on the Saturday night. I remember waking up on the Monday and feeling different, hopeful, more of a pep in my step. The weekend after that, I had arranged to go down to Galway with a couple of friends to get a breather. That's when I met Tara. It was all very unexpected.

I really did believe at that time that it was meant to be. Tara was the first girl I met after Michaela. I'd like to say it was a very easy journey but it certainly *wasn't. It was especially difficult for Tara because getting in a relationship with me was not easy.*

I was still sort of grieving, too. I was trying to navigate all those feelings. There were a couple of times that we felt that it wouldn't work but we stuck together because there was a really strong bond and a really strong love. She helped me grow through this. She's incredibly strong even though she doesn't know that. I know I wouldn't get into a relationship with somebody like me.

But you feel how you feel and thank God we're in this position in our lives now. At 26 years of age, was I meant to just call it quits? We've created our own family. And it's a beautiful, beautiful thing.'

● ● ●

Over time, our sense of loss gave us the desire to do something positive in memory of Michaela. She had good values, ones that we felt were worth sharing with others. Setting up the Michaela Foundation in 2011 enabled us to promote those values and give young people a platform to champion their uniqueness.

Michaela led a life without limits and it was clear that her story resonated with lots of people. We set up summer camps, organised faith and wellbeing retreats, and celebrated young people in their communities through the Wings Awards. So many good things came about because of the Foundation. And it fills me with pride.

Marian suffered the most when Michaela died. She went to bed early, usually at 6pm, and slept on as long as possible. Her days condensed at both ends. Sinéad and Josephine were good enough to stay with her. For a long time, she could not bear to be on her own.

Losing Michaela affected her bubbly personality. She was in a state of non-being almost, here and yet not here. She just existed.

Over the years, Michaela often went to functions with me but as she got older, Marian came instead. She enjoyed those outings, invariably falling into conversation with the wife of a club chairman. Marian is bubbly and outgoing by nature. That side of her shut down when Michaela died.

Her reaction was different to mine. But then you never know how grief will affect someone. Initially, you doubt whether you can survive. How do you live in that world? I was always fit to speak about Michaela, which eased me through that period. Talk became therapeutic for me. And it probably helped that I was used to being in the public eye. Marian had no words to describe how she felt whereas I could express my emotions. You might think it should have been the other way around. Men are not known for speaking about that side of themselves.

Marian did not drive for a long time afterwards. I took her everywhere. She went to the Tara Centre in Omagh for counselling every week. I found that period difficult because her progress seemed slow to me. But I had to be there for her. And at least I felt helpful: I was able to support her in some way. There were some very good people in Club Tyrone who assisted us through that year as well. I will always be grateful to them. Going back to work during that time would have been impossible.

The boys have been great to me, their wives too. I always had someone to talk to, especially if I needed to speak about something that would be difficult to discuss with Marian. They provided an outlet for me to get stuff off my chest. If I bottled all my frustrations, it would be detrimental for my own wellbeing, and catastrophic for our marriage.

Grieving is a slow, slow process. Everybody goes at their own pace. My recovery, if you can call it that, happened much quicker than Marian's. I was further along and yet, at the same time, I could not demand that she progress at my pace.

For some time in the early days, we rarely discussed our difficulties. I let things be. Internally, we were going through the same anguish, just at different speeds. I was inclined to speak about the situation whereas Marian retreated. Sometimes, you are better served keeping thoughts to yourself. No need to share an opinion that might antagonise the other person.

Seeing the world from another perspective is not always easy. When you have been married for a long time – 43 years and counting in our case – you can easily irritate each other. Trivial matters, which you never paid much heed, become a source of conflict. Those problems can escalate if you ignore them. The next time, something even more petty sets off an argument. Then you realise: 'We mean too much to each other to keep going on like this.'

Our ability to empathise has sustained us. I had to make my peace with Marian's reaction and she, too, understood that I was not in the same place as her. My way of coping was different. Just because I wanted to do certain things and go to certain places did not mean I was being dismissive of what we were going through. We had to allow each other time and space to find our own way. And we worked hard to reach that level of understanding. Both partners have to get there, otherwise the relationship is in trouble. I am so grateful to know and love Marian. She is the love of my life and we got through it together.

The Michaela Foundation, which we set up in May 2011, was an issue for Marian. She wanted no part of it. The Foundation became another coping mechanism for me. Out of the darkness, we created something bright. I saw the Foundation as a source of hope and I found it uplifting to know that a young person, who never met Michaela, could connect with her in a way that would help them in their life. But Marian saw the Foundation as a reminder of a terrible tragedy. In her mind, it only existed because Michaela died.

Maybe Marian's response is more typical and perhaps I am different from most. All I do know is that no two journeys are the same. The grieving process is ongoing, wherever we happen to be. We do not run on parallel tracks either. If you were to describe our positions in percentage terms, I was probably 75 per cent of the way along when Marian had hardly reached the quarter mark.

Luckily, we had enough awareness to recognise any distance between us. From that realisation, we can accept

Easy to pick out the baby of the family here! Joe (far left) and Francie (right) are either side of me in the front; Bridie, Barney and Martin are behind us (from left to right); Paddy, Pete and Mary are the three missing from this photo.

A rare shot of us playing marbles outside the house in Ballymacilroy. Barney is on the left, concentrating on the game, while Bridie and Martin watch on from behind. I was probably about eight or nine at the time.

Here I am all set for school. I passed the 11 Plus, which meant that I went to Omagh CBS – 'the Brothers', as we called it. Pete was the first one in the family to go to Grammar school. Martin and myself followed the same path.

Velvet jacket and flares was obviously the fashion in 1976! Marian and I travelled over to Bolton for my brother Martin's wedding. Our big day came two years later: July 8, 1978.

Marking our parents' 50th wedding anniversary with all the family in August 1988. From back (left to right): myself, Peter Junior, Martin, Paddy, Joe, Barney, Francie. In front (left to right): Mary, Daddy, Mummy, Bridie.

After the club split in 1982, we played all our football with Glencull. We held an annual 9-a-side tournament at our local pitch, The Holm. My sons Michael (head turned away) and Mark are the two mascots either side of me in the middle of the front row. Pete Quinlivan, a close friend and neighbour, is back left. Sean Canavan is back right.

The club relaunched as Errigal Ciarán in 1990 and we were county champions within three years. Here we are celebrating that success in 1993. We went on to win the Ulster title as well that year, the first Tyrone club to make that mark.

1993 was a breakthrough year with the county minors and everyone at home was kitted out for the Ulster Final: (from left) Michael, Mattie, Michaela and Mark (standing). Winning that first Ulster title set me on my way as a manager, although we had to wait another five years to get our hands on the All Ireland.

Kevin Hughes (left), Cormac McAnallen (centre) and Brian McGuigan with the All Ireland MFC trophy in 1998. That one, my first All Ireland as Tyrone manager, was 26 years in the making. ©INPHO/Patrick Bolger

Posing with Mark and the rest of the Errigal boys after a clean sweep for the Tyrone U21s in 2000: (from left) Cormac McGinley, Mark, myself, Darren O'Hanlon and Enda McGinley.

Better than winning Tyrone's first Senior All Ireland in 2003 was getting to share that moment with Mattie and Michaela. ©INPHO/Morgan Treacy

Singing the national anthem before playing Mayo in the 2004 National League, with Mark to my left. That was our first game back after the shocking death of our captain Cormac McAnallen – we lost someone of serious stature when he died suddenly at the age of 24. ©INPHO/Keith Heneghan

Michaela was always one of the first in after a game. She was particularly fond of Michael McGee (RIP) from Highland Radio, a fellow Irish speaker. Kenny Curran, then editor of 'The Game', is on the right. ©Damien Eagers/ Sportsfile

We took Sam home for the second time in 2005. This picture with team captain, Brian Dooher, was taken at the Citywest Hotel prior to departure to Tyrone for the homecoming.
©Damien Eagers/Sportsfile

Broadcaster Brian Carthy has been one of my closest friends since we first met in 2002. This picture was taken at the launch of his book *The Championship 2008* at Sharkey Sports in Ardee, County Louth.
©Paul Mohan/Sportsfile

My sister Mary and her husband, Lee, have been hosting the Hartes on All Ireland weekends for as long as I've been going to finals, so it was nice to repay them again in 2008 when Tyrone won the double. Mary and Lee are pictured with the Minor trophy while their son, Conor Mallaghan, holds on to Sam.

I first met Tony Donnelly at school in Omagh CBS, two football-obsessed teenagers, and we have remained best friends ever since. This was taken at the 2008 All Stars in Citywest. Tony was part of the management team that year. ©Brendan Moran/Sportsfile

For us lifelong Manchester United fans, it was a thrill to meet Alex Ferguson at the 2003 People of the Year Awards in Citywest.

Michaela took us on an unexpected trip to the Rose of Tralee in 2004 when she was named Ulster Rose. We all enjoyed a brilliant time in Kerry for the annual festival. Michaela felt at home on the stage.

All smiles in the front room with Michaela during the 2005 season. We were great buds as much as anything else.

somehow managed to get this picture before we left for the church when there was nobody else in he house. I love this image because it reminds me of the time we spent together on that day, special noments only we shared.

Football was another way to move forward after Michaela's death. My first game back pitted us against Donegal at Edendork in the Dr McKenna Cup. I think some people expected me to step away from managing Tyrone but that thought never entered my head. My nephew Davy Harte, Francie's son, is wearing the number 5 jersey. ©Oliver McVeigh/Sportsfile

We had a huge rivalry with Kerry during the noughties and they eventually got the better of us in the Qualifiers in 2012. But the response from the home supporters that day in Killarney was incredible. The way they applauded us onto the bus after the game is something I will never forget. ©Sportsfile

We set up the Foundation because we wanted to do something positive in memory of Michaela. This picture was taken at the launch of Match for Michaela in 2012, a fundraiser for the Foundation. ©Sportsfile

The next generation got their first taste of success in 2016 when we regained the Ulster SFC after a six-year wait. Here my grandsons Michael (left) and Liam (right) with myself and Mark are watching the trophy presentation in Clones. ©Oliver McVeigh/Sportsfile

Sam Maguire was not for Tyrone in 2018 but getting back to the final for the first time in 10 years showed how close we were to the top. My son, Michael, who was team physiotherapist that year, shows his emotions after the final whistle in Croke Park. ©Oliver McVeigh/Sportsfile

My last game in charge of Tyrone came against our old rivals Donegal in Ballybofey. That Ulster SFC Quarter Final was eventually played on November 1 after Covid-19 disrupted the season. ©INPHO/Morgan Treacy

The journey continues in Louth with my assistant, Gavin Devlin. After leaving Tyrone, we started a new adventure in 2021 – beginning with our opening round of the league against Antrim, managed by one of my former players, Enda McGinley. ©INPHO/Lorraine O'Sullivan

Family is what we cherish most and our lives have been enriched again by the grandchildren.

each other's position. Over time, any distance that might have been there has all but gone.

Certain things are still off-limits for Marian. Even now, she cannot go to funerals. So I normally attend on her behalf. I travelled as far as Youghal in Cork when her counsellor's sister died. I am happy to be able to do that for her.

Before Michaela died, Marian went to all the Championship games. During the Minor years, she sat with the children but she has not been to a match since. These days, she might watch on television. Of course, she still wants Tyrone to win because she knows how much it means to us.

Year by year, Marian has reached a better place and we can only be thankful. Not that it has been easy for me to come to terms with her new reality. Distance is important. Every day takes us further away from the trauma and allows more time to heal.

Marian, in Mark's words, has found a way of enjoying life within a certain bubble wrap of friends and family. Marian always had a strong circle of friends and a cherished group of long-standing Loreto school pals. She keeps to herself in certain ways – has no mobile phone, for example – but is rarely idle. Someone like Carmel Coyle, one of Marian's closest pals going right back to their primary school days, has been brilliant to her in every possible way. Carmel helped Marian get back her on feet; she got her out and about again.

And she made important connections through the Tara Centre. There, she built a new circle. She went to different events, joined different groups, gradually spreading her wings. These days, she has a better social life than the rest of us. Her progress has been amazing.

Marian was always a great sounding board. And she still provides great counsel for others despite the challenges in her own life. To be a pillar for someone else is a wonderful quality. She can handle other people sharing their burdens.

Still, it has been a long and difficult journey for Marian. For the best part of a year, she needed constant company at home. In September of 2011, nearly eight months after Michaela's death, myself and the boys arranged to play golf in Omagh. That was her first time alone in the house, day or night. We made sure that Sinéad and Josephine were only a phone call away if she needed somebody. She made tea for us when we came back after the game. That outing, for me, was a major breakthrough.

In one sense, she only took a small step. Yet it seemed like a huge leap at the time. I felt a release, as if it was possible to be somewhat normal again.

Lots of tough times lay ahead. But before we could face the big dates to come, we needed that day in Omagh to happen.

After a death, there are so many firsts you have to get through: Easter, Christmas, New Year; our birthdays, Michaela's birthday; the wedding anniversary, Michaela's anniversary. Late December and early January is the hardest time of the year. So many difficult days are condensed into that period. For a fortnight, they keep coming, one hit after another.

That first year felt like carnage. My head was full, the same thought spinning all the time. There seemed like no escape from the things that were going on in my mind. We were consumed by that sense of loss again. Michaela's absence was the only thing I could think about, how much we missed her. Every day, another reminder. Even dinner became difficult. A meal is usually family time, a gathering of sorts. Often, the beauty of food is the chance to be with others. But, around our table, I kept looking at the empty chair.

Those days were taxing, even though there was little to be done. I was tired from all the stuff that went through my head. But I slept every night, which stood to me. That way, I fell into some kind of routine. And still it seems unreal to me when I look back on that first year. How did I get by?

I suppose one thing that stood to me was my attitude: I tried not to think of each first like a threat. The anticipation of these things is often far worse than the actuality. Mark Twain supposedly said: 'I've lived through some terrible things in my life, some of which actually happened.' Once you get through those days, they are less of a burden: they lose some of their weight.

At the time of Michaela's death, I thought: 'What is the point of life?' Without my faith, I might have been drawn into despair. Knowing Michaela, knowing her belief in God, gave me great consolation.

Michaela is always part of my daily reflections.

Whatever passage I read from the Gospels, invariably it seems to say that there are two choices in life: follow the ways of the world or follow the ways of God.

Life was great before Michaela died. We had a brilliant relationship. But I can connect with her now in a new way. Every day, I feel her presence in my life. No words could adequately describe the way that I feel. Our connection is spiritual, one that no one else could experience.

If Michaela was still alive, she might be in Banbridge one day, Dungannon the next. Now I can contact her any time. I know where she is and I know that she is safe. If she did not make it immediately, I have no doubt the prayers and masses that were said and offered for her across the world got her there.

Michaela had big ambitions. I imagine her still working on plans for the rest of us, figuring out ways to ensure that we are doing our best.

We tend to forget the story of our Lord's agony in the Garden of Gethsemane because of his crucifixion on the cross. But we should remember that part of the story. He sweated blood so that our sins would be forgiven. I often think of the line 'for not his will but the will of the Father'. That passage contains a huge lesson.

Jesus had to suffer and die for us to have access to heaven. If he had said no to the cross, we would have no hope. We might wish for a comfortable existence, but we cannot grow as human beings if life turns out that way. These tragedies that befall us offer the best chance to have growth in the spiritual life. If you can accept that challenge then it becomes a door to a world greater than anything you ever imagined.

There comes a point when you have to pick up your life again. Jesus asks us to pick up our cross and follow Him. He does not ask us to do anything He has not done Himself and, in fact, gives us the strength to do so. Keep postponing that date and it becomes harder to face. That day will come eventually. The sooner you make it happen, in whatever way possible, the better. At some point, you must decide: 'I'm going to do this.'

Avoidance is a coping mechanism for many people but embracing those challenges was the best way for me to deal with them. The words of Wayne Dyer, an American author and speaker, have always stayed with me: 'Change the way you look at things and the things you look at change.'

Football was another way to move forward. A fortnight after Michaela died, Tyrone played Donegal in the McKenna Cup. That game was my first one back with the team and it gave me some sense of normality again.

We played them in Edendork. Jim McGuinness was new into the Donegal job at the time. On some level, I knew that game needed playing but it was a weird atmosphere. The boys stood over to the side on their own. I remember it being a dark and cloudy day, overcast. I think some people expected me to step away afterwards. But that thought never entered my head. Football was my passion and it gave me purpose, things I needed more than ever then.

Each day that passes takes us further away from the

worst day. We can honour the past without getting stuck there. But that process is gradual and I cannot say exactly when the turning point came for me. All I know is that this transformation is possible.

The darkness rises after a while and you start to see a bit more. Then some light gets in. These days, the clouds are in the distance, though they never fade completely. But I am free to look at other things, to live life in the now. I think it gives other people comfort to know that you can get to this kind of place.

Sport gives me a vehicle to do the things that I love. Football is a way of life and a way through life: it allows me to work with others, to live my passions. And sport is ultimately about people. I am a social creature. Whenever I meet someone new, the same questions intrigue me: 'What's behind that face? What does life mean to them?'

I like the fact that you can transfer skills from the sporting environment. Football does not begin and end with the playing of a game. You learn how to engage with people along the way and presence is a big thing in my life. I love exploring new ideas, discovering bigger and better things, and then sharing them.

Yet sport does not define me. Football is a catalyst for all that I want to bring to bear. Life, fully pursued, gives meaning to my world.

I know that Michaela's spirit still exists. On the day she got married, I thought about how much she loved John and her whole family. Now she can love all of us in her own unique way. A heavenly love is indivisible, open to all embraces.

The good days that we shared are never lost. Time and hope and prayer have taken me to a place where I can appreciate them again. Michaela lived her life to be with God. I believe she just got to heaven quicker than the rest of us. Like so many things in her life, I hope and pray she was ahead of the posse on this one too.

I prefer not to think about the moment Michaela died. Still, I wonder what was going through her mind. No doubt she challenged her killers when she walked into the hotel room. That was the kind of her. I can imagine her disgust: 'What are you doing? How dare you.'

While she did not die in peace, her pain was short-lived. The PSNI officers who went out to Mauritius told me that she was gone in a minute or less: dots around her eyes indicated as much. I try not to dwell on the detail because I choose not to picture her dead. In my mind, she remains vibrant. There was too much happiness in those final days we had together for me to be drawn down into that well.

But I knew that Marian would find things harder. She carried Michaela. A mother's bond is so much more intimate.

Marian probably cannot distance herself from the horror of what Michaela endured. Maybe my consolation is that something worse might have happened before she was killed, which is important to me.

I would love for Marian to be able to speak more freely about Michaela again. Like the rest of us, she wants justice for what happened but I know, ultimately, that day may never come even as we continue to fight that cause.

Michaela's death impacted the boys in different ways. I wanted to show them that it was possible to cope. Maybe that sense of duty gave me the strength that I needed. Like us, they had to find their own way to deal with the grief.

Mark went through a lot on his own. He carried a huge burden for the family by going to Mauritius and then heading back out for the trial. For a long time, he found it hard to refer to Michaela by name. There was too much emotion attached. He talked about the Foundation rather than the Michaela Foundation. Mention of her name brought back too many painful memories. Among the family, Mark never spoke about his feelings because he felt it might upset others.

Mattie was different, always well fit to talk. He wanted to share. Mark and Michael wrote letters to Michaela and they put them in her coffin. Mattie felt that he had already said everything he needed to say. She knew how much he thought of her.

Michael is quiet by nature and tends to be his own man in everything that he does. I think it was more complicated for him to deal with Michaela's death. He had only been married to Josephine a short time and they were about to start their own family. So he had to deal with a lot of conflicting emotions. Michaela should have been following the same path that he was on. Inevitably, I suppose, some guilt sets in.

On the night of Michaela's first anniversary Mass,

January 13, 2012, we welcomed our first grandchild. Liam's arrival was a complete blessing: he gave us all a great lift. But there was something bittersweet about it for Michael and Josephine because they had something that Michaela and John were denied. So it was hard for him, meeting John at that stage, and he still struggles to let go of that guilty feeling.

Liam will never know what he did for everyone in the family. He was such a positive distraction at a really painful time. Pretty quickly, he became the most travelled baby in the country. Anytime Marian wanted to get away, Liam went with her. He was everywhere.

Michael became a huge support when I got back with Tyrone. By then, he was a physiotherapist for the team. Having a family link every night at training meant even more to me at that stage. We were together in that environment, our own little bubble. And we could relate to each other in a way that nobody else could.

But no amount of football can stop reality. Our daughter was killed on her honeymoon and two men were facing trial for murder. The court case came at us quickly after her first anniversary.

For us, it seemed open and shut. All we heard from the time of Michaela's murder was how embarrassed the Mauritian authorities were. They assured us that justice would be done. Even their prime minister spoke out about the case, saying 'no effort will be spared'.

As soon as Mark landed out there for the trial, he realised things were not going to be straightforward. We were naïve, looking back. At the time, we thought: 'What we want we can't have but we can have the next best thing in terms of justice for Michaela.'

As far as we could see, Mark was going back out to Mauritius to witness a short trial and come home. By the time he got there, a different agenda was in play. The defence team were trying to pin things on John. They turned the case on its head. Suddenly it seemed like we were on trial. They questioned Michaela's character; they questioned the kind of people we were.

I spoke to Mark every evening on the phone. Again, he showed immense courage to face that gauntlet every day. Marian needed me at home but I doubt I would have been able for all that turmoil. Josephine, Michael's wife, was heavily pregnant at the time. Mattie wanted to go to Mauritius but we talked him out of it, thankfully. He was too young. So the responsibility sort of fell on Mark, not that we discussed it formally. Things just worked out that way. I knew he had the strength of character to deal with everything but he still had to do it. Mark is calm by nature, self-assured, and he knows how to be practical. His world had been rocked before: the death of Paul McGirr in 1997 left a serious mark. Then we lost Cormac McAnallen in 2004. Mark believes that those experiences of loss, grief and hurt left him a bit more prepared for what was coming. The trial, and all that went with it, was as significant a period of time as anyone might ever encounter in their lifetime.

Things got ugly during the case, and Mark was glad that the rest of us were back home. All the time, he could see the dissolution of the key points. At least Mark felt able to cope with what was going on in the courtroom. But I know by the way that he talks about it that the trial was a horrible experience. He had to listen to some terrible stuff. Most days in court, the men charged with Michaela's murder were just a few yards away from him.

We were reliant on media coverage for a lot of our updates, which made life harder. Mattie decided not to follow the trial in the media. He made his mind up when he spotted someone browsing through the coverage in the shop one day. Mattie knew the guy and when your man spotted Mattie, he put the paper under his arm. Those little things get to you. Maybe I found it easier to detach from what was going on in the press. But, in Mattie's eyes, the newspapers were treating the whole thing like entertainment. And they published really sensitive details about Michaela and John, stuff that needed to be contextualised. A lot of the coverage was disingenuous. For the first time, I saw Mattie get really angry.

As the case unfolded, the facts got lost in the drama. The defence lawyers turned the trial into a circus, doing everything they could to take the jury's attention away from the evidence. They tried to depict John as this famous footballer from abroad, a Ronaldo-type figure, who lived a life of prestige. Discrediting John meant the real culprits were no longer in focus.

I know that the husband is considered a suspect when his wife is murdered, but that thought never entered our heads. The facts alone showed it was impossible for him to access their room at that time. Thank God he did not have a key to get in. The police might well have pointed the finger at him. As far as I am concerned, they caught the culprits. If Michaela's case was heard at home, it might have run for a fortnight.

Instead, it dragged on for seven weeks. Everyone is entitled to their defence and none of us wants to put an innocent person in jail, but the evidence is overwhelming. Michaela walked back into her room at the wrong time. She found two hotel workers rifling through her stuff. They were stealing. And then they panicked. Bad enough that she caught them, but what next? Michaela would have reported them, no doubt. And those intruders probably felt that they could not afford to be exposed. I believe she was killed because those men wanted to keep her quiet. To save themselves, they took our daughter's life.

If I met her killers, I would ask them how the whole thing unfolded. I have a fair idea but want it confirmed. The detail of what happened matters to me. And then I would ask them one question: 'Are you not sorry that you went to such lengths to cover up a stealing ring?'

Whether they set out to do what they did that morning, I cannot be certain. But I am inclined to think not. And that fact is important too. Because I would love to hear them say that they did not set out to kill. That statement alone would mean they recognise their wrongdoing and appreciate the impact their actions have had on other lives. They need to realise the sorrow that we have suffered.

As the case went on, we could see that there were bigger forces at play. The Mauritian authorities became more concerned about what a guilty verdict would mean for their country. What would the rest of the world think about a Western girl being murdered out there on her honeymoon? How could anyone contemplate two killers living in paradise?

There was governmental pressure on the outcome. Mauritius, I felt, wanted everyone to think that we were troublemakers. And the result was a gross miscarriage of justice.

Mattie was philosophical about the outcome. Michaela's killers being brought to justice was not going to change anything for him. Nothing could bring her back. Mattie was always conscious of the bigger picture in life. He followed politics closely from a young age. So he was well aware of the hurt and pain that people had suffered as a result of the Troubles. I know he gets cross thinking about those men in Mauritius. So he chooses not to go there. He prays for them instead. Because of his faith, he feels he has to forgive them. Jesus died for our sins and offered his forgiveness to everyone. God calls us to do the same. Who are we to hold it back from others? Afterwards, Mattie made a conscious decision not to let the trial define him as a person.

Michael's response was more reserved. He felt kind of emotionless about the outcome. I know he was worried about what it might do to him if he became fully invested in the trial.

Like Mattie, looking at the newspapers was difficult, particularly when it seemed like the worst days were behind us. The story had moved off the front. So you think it might be safe to read them again. But then, page seven, something else crops up, another hit to the system.

Nearly everything we went through played out in public. And it makes you angry because you need privacy to deal with those moments properly.

For Mark, resolving Michaela's murder is a deeply personal issue because he was witness to what happened during the trial. And, like me, he still wants justice. We both believe that that day will come. But we know that the system is complicated: nothing comes easy. Behind the scenes, there is a lot of corruption. All we can do is keep fighting.

At this stage, the case is ingrained in our psyche. We cannot give up. I often think to myself: 'There's right and wrong, and we were wronged.'

You have to trust that some day, in this life or the next, justice will be served. We know that Michaela would fight just as strongly for any of us. She was tenacious. As Mark said once: 'If that had been me, Michaela would have attended my trial and backed me up. I'm just doing what I know would have been done if the shoe had been on the other foot.'

That fact gives him comfort.

Who knows what kind of life Michaela's killers lead? We are lucky in one sense: they do not pass our street. Daily life would be so much more difficult if I lived in Mauritius. Yet the fact that they do live freely gets to me. I find it hard to think about.

If we were obsessed by her case it could shatter our family. I hope, in time, that justice will prevail but the situation is not eating me up: the quest does not dominate my thoughts.

Mark feels the same way. He knows that his life could be consumed chasing the case and then his own marriage might suffer. There are days when he feels like really going for it, maybe moving to Mauritius for a while to ramp up the campaign. But his nature keeps him in check. Mark is as balanced as they come. The pursuit of justice cannot come at the expense of the entire family circle.

Revenge is not my overwhelming urge. My faith tells me to leave this in God's hands. Everybody goes blind if we take an eye for an eye.

I never questioned why Michaela was killed. Life is God's gift. Without that perspective, I probably would question her murder. The lives that He has given Marian and I are His gifts to give and His to take. I cannot contemplate life in any other way.

Michaela's 27 years on Earth, our gift, is more important than the fact that her life ended early. God has taken Michaela from us, in human terms. But, in spiritual terms, He has given us something greater. He changed what it is that we have.

You might think me crazy: 'How could you look at it that way?'

Never once did I feel angry with God; I never doubted my faith. The way that I view the world, I can only be true to my beliefs if I accept that people have free will. To me, free will is God's greatest gift. What is faith without conviction?

I think my convictions give me the strength to deal with difficult emotions. Maybe faith works twice over, sometimes a shield and more often a support, because we all need something that makes us feel less fragile when our world seems close to collapse. And prayer is always there for me.

Naturally, I find it hard not to get angry about what happened to Michaela and the people who caused her death. Ultimately, we want justice for Michaela, but who knows when that day will come. So I have to keep my feelings in check. My wellbeing cannot depend on the outcome of a case that could run for many more years. Life has to be that way for me or else I think I would find it hard to move forward.

My outlook has always been positive. I rarely dwell on the past. Would you rewatch a morbid movie? Why not recall uplifting moments instead? Because they do exist. You cannot erase the bad things: they were just as real. But you can park them.

Some might think my approach is oversimplified. I just believe that you can honour both aspects and start living from a positive place. Why let the negative dominate your life?

Death is not an end, but a part of life's journey.

●　●　●

Mattie's big day in 2015 became a target for Marian. She used to say to him: 'If I only go to one more wedding, it'll be yours.'

As the next one after Michaela's, that date became significant for everyone. Was I anxious? Strangely, I felt at ease, even though that day left us exposed again.

Family get-togethers are tough for us all. The hardest ones, odd as it might seem, are the times when everyone is there. Mattie feels that the three of them together reinforces the fact that one person is missing. If one of the boys is elsewhere then Michaela's absence is not as apparent.

Marian is in a much better place now, but life is not always straightforward. Innocuous things, the kind that would not even cross my mind, can still cause her a lot of bother. We went to see Brendan Quinn in concert one night. Both of us are big fans. Some people we knew happened to be there too, sitting near us. I paid them no heed, but Marian is private by nature and sensitive about being seen in public. Those situations where she might end up talking to someone for the first time since Michaela's death make her feel apprehensive. She prefers to be anonymous. I thought we might have to leave because she was getting more anxious.

Just when I thought she had calmed down, on came 'Caledonia', which Michaela loved. I had to look away, praying for the song to end. I knew how much it was upsetting her.

Often, our instinct is to run away from painful emotions. Marian probably felt like walking out at that point. I knew by her body language. Experience has taught me that reason is no use. Just listen. You can be present with someone without having to speak. I take on board what she says and try to feel for her as much as I can.

I love hearing 'Caledonia', which is the sad thing. That song brings back happy memories: I see Michaela smiling, her face lit up. The concert identified an issue to me that I thought had been left behind.

Marian is going through a process that I started a long time ago. I have been in those places. She might only be a few miles in, whereas I have spent years on this road.

I could not understand why every step was such a challenge. Over time, I have become more understanding. I cannot demand that she sees life through my eyes. Thankfully, she appreciates that I am in a different position. I cannot be ultra-emotional about everything.

I can see how Marian is progressing in other ways. She has overcome the fear of people talking to us about Michaela. That said, we stay in our seats during concert intervals: Marian is not one for small talk.

Another time, we went to see Ray Lynam. Tony Donnelly happened to be in the same row. We got chatting to Tony during the break: Marian was in her comfort zone then. So we sat beside him for the rest of the night. Tony's company was invaluable because it put Marian at ease.

The way we socialise has changed but Tony is great. He knows the craic. If we go to his house for dinner, he knows not to mention Michaela. Fine if Marian talks about her. And even then Tony knows not to prolong that conversation because he might put Marian in an awkward position.

Tony stepped away from the Tyrone scene in 2014. So we had to make a conscious effort to keep in touch. We go for meals regularly. The general rule is we get 15 minutes of football talk at the start and no more. Sometimes Marian will dominate the conversation and talk away, chat about her work with the Tara Centre. And she likes the funny stories, too. I can see her personality returning when we get together.

Grocery trips can be tricky, though. People feel comfortable approaching me and a stranger will often share his darkest moment in the strangest place.

We were in Sprucefield once when another shopper came over to us. 'Lovely to meet you,' he says to me. 'I have something in common with you.'

Alarm bells went off in my head: I knew what was coming. At this stage, Marian is cute enough to make herself scarce. Anytime someone makes that sort of introduction, she drifts away towards another aisle, as if out shopping on her own.

Before, she simply would have walked away. And might have seemed rude doing so. Talking about Michaela was wrong, in her mind. She got cross if someone mentioned her but the people who approach us have the best of intentions. In their minds, it would be insensitive not to mention Michaela.

I understand why people want to talk to me. That particular man was genuine: he had lost his daughter to leukaemia. Like me, his faith was important. He wanted to sympathise.

At this stage, thankfully, Marian and I have the best of both worlds. She loves visiting friends, going out for lunch, getting her hair done. I enjoy the time that I get to myself. But only during the day – I cannot be alone in the house at night. I stay with Mark and Sinéad if Marian is going to be home late. I never liked the dark.

I thank God for the fact that we are all moving in the right direction. Who knows where life will take us from here – is there even an end point? We have to carry this loss wherever we go. And I often think our own problems would not seem so bad if we heard everybody else list their troubles. You might be glad to carry your own cross.

For me to think outside the normality of my life is a big challenge because I only know my own private world. Mostly, I led a privileged existence: no major problems, no serious afflictions; healthy happy family. And time for all pursuits.

Others have battled alcohol, come to grips with psychological problems. I admire them. Perhaps their lives are more rewarding because they found a way back from the dark side. My challenges came later in life. I lived through the darkness and learned how to move away.

I firmly believe that you can choose to be happy. To me, that realisation is the great discovery of life. I make the same point whenever I am asked to give a talk. What is your first thought each morning? Is it: 'Good God, morning' or 'Good morning, God'?

This simple point makes complete sense to me. The day is long if it feels like a burden as soon as you wake up.

Regardless of what life throws at us, we have the power to choose our own path. We can be actors or reactors. If you have the presence of mind to be an actor in your own life then you can make better choices. We can choose to be angry or frustrated or bitter, or we can choose quite the opposite. But each of us has that choice.

I went through so much dealing with Michaela's death, there was hardly time to think. Those early days were incredibly intense: I lived every second. And, at the time, things were happening too fast for me to process them.

Grief is such an intrusive emotion: it reduces your capacity, leaves you bare. Whole chunks of time are lost to me, days that passed in a blur. We fought so hard to get through that period, it was enough just to survive each day. Then you wake up and start all over, fighting for survival again. The worst moment of our lives played out in the most public way imaginable. We were fragile, our lives in turmoil. How do you regain your senses with the world watching?

We were at a remove from a lot of things throughout that period. I can appreciate now, looking back on it all, how much work went on behind the scenes. The club were amazing: Peter Canavan was among the marshals for the wake and the funeral. It was something else to see him out directing traffic in a high-vis vest. Those moments make you realise what life is really about.

We received incredible support and MCD's input was typical of the unbelievable generosity from so many people and businesses. My eldest nephew, Conor Mallaghan, had a connection with them through Damien O'Donohue. They helped us with the music and provided thousands of euro worth of equipment: barriers, toilets, screens, speakers and the like.

Through MCD, we were able to get Mary Black too. At the graveside, Mary sang 'Our Lady of Knock' and 'Song for Ireland'. She was superb.

But not everyone was that thoughtful. Much later, I found out that the national broadcaster made life difficult. Conor also acted as a link between us and the media along with Eoin Conroy. Deric Henderson of the Press Association was brilliant to deal with. Broadcaster Adrian Logan was a great help too. Before the funeral, they held a meeting with all media to let them know how things would run. Seemingly, RTÉ took issue with our approach. Their attitude seemed to be: 'Who are you to tell us what we can and can't do?'

The big thing for us, for Marian especially, was that the funeral would not be broadcast. Again, RTÉ took the hump. We set up screens to relay the footage for people outside the church and they reckoned there was nothing to stop the television cameras from being pointed at those screens. Their arrogance sickened me when I heard about what went on. It was not in keeping with the general tone up to that point.

There were other incidents. RTÉ were among the first media outlets to land at our house when the news broke about Michaela. I thought one member of the team, whom I knew, was just there to sympathise; next I heard he was on the news making out that he had had dinner with me as if it was just another *ordinary* day in my life. Then he wanted a sit-down interview, one on one. By that stage, we had agreed that I would speak to the media outside the house. Adrian Logan did the interview, which was syndicated. That way, everyone would get the same feed. But this person wanted his exclusive. And, when it failed to materialise, he let others know how unhappy he was about the situation. Suddenly, it was about him and his exclusive! The same person, a few months later, called me more than 60 times over the course of one weekend. I would have expected such calls to end after two or three attempts. Next thing, his car pulled up outside our house. Needless to say, given all that had happened, there was no desire to answer the door.

Then there was that episode with *The Mirror*, when one of their reporters called to the house on the basis of a goodwill gesture. It never crossed my mind that someone would do something like that. Those incidents have stayed with me.

People still wonder about my fallout with RTÉ, how I became so entrenched. Without knowing the full story, it can be hard to make sense of things. As far as I am concerned, RTÉ brought this situation on themselves.

I first met Brian Carthy in 2002 when I took over as Tyrone manager. He was a total gentleman and we quickly developed a close friendship. Michaela became very fond of him as well and she was always a great judge of character. If you needed anything, Brian would be there, generous to a fault. Trish, his wife, has been very good to run a Michaela camp in Dublin over the years.

They were guests at Michaela's wedding and he was one of the first people I contacted when she died. Apart from our friendship, I greatly respected him as a journalist. I saw the rapport that he had with other managers and with people at every level in the GAA. He was never less than fair and had no problem asking the hard questions either.

May 7, 2010, I wrote about Brian in my *Irish News* column on the occasion of his 30th year with RTÉ. The piece read: 'In the world of Gaelic games, we have been blessed with marquee broadcasters and commentators who have brought us the action from venues such as Croke Park, Semple Stadium, Casement Park and Clones into virtually every home in the country. Indeed, RTÉ Radio has been fortunate to have become synonymous with such names as Micheál O'Hehir, Micheál Ó Muircheartaigh and Brian Carthy.'

I elaborated on the contribution of the three commentators: 'Whilst the late Micheál O'Hehir also brought his skills to the world of television and other sporting spheres, especially horseracing, Micheál Ó Muircheartaigh and Brian Carthy have continued to create vivid pictures of Gaelic games in the minds of their vast array of listeners through the medium of radio. Ó Muircheartaigh's career and the achievements of his colleague in RTÉ, Brian Carthy, ensure the future of RTÉ Radio Gaelic games commentary is in safe hands. Brian has spent almost 25 years commentating and reporting on games at all levels in football and hurling. With Brian's distinctive tones and wealth of additional relevant knowledge, the listener is treated to much more than an outcome on a scoreboard.'

A few weeks after I wrote that article, Mark brought my attention to reports in newspapers about Brian Carthy being demoted to the role of pitch-side reporter. Brian and I never discussed his situation with RTÉ.

Mícheál Ó Muircheartaigh retired in 2010 and Brian seemed his natural successor. Only in April 2011 did I read that Brian was not considered for the League Finals. RTÉ had released the information to the media before Brian knew anything about it. At the time, I wondered why RTÉ would undermine their own man. And so publicly.

As the weeks passed and the Championship got under way, I could see that Brian was getting less and less commentaries. I thought it was insulting. And I felt compelled to support Brian. So, I set out my views in a letter to RTÉ. Nobody asked me to intervene; I was acting on my own volition. Loyalty is something I value highly and Brian had been treated poorly in my eyes. To me, it seemed that RTÉ had lost sight of what he brought to their coverage. And I wanted his employers to know how much he was valued by myself and others in the GAA. I have no regrets about what I did. Either you believe in something or not. To me, these things are black and white.

I was addressing the man's record and the quality of his work. And I felt my opinion was one worth listening to. I had been working with the media for 20 years at that stage. RTÉ could have responded to my letter in a professional way. Instead, they put that letter into the public domain, as if I was just full of hot air. They treated me with disdain.

I sent my letter in late May 2011, in the hope of getting a meeting, just to have a conversation with the powers that be. Maybe I was naïve getting involved in another person's dispute, but it felt like the right thing to do. If I had my time over, I would write that letter again. It was about a man's professional career. You cannot compare that situation with an amateur player competing for a place on a football team.

Whether RTÉ appreciated my input or not, they could have acknowledged it at least. Not for one minute did I think that I could tell them what to do. I was painting a picture of the value of the man that they had. Plenty of other managers lent their support: Brian Cody, Conor Counihan, Kieran McGeeney, Justin McNulty, Mickey Moran, Kevin Walsh.

After my letter went to them, I heard nothing back before we played Monaghan in the Ulster Championship on June 5. So, I decided not to cooperate with RTÉ at that game. Word got out afterwards and they reacted almost immediately. The following day, which was a Bank Holiday Monday in the North, a letter came to my house. Suddenly they were fit to send a motorbike courier having ignored me for more than ten days. They were only worried about the optics because the papers had got wind of the story. Their quick response, at that stage, seemed like another insult.

The standoff with RTÉ came to an end once we received a response on the issue. But, with the matter resolved and the managers on board again, RTÉ compounded the situation. Next thing, the content of my letter appeared in the *Irish Independent* (Saturday, June 11) under the headline 'Mickey Harte, Brian Carthy and THAT four-page letter to RTE'. They waited for the most opportune moment and hit back by getting their own spin on the issue into the papers. They later claimed that the leak must have come from my side, which further infuriated me because I knew that not to be true. I only sent two copies, both to the appropriate people in RTÉ: one to Noel Curran, the Director General, and the other to Tom Savage, the Chairman of the RTÉ board. The letters were marked private and confidential. Nobody else got a copy – I contacted the other managers by email only. The leak could only have come from someone in RTÉ.

RTÉ doubted my word and doubted my character. And they were underhanded in the way that they went about things throughout. I felt a sense of betrayal from the people on the other side. Right is right, in my book, and wrong is wrong, regardless of the consequences.

It was the first time that I saw how devious RTÉ could be, but my experiences since have taught me how dishonestly they operate when pursuing their own agenda. Nobody has been held accountable for leaking my letter. Noel Curran has now moved on from RTÉ without ever offering me any explanation as to how this private and confidential communication was leaked to the media. And as far as I am aware there was no investigation into how it occurred or who was responsible. So much for their current slogan, 'The Truth Matters'. Let them tell the truth now about their behaviour towards me and my family.

Then came *The John Murray Show* on Radio 1 and

that horrific skit. I was shocked. That changed everything. I could never have any dealings with them again.

I missed the programme when it went out live. So, I had to listen back afterwards. Disgusting was my first thought. I could not believe that Murray and his producer could stoop so low. They were mocking me, referring to the Dalai Lama because I had attended his conference in Limerick and making out that I was dictating what they should cover on the programme. They also used my voice out of context. Then they brought Michaela into it by playing 'Pretty Little Girl from Omagh'. To play that song showed their complete lack of sensitivity. How crass can you be? Michaela was dead a mere matter of months.

But I also thought it was par for the course from RTÉ. That episode really confirmed my opinion about how they operate. To me, it seemed as though they could do as they liked. Playing that skit showed just how detached from the real world RTÉ had become.

I rang Murray a few days later.

I spoke calmly for the most part, no shouting or ranting: 'Do you even know me? Do you know anything about me or my life? Do you know what my life looks like right now? I got up and walked past my daughter's room, which hasn't been touched since she was murdered. I went to her grave and replaced the candles, gathered the letters and mementos people had left.

'I came home to more letters and parcels from people sympathizing and telling their own story. Then I went to Paul McGirr's anniversary mass, a young footballer who died tragically during a game playing on a team that I manged. Did you think about the impact your behaviour could have on somebody else? Did you think about the nature of the song that you played? Have you thought about how insensitive that could be to our family?'

There was no cursing, no tearing strips off him. A younger me might have called him all the sods of the earth. I was still raw at that time. So soon after Michaela's funeral, RTÉ thought I was fair game. They made little of my family. And they thought they could walk all over me. I have seen this kind of thing happen lots of times with RTÉ since: insulting you one minute and then the *plámás* to get you back onside.

Not many of the family heard the skit when it first aired. There was probably too much going on in our lives at the time. Mark was furious.

RTÉ eventually took down their deeply offensive broadcast, which said everything, although the damage was done at that stage. They put out plenty of feelers afterwards, but nobody came directly from RTÉ with an official apology. Somebody from their production team left a voicemail to say that he was going to leave flowers on Michaela's grave and call in for coffee. No flowers appeared; no visitor came.

At this stage, nothing RTÉ do will repair their relationship with me. The time to sort out things has long since passed, not that their efforts have ever felt sincere. I never got the impression they were truly sorry about what happened. They wanted things sorted in a way that suited them. Over time, it seemed to me that some within RTÉ were competing to be the one to make the breakthrough.

One individual tried to intervene behind the scenes. All of a sudden I was hearing from people who worked at the Tara Centre in Omagh, where Marian attended counselling, how it would be a good thing for me to start speaking with RTÉ again. Sometimes, two plus two makes five.

Under the headline, 'Tyrone Stance has Decency on its Side', *Sunday Independent* journalist Eamonn Sweeney wrote about the situation in 2013:

> *I'm glad to see that Tyrone footballers will be boycotting RTE coverage for the third championship summer in a row. Not because I've anything against the RTE sports department but because it's good to see people sticking by their principles.*
>
> *We're talking about respect. Back in August 2011, only a few months after Tyrone manager Mickey Harte's daughter had been murdered in Mauritius, RTE's John Murray Show broadcast a sketch which lampooned Harte as a kind of idiot for going to see the Dalai Lama and included the song, 'Pretty Little Girl From Omagh In The County Of Tyrone'.*
>
> *It was horrible stuff. But the worst thing about it was the ignoble motivation behind the skit. Harte was, at the time, one of a number of inter-county managers who had criticised RTE management for not promoting GAA correspondent Brian Carthy.*
>
> *So the sketch smacked of sycophants having a go at Harte in order to ingratiate themselves with their bosses.*

Or, worse again, of Mickey Harte being taught a lesson about what happened to people who dared cross the national broadcaster. Gotcha Mickey.

It took RTE three days before they decided to furnish an apology, an apology which you'd have to say didn't exactly reek of wholeheartedness

Actually, it's unbelievable stuff. A group of people decided to take the piss out of a Tyrone man whose daughter had been murdered by playing a song about a girl from Tyrone.

Think about it. Murray continues to purvey his brand of wacky fun on RTE Radio. Meanwhile, Mickey Harte and his family have had to get on with their lives.

So it's strange to see the Tyrone boycott being portrayed as something surprising or even unreasonable. In reality, the team and the county can do nothing else. Respect for Mickey Harte and the memory of Michaela McAreavey leaves them no choice.

The RTE boycott, far from being an infringement of press freedom, is actually a tribute to the integrity and spirit of the Tyrone footballers which says a lot about the kind of people they are.

That column resonated with me. I have no problem speaking with people who work in RTÉ – myself and Brian Carthy remain the best of friends. My issues are with the institution and those people who allowed that institution to behave the way that it did. Those who had the authority to deal with this situation failed in their duties. A lot of those people, I will never meet. But that is their legacy.

Some think that I am too stubborn. I suppose it depends how you look at the world: principles are important and if that makes me look obstinate then so be it.

I know my own failings: a quick temper, pride, some-times over-competitive. And I can be judgemental. But I know the difference between mercy and justice. Mercy means that we can forgive. There are consequences, though, when you treat people in a hateful way.

• • •

For most of my time in charge of Tyrone, I enjoyed a good relationship with the county board. Dominic McCaughey, Tyrone secretary, was always helpful and extremely efficient. But there was a serious rupture in 2015 when the RTÉ debacle raised its head again.

Róisín Jordan had been elected chairwoman in December 2014. The story attracted some media attention because she was the first woman to hold such a position in Ireland. Little did I think that RTÉ would use this development to their advantage. But as soon as I saw them running a feature interview with her on the main evening news, I sensed they had more than one angle. And their subtle manoeuvrings quickly turned overt. Suddenly there was talk of our sponsor walking away unless I ended the standoff with RTÉ. I do not know if this was true but that approach never washes with me. And whoever was pulling the strings should have known better.

'Let the sponsors go, then, if that's the case,' was my attitude. 'We don't need them. We'll be all right without them.'

At that stage, we had played the Dr McKenna Cup wearing their company logo on the jerseys. It felt like a gun was being put to my head: I had to speak with RTÉ or else permit the players to do so. For a tiny minority in the county board and Club Tyrone, RTÉ was now more important than the Senior manager, one of their own.

A delegation, including some members of Club Tyrone, met RTÉ without my knowledge but some on the county board were unhappy about that meeting. Behind the scenes, these people were trying to broker a deal. They completely overstepped the mark and showed total disrespect to me. It was wrong on all counts. If, as I understand to be the case, a county board officer went without the imprimatur of the full board, they were undermining me. Members of Club Tyrone getting involved only served to damage my position. Involving themselves in a situation to do with the Senior manager was not their role.

A prominent member of Club Tyrone told me that an RTÉ journalist was working behind the scenes, advising them that it would be beneficial for the county to have me talking to RTÉ again. I believe the same journalist attended at least one meeting between this Tyrone delegation and RTÉ. I found it incredible the lengths RTÉ went to: they used their institutional influence to force the situation in their favour.

Football should have been our main concern. But we spent more time discussing off-field matters than figuring out how to become a better team. That aspect of things annoyed me most about what went on.

And I felt that RTÉ were playing us. Instead of making amends with me, they curried favour with Róisín in the hope that she would heal the rift. RTÉ, in my experience, get others to do their bidding when they have caused offence. I could see the game being played and all the talk about our team sponsors only confirmed my suspicions.

I was taken aback when I realised how much pressure was brought to bear. You could feel it coming on from all sides. Some senior people in Club Tyrone were told that the team were losing out because of my refusal to speak with RTÉ. I had a hard time convincing them that RTÉ were at fault for this situation, not me. Even among the Tyrone public, people were beginning to wonder. You could walk into the shop and someone would start up about it. The story kept getting airtime. And, if we lost a game or a tight decision went against us, the RTÉ situation became all the talk again. Tension was building all the time.

Support from the players and the immense leadership and loyalty shown by Mattie Donnelly kept me going through the most difficult days. I never lost them. And they are the most important constituency whenever you have a rocky period. The players always backed me, which a lot of people outside the camp failed to realise. They misread the situation.

I remember saying to the players at that time: 'Boys, I've my reasons for not speaking to RTÉ but you don't need to be dragged into it. If you want to go and speak to RTÉ, go and speak to them.'

The players made their own decision. And they opted to stand full square behind me, which meant a lot.

At times, it felt like I was fighting on all fronts in 2015. And nobody really knew how hard I had to fight.

Setting out that year, I was coming off my worst season in charge of Tyrone. 2014 was horrible. We went out of the Championship in round two of the Qualifiers. To bow out at that stage, against Armagh, was a sickener. I spent most of the summer kicking my heels. Inevitably, I suppose, people started questioning my position. Winning Sam Maguire was the new bar for Tyrone. So we were failing in some eyes. I found that verdict hard to stomach given where we had come from. It's amazing how perceptions can change in such a short period of time. Our failure to win Ulster since 2010 was now being held against me.

The greatest team in Tyrone's history had broken up. We were building a new side while competing close to the top. But patience was in short supply. Relegation from Division 1 of the League could hardly have come at a worse time.

A number of players subsequently opted out of the panel. They complained about lack of game-time yet they never afforded me the chance to discuss their situation. Fringe players, when they get together, can quickly reach the same conclusion: 'I'm not getting a fair chance.'

A team is about what you bring, not what you take.

I made this point in an interview at the end of 2015: 'There is something about the people who stay and bide their time and have the patience. They are probably the people who will serve you best in the long run anyway.'

I sometimes hear players say things like: 'I need more than 20 minutes. Give me 40 minutes and you'll see what I can do.'

That kind of mentality puzzles me. I say to players: 'If you get 20 minutes, they're precious. What you do in 20 minutes will tell me whether you're worth 40.'

But some players find it easier to convince themselves the manager is to blame.

Three weeks later, the storm clouds gathered again in Ballybofey. Donegal beat us in the first round of the Ulster Championship. Mid-May, and we were heading for the Qualifiers. That defeat left us contemplating another long road to make something out of our season.

Meanwhile, the Tyrone Under-21s were on the way to winning their All Ireland. They beat Tipperary in the Final at the beginning of May. So here was a ready-made management setup to replace me: Feargal Logan, Peter Canavan and Brian Dooher. They were seen as the dream team to take over the Seniors. Everything seemed to line up nicely for those who wanted me out.

Publicly, it was obvious my position as manager was under threat. Privately, I had bigger issues. I spent 30 seasons in charge of Tyrone teams and one game is all I missed in that time. April 5, 2015, I could hardly get out of bed.

Kerry came to play us in Healy Park that day: final

round of the League, our Division 1 status on the line. No trophies or medals were at stake. For the players, it was about standing up for their county.

Before the game, I made it as far as Kelly's Inn to meet the team. I managed to give the pre-match pep talk despite my weakened state.

'We need to stick together,' I told the players. 'I wish I could be with you but sometimes life dictates that you can't make it.'

My energy levels were too low to stand on the sideline. The players knew something was up without knowing the seriousness of my condition. At that stage, I faced an uncertain future. If my health continued to deteriorate, my football days were numbered. I spoke that afternoon in Kelly's not knowing how much longer I could carry on as manager or what my ultimate prognosis might mean for the future.

Cancer makes no allowances for inter-county football.

January brought the first sign of trouble: specks of blood in my urine. At training one night, I had a quiet word with our team doctor, Damien O'Donnell, a GP in Coalisland. The fact that I could speak to him casually about it probably made things easier for me. Otherwise, I might have left things for a while.

Damien arranged some blood tests but there was no major concern on his part. And nothing showed up on the tests when they came back. Again, I might have been tempted to let things go. But the doctor decided to send me for a checkup in Craigavon. At the hospital, I underwent a cystoscopy, which is a procedure to look inside the bladder. A thin camera, called a cystoscope, goes in through a catheter – an unpleasant experience.

At least we now knew the problem. The medics discovered a non-invasive growth in the wall of my bladder. And yet I was lucky: the cancer had been detected early.

Things moved quickly then. For six weeks, I underwent chemotherapy. At that time, the preferred medication was in short supply worldwide. So I had to make do with the next best available. Only it failed to work. Second time around, same result.

By now, I was facing the stark possibility of my bladder being removed. And, in that event, there were two possibilities left on the table: bladder reconstruction or a permanent colostomy bag. Either option was a life-changing prospect. A major operation like that would have put me off my feet for three months.

While I was contemplating the future, the chemotherapy treatment continued. But the odds had significantly reduced. Starting out, I had a two-thirds chance of success, but now that figure was closer to 15 per cent. I prayed a lot during that time. I was in trouble.

I could cope with cancer, but the practical implications were harder to contemplate. All I could think about were the challenges of daily life: if I lost the sensation of when to go to the toilet, would I need to set an alarm every couple of hours? And the truly awful thought? No more football. Most of the time, stepping away from the game was my biggest worry.

Marian was better placed to look at the bigger picture: she could stand back a bit, emotionally. Your health, ultimately, takes priority. I was too caught up thinking about the consequences whereas she took a practical view: 'It's still not the end of the world if you have to go for surgery.'

Even though Marian is a worrier by nature, she remained strong throughout. I felt as though she was bearing some of the burden for me. My illness became a focus, something that occupied us almost completely. So it became a positive distraction, strange as that sounds. And Marian seemed to take it all in her stride. The worst-case scenario sounded disastrous to me whereas her attitude was bullish: 'This can be sorted. There's no point in panicking.'

She had conviction but I was full of doubt. For all her confidence, I knew that things might not turn out okay.

Every three months, the medics took a biopsy. And those procedures are risky because the bladder can get punctured in the process. After the first operation, I endured a lot of pain. The biopsy causes trauma because they take away some of the lining from your bladder. As a consequence, you feel ferocious pain when urinating. At times, I was curled up in a foetal position, clutching a relic, praying for the pain to pass. My sleep suffered too. At night, I was up every hour to go to the bathroom. Living like that takes its toll.

But I probably only realised afterwards how much the treatment was affecting me. At the time, you just get on with things. Really, you have no time to think. Perhaps our ability to keep going is part of the body's coping mechanism. We seem to find ways of adjusting when our circumstances change. I suppose we must be resilient by nature.

I dealt with the cancer the same way that I approached most things in life: I was prepared to do whatever it took to succeed. Only this new game made new demands of me. So my diet became a big focus.

Around that time, I first met John Price. I was working for Bank of Ireland at one of their Enterprise Town events in Tallaght. John was a passionate advocate of wheatgrass juice, which he believed had helped him overcome cancer. He talked about all the health benefits and showed me this machine for extracting the juice. The more that he spoke, the more convincing his pitch.

John explained how to grow the wheatgrass. So I took some organic seed and compost to start my own little enterprise at home. I started taking the juice each day, a habit I have kept. These days, Derek and Anna Walker are my source for wheatgrass seed, a couple from Donegal whom John put me in touch with.

Still, diet alone was not going to heal me. And there were lots of days when I just had to put up with the pain.

Round six of the League, we played Donegal in Ballybofey. All week, I had been nursing a head cold. The weather was raw and we got hammered up there. I remember the date, March 29, because I was in theatre the following day.

The previous Thursday, I had been in hospital for the cystoscopy. My consultant told me he had a slot for treatment on the Monday. I jumped at the chance: to get in that quickly was a major boost. Even though I was feeling less than 100 per cent, I went through with the procedure. I knew I might be waiting a long time to get into theatre again.

Five days later, I was still in hospital. My temperature soared after the surgery and it took me the rest of the week to recover. Every other procedure I had during my treatment, I went home the next day.

While I kept my diagnosis private, there were stories doing the rounds. People see you visiting an oncology department and draw their own conclusions. Word spreads quickly in a small place.

For most of 2015, the outcome was uncertain. I had no way of knowing if the treatment would be successful. So I could have done without any extra pressure. Football was a source of light, a release from all that stress. The last thing I needed was more questions about my position as manager. Influential people within Tyrone made life difficult for me. And they could not have been unaware of my health issues. Maybe they thought it was time to turn the screw.

Regardless of what was going on behind the scenes politically, my future depended on my health.

We set sail for the Qualifiers in June. Three rounds in, we were drawn away against Tipperary.

July 18 was one of the worst days I went through with cancer. On the journey down, I had serious pain across my back and along my side. I started to feel sick and then I vomited at the front of the bus, which was awful, the embarrassment of it.

We stayed overnight in Tipperary before the game. As soon as we got to the hotel, I went to my room. But no sleep would come. The pain was that bad.

Gavin Devlin took over. He had to continue

preparations for the match without me. Mark called out to the hotel the following day. I was still in bed, the game only two hours away. He was really worried when he saw me. Himself and Gavin were unsure what to do.

The thought never crossed my mind, but Mark wondered if I was fit to go to the game. By then, the team were having their pre-match meal. And I was still in bed, in real pain. Mark said to me: 'I don't know if this is the right place for you.'

Then the team doctor looked at me. Ideally, I should have been resting up. But an injection would get me through the game without any major consequences.

Even after I got the injection, it took me a while to come right. I was hunched over going to the bathroom. Mark had to help me put on my shoes and trousers. Then I walked out of the room and went down in the lift to meet up with the team before they boarded the bus. Gavin had taken the pre-match meeting and I came in to speak at the end. The players were oblivious to how I was feeling but instinct, my adrenalin for the match, probably masked the pain.

I delivered my words with typical conviction: 'Boys, we are down here to do a job.'

Once the painkiller kicked in, I felt okay. I spoke again in the dressing room, gave it a really good blast. At that stage, I was like Lazarus rising from the dead. And I stood on the line for the full game.

But my body language gave me away during the match. I was still hunched over, wincing from time to time.

The injection had worn off by the time I got home that evening. I had one hell of a night. Never mind sleep, I could hardly lie still in bed. The pain was unrelenting no matter what way I moved.

Next day, I was back into hospital where they quickly uncovered the problem. The pain stemmed from a tube running between my kidney and my bladder. Imagine a Bic pen with the ink holder swollen inside the plastic casing. The fluid in my system was unable to get through fast enough.

I needed a stent, which meant another operation. The stent was inserted into my kidney and a hook on the end kept it in place, to prevent it from slipping out. But I had this constant irritation around my bladder. And I was restricted in what I could do: I started bleeding while playing golf one day.

Originally, the stent was to stay in for three months. But the problem persisted. So it stayed in for another three months. What a relief, then, when the stent finally came out.

The psychological impact of bladder cancer is awful. No one, least of all a man at my age, would feel comfortable being treated in such a sensitive area. To be honest, I found it wild embarrassing at first. During the cystoscopy, there would be two or three female nurses around me. Maybe a female doctor as well. You have to get over yourself quickly, leave your hang-ups at the door. Serious illness changes your perspective on life. I think you develop a lot of humility going through this kind of treatment.

Really, I was blessed they caught my cancer early, before it became invasive. My own GP, Dr Tania Gribben, said to me: 'If you're going to get it, this is as good a place to get it as any.'

Then again, only for Damien O'Donnell, our team doctor, chances are I would have left it for a month or two. The blood appeared in my urine only every now and again. I might well have convinced myself that everything was okay. With Damien, I had easy access, no need for an appointment.

I had another stroke of fortune when I went for my first cystoscopy. The surgeon, Mark Haynes, had a slot available within a few days. So everything happened quite quickly. And the faster you do things, the better.

Aidan O'Brien, another consultant in the urology department, I had actually met previously, not that I knew it at the time. About a month after Michaela died, I was walking down to her grave when he introduced himself. Michaela, he told me then, taught his daughter at St Patrick's Academy in Dungannon. I had long since forgotten this encounter until I met Aidan again at the hospital. He gave me his phone number.

'Ring any time you want,' he said.

I had the best of care. The nurses arranged a private room because there would have been a posse of people around and that was the last thing I needed. Catherine Smiley, a sister of the Down referee Ciarán Brannigan, was the nurse in charge. She, along with Karen O'Neill and Janice Holloway in the outpatient department, looked after us so well, which we greatly appreciated. Having a private room made life much easier, especially for Marian.

Believe it or not, there were some lighter moments. I

remember going down for surgery one day on the trolley. They were wheeling me through a corridor when some boy walking past let out a roar: 'UP ARMAGH!'

All I could do was laugh. I know it seems crazy to think that someone would react that way, but this mad little world we live in can only make you smile sometimes.

Getting through 2015 did not mark the end for cancer and me. One year after my diagnosis, I still had a long way to go. After the initial treatment, I went through a maintenance phase and a biopsy was taken every three months.

Every three weeks, I went into hospital for the maintenance programme. Benign as it sounds, the treatment is severe. The chemotherapy was inserted straight into my bladder through a catheter. Two hours later, I peed it out in a bathroom no one else could use, which tells you how potent the medication was. I had to pour bleach into the toilet bowl afterwards.

And it is painful. Some people cannot hold on for two hours. The most common side effects are flu-like symptoms. You can get aches and pains in your joints as well. Sometimes, it makes you sick. After my treatment, you would think I had a bad cold. I took paracetamol to relieve the pain but I always ran up a temperature. I would be fine the following day and I was fortunate in that sense because it could have been far worse.

The maintenance treatment continued for the best part of two years. The prognosis, although still unclear, was at least less uncertain.

Hindsight makes that time seem like such a different place. Some said I looked shaken but most tended to tiptoe around the issue. I suppose people are conscientious about whether you want to speak about cancer. If someone asked, I told them. Others might be more private but I felt okay talking about the subject if it came up.

They say that the best way to tackle cancer is to live rather than retreat. No doubt football played a big part in my recovery. I was able to get out and be social. I had a purpose beyond cancer.

At no stage did I consider throwing in the towel with Tyrone. I felt others wanted me to, especially when the situation with RTÉ resurfaced at the start of 2015. Maybe some people figured that I would have been fed up and walked away. I always say: 'Anyone thinking that way doesn't know me well enough.' Ultimately, I think my health would have suffered if I had capitulated.

But there was more to my recovery than football. I prayed a lot, which gave me peace of mind. And I have no doubt that the wheatgrass juice played a part. Really, it was a combination of factors – chemotherapy, diet, prayer – that enabled my body to heal.

I was lucky in that I avoided major surgery. My quality of life would have been severely diminished.

Finally, I got the all clear at the end of 2017. And, by that stage, Tyrone had taken a turn for the better as well.

Football-wise, Tyrone needed to get back to winning major trophies in 2016. We redeemed ourselves by reaching the All Ireland Semis the previous year, going further than any other team from Ulster. But we had nothing to show for the season. A run in the Qualifiers can only do so much for you. Titles affirm progress. And it cuts me deeply when Tyrone are not Ulster champions. I struggle to watch other counties winning the Anglo Celt. That prospect never sits well with me.

2016, then, proved a turning point. We went through the League unbeaten, going straight back up as well as winning the Division 2 Final at Croke Park. But the victory against Donegal to regain Ulster was the moment: it showed a new resistance, a new resolve in the team. Meanwhile, the Under-21s lost their provincial title. The landscape around me had shifted again. And who would have predicted such a transformation at the start of 2015?

Still, my position remained a topic of debate. The team were getting close to the big prize but 2017, officially, marked the final year of my term. So I asked the county board for a one-year extension to dispel any notions that 2017 would mark the end. Players behave differently when they think you might go at the end of the season.

The board turned down my request: they wanted to wait until the end of the season. And I could understand their point of view. But some members failed to realise that my status would continue to be a talking point until the issue was resolved. The media kept asking the question. So long as my position seemed uncertain, there was cause for them to speculate. And I found it a drain. At times, I had to justify my existence.

2017 was a strange year in a lot of ways. I knew we were on the verge of doing something special: our provincial success was one of the best in Ulster Championship history. We put together the highest-scoring winning team since records began in 1940. Every victory, including the All Ireland Quarter-Final against Armagh, came with a high degree of comfort on the scoreline. Yet we were castigated for being ultra-defensive.

A vocal minority continued to doubt us. And they wanted me gone.

Our season ended in disappointment: a 12-point defeat to Dublin, beaten all ends up. At that stage, it was easy to make the case for my removal. But our year could not be defined by one result. Although we failed to make the League Final, we won our first four games. Then we defended our Ulster title, which was the minimum requirement. And we consolidated our position in the top four.

You had to look at our entire season to see the true picture.

I went back to face the county board seeking a new three-year term. I was too close to winning Sam again to simply walk away.

And, in fairness, my meeting with the board was cordial, by no means a grilling. I gave them my views, outlined our progress. There was disquiet about the Semi-Final but I felt some officers were merely reflecting public opinion. People forget everything else if you play poorly in a big game.

So I had to enlighten them. Football is not always about the last match: look at the trend. According to some, Tyrone have been through a lean period since winning the All Ireland in 2008. But, by the end of 2017, we had won four Ulster titles, more than any other county. We played in the 2013 League final against Jim Gavin's Dublin, only beaten by a point. We sailed through Division 2 undefeated in 2016. Five years running, we won the McKenna Cup.

Never mind the All Irelands we won in the noughties, our most recent campaigns were more than strong enough to warrant more time in charge. Obviously, the officers were convinced by what I said. Twelve months after turning down my initial request, they decided I was worth three more years at the helm.

News of that decision by the county committee broke in early September, less than a fortnight after the Dublin defeat. So it caught some people by surprise. But I needed more than a brief extension to keep the wolves at bay. An additional year would only have left the same questions hanging over me.

At that point in my career, I was working to help other people taste success. Too many good players were walking around Tyrone without All Ireland medals. I desperately wanted to change that situation, to see the likes of Mattie Donnelly and Peter Harte and Ronan McNamee gain the ultimate reward, the prize their talents deserved.

Another All Ireland was not going to change my life. But I still had the same drive. I would look at my grandchildren and picture the smiles on their faces if they got their hands on Sam Maguire. I saw what it meant to my children. So I wanted the same thing for the next generation.

There were other motivating factors, of course. No more than any other Tyrone fan, I wanted us competing with the best teams in the country. Easy for any county to drift and become an also-ran. Then there are the records. Down made no secret of having their five wins. We might well have had five by then.

I love the fact that Tyrone top the McKenna Cup roll of honour. 2008, we lost in the first round, and still won the All Ireland. We played ten games to win Sam in 2005. During my time as manager, Tyrone were Ulster champions six times. And, as 2018 approached, we had the chance to do three in a row for the first time.

All these thoughts were playing around in my mind. Ultimately, I believe every man must know his why.

First and foremost, football is about winning, and Tyrone people seldom appreciate the way in which you lose. To win, you have to master the way football is being played in your era. No good harping on about the past. Every team adopts a similar style in the modern game but catch and kick is not an option. That approach is all about personal battles and to hell with the team. Honestly, it bores me.

Sport is a process. Make sure you win more than you lose. Then, of the ones that you win, win with a bit of style. The pinnacle for any team is winning while playing great football. How we play has changed over the years, but my football philosophy is much the same. The challenge for any manager is to keep the players engaged. So I have to find different ways of communicating the same message. And I love that challenge.

Core values – hard work, first touch, team ethic – are non-negotiable. Work rate is self-explanatory. Getting the basics right is an obvious requirement because you lose precious seconds trying to get the ball under control. Time wasted limits what you can do in possession.

Then you learn to play with your head up, to do what is right for the team. A player must adapt, steel himself for every situation. You learn to play with intensity and controlled aggression. As the manager, I keep reminding them of the same things: 'be match alert, on your toes, talk to your teammates.'

Say those things day in and day out and still you need to repeat them every half time. Players forget.

Success rarely travels in straight lines. The speed bumps were more obvious as we turned to face 2018. Our squad contained a lot of serious athletes and we needed to get them playing in a way that suited their athleticism. No good kicking high ball on top of small forwards. The running game was our strongest suit but we needed to get the right balance between defence and attack. Besides, Dublin were by far the best team in the country. Everybody was failing to a find a way past them.

Me being the longest-serving manager in the game did not mean I was unfit to do the job. Good experiences retain their value.

My age never concerned me. So what if the players are younger: I could mix with any of the lads on the panel. I used to get annoyed when people said Tyrone were suffering from same-voice syndrome. Such criticism implies a lack of thought on my part. That suggestion always insulted me. Management has never been a static role; you move with the times.

I firmly believed we could take the Dubs in 2017. The evidence was there from our previous meetings in the League. They needed a last-minute free to level the game when we last met them. And we had them on the ropes that evening in Croke Park, five points up, playing against the breeze.

Still, our position in the pecking order remained uncertain before we met the Dubs again. Okay, we won Ulster in a canter and beat Armagh by 18 points in the Quarter-Finals. But those games were played on our terms against familiar opponents from within our province. Dublin, back-to-back champions, were chasing three in a row. Could we rock them?

Going by the beat on the street, we were well primed. To me, that analysis was flawed because we were being measured by our previous performances in the Championship when Dublin were the only assessment that mattered.

Contest a Semi and you expect to make the Final. You begin painting a picture of the big day, thinking how you might prepare. What will the day look like? How will we feel? Your imagination takes over.

As the Dublin game drew near, I felt the team were in a good place. Motivation was certainly not an issue. I kept telling the players: 'Their boys have medals rattling in their pockets. They have been on the circuit, meeting sponsors, promoting cars. Could they possess the same hunger as us?'

Every night at training, you could sense the mood within our camp, everyone flat out. I often feel that team spirit is the secret ingredient. Because sport is about more than pure skill and athleticism. And you can see that spirit within a team: players are happy in each other's company. They can challenge each other on the pitch without compromising their off-field relationship.

So I hammered that message as well. I told our boys, over and over: 'I know our team spirit is stronger than theirs.'

Tactically, I knew we could frustrate Dublin. But playing on the counter-attack requires a lot of discipline. The mass defence looks like a basic setup, everyone behind the ball. Often, the mass conceals a pattern. And there are lots of moving parts, different players stepping into different lines, always covering for each other. Then, if you do win a turnover, the trick is to release men to go forward at the right time. And that phase of play – angled running, slick passing, heads up football – requires a certain amount of discipline as well. At every stage, the goal is to get the ball to the man in the best position. I like to think we pioneered a lot of those elements. Even the Dubs have discovered that pulling 15 men inside your own half is not such a big deal. Provided it serves a purpose, of course.

So I had total faith in our game plan. We could stifle Dublin at one end and then use the pace within our team to exploit them on the break.

But any plan can be made to look brittle by a hard punch. Dublin hit us for a goal within five minutes: Con O'Callaghan straight down the middle. Our discipline, in that moment, deserted us. Against a team as good as Dublin, that lapse was fatal.

O'Callaghan's score was our own making. An attack broke down and we were caught out of position. At all times, somebody has to mind the house. But nobody filled in for Colm Cavanagh when he joined that early attack. These things happen in a game when the blood is up.

And yet the match was too young for us to consider abandoning our defensive shape. Changing tack at that moment would have left us more vulnerable. At half time, we had a chance to adjust. After the break, we pushed forward, going at Dublin instead of trying to catch them on the counter. We had five attacks in eight minutes, enough chances to get within two. Then we could have sat back and frustrated them.

Afterwards, the consensus view, that we let Dublin play in front of us, was hard to stomach. Their early goal forced us to retreat. Plus, we failed to do ourselves justice, which grated most of all. While coping with those feelings, you have to deal with the backlash. Inside the camp, there are always players thinking they would have made the difference had they got on.

You travel a long way to get away from the vitriol, to hear an objective assessment. At least I know what to expect in those situations. Gavin Devlin, my assistant manager, had greater difficulty dealing with the aftermath. I went through the same process with the County Minors. Everyone has to go through it, but these feelings will pass. Within a week, another team will be ripe to pick apart.

The crowd are all over you when the team is going well but losing teaches you not to take too much from any victory. Experts tell us how and why we went wrong, though few predict that run of events beforehand. So I warn the players about what will come their way. The final whistle does not mark the end of the torment. Everyone gets doubted afterwards, every detail unpicked.

Two weeks after Dublin, we gathered the team for a meeting, a debrief, essentially. I went through the game at length and the players could see how the margins were much slimmer than they appeared on the scoreboard. I reminded them of an important statistic: the football we played in 2017 made us the highest-scoring Ulster champions of all time. I wanted the players leaving that session feeling upbeat. Our approach served us well for most of the year. The Semi-Final was just a wobble, another part of the journey. One pothole does not mean the whole road is a wreck.

My path in life has taken lots of unusual turns and football often leads to chance encounters.

I get to meet all kinds of people. And for all sorts of reasons. Tyrone football, naturally, is a common connection.

Before we played Armagh in the 2019 McKenna Cup final, a group from the Roger Casements club in Antrim visited our dressing room. Paul McKeever, who played with Antrim and refereed at inter-county level, was the link. The McKeevers made contact the year before through John, Paul's brother, who teaches alongside Peter Canavan at Holy Trinity in Cookstown. Paul had been diagnosed with cancer and was due for major treatment when I first met him.

Sadly, he was in a hospice when I next visited. He died in November 2018, leaving behind a young family of his own. I was glad then that his two boys, Ryan and Conor, were part of the group who met with us in the Athletic Grounds.

I feel our players benefit from these interactions. To spend time with people who have suffered loss is always a humbling experience, keeps you grounded. And it can actually feel like an uplifting experience. As the group left our dressing room, ten-year-old Ryan said to me: 'Go out an' win it now. That's what my Daddy would say.'

That gave me a great kick: I knew he meant every word of it.

Another time, Michael's wife Josephine, who works as an occupational therapist, arranged for me to visit one very memorable woman. Josephine got to know about her through work. This woman had been unwell for a while and, between one thing and another, a suitable date was hard to pin down. Then we got word that she was home from hospital. Finally, we were set.

But her family decided to keep the news from her until the night before. They said nerves would have got the better of her otherwise.

Well, when I landed! There she was, 70 years of age, togged out in the full Tyrone kit: jersey, togs and socks. And she was shaking with excitement. The woman could hardly believe her eyes. I felt like I was after walking into a family party. The family took photographs and I signed my name on a glass with a black marker – she wanted something to remember her day. I could see by her that she savoured every minute.

She even had the house painted red and white. And there were pictures around the place of everything that Tyrone ever did. Her home was like a shrine to Tyrone football.

Someone asked her if she had slept the night before.

And she says: 'I couldn't sleep. I can't believe that Mickey Harte's in my house.'

Amazing the impact sport can have on people at every age. Me being there meant so much to her. She was so taken with the whole idea of Tyrone, our county, doing well. I felt so humble that someone would think me calling to her house was such a big deal.

We chatted football and games of the past. These experiences are unique to Gaelic games. Someone meets you for the first time and feels great. I get just as much from those encounters. One thing I do know, from reading the Gospel and from living this life: in giving you receive. To be able to brighten someone else's day is an amazing gift.

I often say to players: 'Football is not just about you. And this is not just about now. This is about the history of your area, your parish, your club, your community, your people.'

Being part of the GAA means belonging to something special, something unique. Call it tradition. I think of the people who went before us who worked hard to provide the pitches on which we play and the facilities where we train. Here, in the Six Counties, people have lost their lives because of their affiliation to the GAA. Always be conscious of what it means to the people you represent. Cherish your heritage.

Other times, I get requests to make phone calls, especially when a family member is sick. But I much prefer to meet with the person. Those trips hardly cost me a thought. All I give is my time.

The reactions I get are hard to believe. One man wanted to be buried with a picture of himself and me, which was taken shortly before he died.

A man I met in 2018, another Tyrone supporter, was in a bad way with cancer. He was living in Fermanagh. So I got the address and called to the house. His wife and daughter were there when I called and we had a great conversation. This man, originally from Trillick, had played football back in an era that I was familiar with. So we traded stories and talked about the old times. I had a signed Tyrone jersey with me and presented that to him, a small gesture, but his family loved it.

Those visits move me: they are heartening and yet poignant at the same time. That man was confined to his bed when I called. So I left the house knowing I was unlikely to see him again. I know people appreciate me calling but I think it is a relatively small thing to do. If they get something from it, great. I feel in my heart that these visits are the right thing to do, not that they make me special or anything. Because I get just as much from those conversations.

Since Michaela's death, I have met many other families touched by tragedy. Sometimes, I seek them out.

I found out about Adrian Doherty through Radio Ulster. Oliver Kay, the football writer, was being interviewed one day about *Forever Young*, his book on Doherty's life.

Until I read the book, Doherty's name was new to me. He hailed from Strabane and went on to play with Manchester United. But he was a forgotten hero. His story naturally appealed to a life-long Man U fan.

But he met a tragic end. Doherty's life fascinated me. He was a free spirit, the polar opposite of what you might expect from a modern professional soccer player. People likened him to George Best yet he saw himself as much more than a footballer. He preferred to go busking in Manchester rather than watch games at Old Trafford.

His football career ended prematurely through injury. And he simply moved on, refusing to see himself as a victim. Spiritually, he felt fulfilled. I loved his attitude to life.

He died at 27, a significant age for me because of Michaela. I wanted to meet his parents, to spend time in their company. I felt it would be good for us. Turned out they were still living in Strabane.

Fr Michael Doherty, a priest I knew, was mentioned in the book. So I got in touch with him and he gave me directions to the family house. I arrived unannounced, knocked on the door. I figured that way was best. His parents were country people like me. And they were pleased when I called.

I told them how much their son's story resonated with

me. Really, I just wanted to say hello, empathise with them in some way.

We chatted for an hour and more. They were glad that Adrian's story was out in the public domain, that others had the chance to read about their son. To me, it seemed like he had been let down by the system. They felt that the book afforded him some recognition, even if it was long overdue.

There was a kind of instant connection between us. Our lives had known similar experiences, travelled parallel roads. Here was another life with a major challenge. We shared an unspoken bond, a spiritual link that needed no words. Afterwards, they sent a card to the Tyrone GAA Centre in Garvaghey, thanking me for the call.

Having been on the other side of grief, at this stage I know what not to say in those situations. Some people speak without thinking and they come out with the most ridiculous things.

One person came to me when Michaela died. 'They say it gets better with time,' he began. 'It doesn't. It gets worse.'

At least I can laugh at that memory now.

One phrase has stayed with Marian: 'If we knew what to do, wouldn't we be doing it?'

Francie Mulgrew said that to us at the time, wise words from a good friend. He got married the same day as us and was involved with me managing underage teams in Errigal. Sadly, Francie died in 2020. His words always rang true.

So many people say the wrong thing in those situations.

Never tell a grieving person that you know how they feel. You never do. They might not even know themselves. You only know what grief is like for yourself.

'How are you doing?' is the typical thing people ask. Yet that innocent question is often the worst thing you could say.

I really want to tell them: 'How the hell do you think I'm doing?'

Words seem shallow in those circumstances. Be genuine. Give the person a hug and promise to say a prayer for them – nothing else will be any use, really. The most important thing is to be there because that shows you care.

I say very little when I meet other people who have just suffered a loss. Your presence is what counts. My words, not so much. I want to show them that there is life beyond your bleakest moment. However distant or remote that brighter place seems, it does exist. I know. I found it.

One thing I have learned from spending time with grief is that we all cope in different ways. My grief is not the same as my wife's, and mine is not even the same as it was yesterday. Grief hits us all at some point but nobody knows how they will feel until the moment comes. Pain is subjective. No one has a licence to presume what another person is going through, even if you have suffered a similar loss.

Everyday greetings work in most places, but not here.

Instead, say: 'I'm calling to be here with you. I'll keep you in my prayers. I just want to be here for you.'

Be true. Be genuine. Awareness is everything: the more we think about the words we use, the more likely we are to share the right ones.

Typically, a family friend gets in touch after a tragic death and we make arrangements to meet. The expectation is that I will do all the talking but my mission is to find out what they have to say. So I turn the situation around, ask them to share their experiences. At that point, I know they need to be heard.

I once met a couple from Donegal. They had lost their young boy to a tumour. I could see the sadness in the mother's eyes; they were such lovely people.

I try to be as honest as possible with everyone I meet. The first thing I tell them kind of takes them by surprise. I usually say: 'I don't expect you to understand this at the minute. In fact, I would be surprised if you did.'

Then I talk about my journey since Michaela's death. One of the major things with grief is to be able to get to a point where you can appreciate what you had rather than be suffering for what you lost. Everyone gets stuck at some point: we tend to fixate on our loss.

I only try to give people an alternative way of looking at their situation. There are no guarantees, no magic words of comfort. All I can give them is some hope, the possibility that they might rediscover some joy in their lives, to move beyond the darkness.

Not three months after Michaela's death came the terrible news about Ronan Kerr. He was from Beragh, Marian's home place, and had attended Omagh CBS. Mattie knew

Ronan from school – he was in the same year as Ronan's brother – and always spoke well of him.

Ronan was an officer with the PSNI, only 25 years old. His murder rocked the whole community. He was killed outside his home by a car bomb, an unthinkable act. And all because he was a Catholic serving in the police force. How could you get your head around it?

Nationalist people generally viewed the police service with suspicion, which was understandable given our history with authority in the North. For someone like me, who so strongly identified as a Catholic and a GAA man, carrying an officer's coffin was unheard of.

But I just sensed that it was the right thing to do. I knew what it was like to lose a child; I could identify with that hurt. And I felt so much for the Kerr family.

Both communities were united for once, which was such a positive thing at the time. And the GAA came out in force to condemn what had happened. It was the first time that we saw the GAA take that kind of stand. I think everyone recognised the significance; it was a powerful moment.

Some time after the funeral, I got a letter from Manchester: Alex Ferguson had taken the time to write to me. I could hardly believe what I was reading.

He wrote: 'I was always impressed by your achievements with the Tyrone team and how long you've been there. I meant to write to you after what happened to your daughter. I knew I had to write to you after Ronan Kerr.'

He left a contact number for me to get in touch. I remember calling him and he said to come over to Old

Trafford. So we got tickets for a derby game through Martin Logan, a great friend of mine from Galway who spent most of his life in Manchester. Myself and the boys went across in October 2011. But we picked the worst day possible: City beat United 6-1.

I called Alex a couple of weeks afterwards and told him about the game we had been to. He said: 'I hope you don't think it's like that all the time.'

But the trip gave us a lift, something we badly needed. And the boys got a real kick out of it.

I was taught to profess my faith. So I see it as my duty to share those beliefs, to spread the word of God.

Ultimately, God is not going to talk about All Ireland medals. I imagine him asking me: 'How did you help people get closer to me?'

Just because my faith guides me does not mean I will always do the right thing. There are times when I must challenge myself. None of us are perfect. But I know what I should be doing. I have to ask myself: 'Am I living up to my ideals?'

I reflect on that question all the time. Because I could easily go with the flow and take my lead from the crowd. My faith challenges me to dig deeper, which means going against the grain at times.

Thankfully, I never lost sight of my faith at any stage. Even in younger days, when life was busier, I sensed an inner presence that kept me calm and content. I never felt idle. There was no yearning for action. And I always had good people around me.

What do you grasp when trouble comes? Prayer is my pillar in good times and in bad. The chapel is always a place of peace for me. I go there seeking solace, knowing that I am never alone: my faith never fails to support me.

Luckily, my parents planted a seed. They cannot grow if you neglect to sow them.

Marian and I made a conscious effort to do the same thing with our children. They grew up in a similar environment: prayer was a normal part of their life. We kept a copy of the parent's prayer in the house, which served as a reminder for us about those values. Marian and I were raised in loving homes; both of us inherited a strong template for family life. Our parents taught us parameters, the difference between right and wrong.

And our children spent a lot of time with their grandparents. So the faith was passed down in numerous ways. I think if you force-feed religion, children are more likely to reject it.

Maybe faith is a bit like grief: we all experience it slightly differently. Pick a line from the Gospels and its meaning may not be the same for any two people. I make the same point wherever I speak: 'These things may not resonate with you now. But hopefully you can take something with you that might help you in your own journey.'

I only know the answers to my own questions.

And still I have much to learn. Each day, I set out to live the life of a good Christian, to become a better Catholic. That thought remains foremost: changing your mind has never been on my agenda.

Where would I be without my faith? That question helps me reflect on life with a sense of hope. Michaela's murder rocked us in an elemental way. And yet, I can bring myself to say that a lot of good has come from her death. Just because such thoughts are hard to contemplate does not make them any less true. There have been positive changes in our lives and I thank God for each one of them. The impact on Mattie has been nothing short of a miracle.

Mattie always believed in God and, like the rest of us, faith was an important part of his life. But his generation is different to mine. The word 'faith' can mean anything now whereas we knew it to mean Catholic. And it was part of our culture: we lived and breathed it, a faith that was caught rather than taught.

Society has changed. Atheism became prominent through the internet and the popular media during the mid to late 2000s. Faith became outdated because science seemingly had the answers to everything.

Mattie would get asked questions in school and especially in college: 'Why do you believe these things? How can you think about trusting the bible? Did Jesus even exist? What about all the other religions? What about all the science?'

Without having all the answers, he got really irritated. It made his faith seem shallow. He was studying History and Politics at Queen's at the time, his first Master's, so he was used to following evidence, searching for what was real. These questions frustrated him because he knew they were legitimate. And it pushed him to the brink of not believing in Jesus.

What happened to change that was remarkable. Football became like a religion for him at that time. He gave himself almost entirely to the game: in the gym four times a week, plain chicken for breakfast, three protein shakes a day. And all to play Senior Reserve for the club. Everything else came after football. He would train in the morning before going to work and do another session in the evening. Of all the boys, Mark was blessed with the most ability. And Michael always had an eye for a score. Mattie probably felt he needed to work harder at his game to be competitive. So, he dedicated himself to being in the best shape possible.

But injury struck: a ruptured cruciate ligament. He spent months out of action rehabbing the right knee. Shortly after, his hamstring went in the bad leg, a common thing post cruciate unfortunately. And then Father James Devine came into our lives. The timing seems providential now.

Fr Devine, a young priest from Derry, has had a major impact on both of us. He was a deacon in Limavady at the time, where they ran a faith-based summer camp called HOPE: Help Our Parish Evolve. His search for a patron brought him to my door. For him, Michaela embodied the values for every life of faith.

He sent me a handwritten letter, which ran to six pages. I was impressed that he would go to so much trouble. I gave him my blessing and through that connection, Mattie got to know Fr Devine as well.

We invited him to lead a retreat for us at the Michaela Foundation, where he offered a mass. He was newly ordained then. Mattie was just blown away. Fr Devine said the mass like he meant it, like he truly believed he was bringing Jesus Christ to the altar in the Eucharist. The reverence and importance of what was happening was so clear. This was something different.

Mattie then got to asking him questions, the same types of questions he was being asked by his friends. Only this time, there were answers, intelligent answers. Fr Devine was able to give a convincing and articulate argument for the Catholic faith.

Next thing, Fr Devine floated the idea of going to Fatima. And Mattie was ready to make that trip as he wanted to learn more and give the faith a real go. Catherine, then his girlfriend, went with him. She saw first hand how much his experience there affected him. Over the few days his life was completely changed. He learned the story of what Our Lady did in Fatima, the miracles witnessed by 70,000 people, and was able to grill Fr Devine for more answers to explain the Catholic faith.

After hearing what he had to say, Mattie let the idea that this might all be for real into his head and opened up to God. At one stage during Adoration, he was hit with the full reality of Jesus' presence in the Eucharist. As he says, the power and love of God hit him like a tonne of bricks, rocked him to his core. He realised this was all for real. After all the years of mass and Church, it finally clicked.

That made him realise he had to go to confession. He knew enough now not to receive communion until getting rid of some of the stuff he had done in the past. Having not been to confession in a long time, he knew he had to make things right. The next day he made the first real adult confession of his life, pouring it all out, letting God forgive him in the sacrament.

He went into adoration after and fell into floods of tears. Whatever happened, he was sobbing like never before. Nothing like it has happened to him since. Mattie had this sense of being so sorry for everything that he had done wrong in his life. And then he felt complete peace, a true joy. What was weighing him down and holding him back was gone. People scour the earth looking for that peace and joy when it is there for us in confession and in the Eucharist.

One of the last nights, he helped to carry Our Lady in the nightly procession around the shrine. That was a big moment for him, a real moment of healing. The last woman he had carried on his shoulders was Michaela at her funeral.

I cannot think of this episode as anything other than a major encounter with God. He came back from that pilgrimage on fire. He was transformed, like a man who had discovered his true calling in life. I remember him telling Marian and me: 'I don't know what's happened here. All I know is that this is all real.'

Marian was a bit taken aback by what he told us. But he made total sense to me. I could feel this burning energy coming off him, as if he had been infused by some divine power. And he started to make some really significant changes to his life.

Mattie was teaching religion in secondary school at that stage. So he knew how hard it was trying to discuss serious matters with teenagers who were utterly sceptical of the faith. But the more that he knew about his faith, the more he could answer their questions and engage the students. They were hungry for it. Everybody asks the big questions at some stage: Why are we here? What's our purpose? What do we believe? Why do we believe it? Now Mattie was fit to say why we should believe. He had answers for the most difficult questions.

But more than that, he felt a genuine love for his students. He started to pray for them and their families.

Mattie is convinced that he is a better man, a better husband, a better father and a better teacher because of what God has done in his life.

Gradually, Mattie incorporated more aspects of his faith into daily life. Best of all, his faith journey has brought us closer together as father and son. I know from conversations with him that my support was important. After Fatima, he decided to quit playing football. And he feared that I might fight him over it. But that thought never entered my head. I only wanted the best for him, like I did for all our children, and I could see that he was going down a path he needed to follow. Then I started to walk with him.

Adoration became a critical part of his practice. Years ago, I was a Eucharistic Minister in the parish, which meant that, with the priest's permission, I could expose the Blessed Sacrament. So I would go with Mattie and Catherine to the chapel. At first, I found the hour long.

With each practice, the time seemed to go quicker. I felt the benefit of that time in prayer. Those hours became a complete gift. The silence allows for so much space in your head: you become free to focus not on your troubles or problems but on Jesus and what He has done for us. We kept going through the winter, wrapped in padded Tyrone jackets, hot water bottles on our knees.

Psychologically, the silence frees you to look inside.

Mattie really opened my eyes. I would love to have discovered the faith in the same way at 26. He has gone on to complete a Master's in Theology and is now going for a PhD. I discovered through him an incredible intellectual depth to what we believe. It turns out the historical evidence for Jesus and the bible is better than any ancient document, that science is completely reconcilable with faith. Either Jesus is God or not. As the writer CS Lewis put it, 'Jesus is either a liar, a lunatic or the Lord.' So he cannot just be a good moral teacher. Anyone who claims to be God has to be one of those three things.

The changes he brought about in his life made sense to me. Secularism, this 'me me me' culture, has become the new faith. The world suggests that you can become your own god. Have whatever you want: drink, drugs, sex, money. Take as much as you like. And pursue them however you wish regardless of the consequences. Deep down, is that kind of life really fulfilling?

Secular society has largely lost sight of what is most important. Obviously, I put a lot of time and energy into football. And I can be single-minded. But I carried on the rest of my life as best I could. Having children makes you realise, maybe for the first time, that the world does not revolve around you. As much as football means to me, family is foremost and faith underpins every aspect of my life.

Mattie's experience even spurred a marriage proposal. Within a few weeks, himself and Catherine were engaged.

To me, their relationship is one of Michaela's enduring gifts. She guided him about his girlfriends, advising what qualities he should look for in a woman. For a young lad, he was well fit to heed her advice. But his regard for Michaela's opinion was such that he feared no one would ever meet her requirements.

I remember him saying to me: 'I'll never meet a girl that will fulfil the standards Michaela would have.'

And I said: 'I bet you will. I guarantee you will.'

He doubted me for a long time. Sadly, only when Michaela was gone from our lives did my prophecy come true.

We held the first summer camp for the Michaela Foundation in 2012 and Catherine was among the volunteers. None of us knew her beforehand, although she lived just six miles from Glencull. She was a cousin of my nephew Petey Harte, Barney's son. Petey's mother, Joan, is Catherine's aunt. That connection drew her to the camp, which we held in the local primary.

At St Malachy's, Mattie and Catherine struck up a rapport. They found much in common: love of family, a strong faith, appreciation of community. I felt Michaela was an invisible force guiding them together. Like Mattie, Catherine is a Pioneer. Here was a woman who met Michaela's criteria.

But, before they became serious, Catherine's aunt cautioned her: 'He's a Harte. He'll be late. They only speak the language of football.'

We can only laugh. While not entirely fair, there is more than a tinge of truth in that verdict.

About five weeks after that camp, they started going out. I was thrilled for Mattie. He had found the kind of person he wanted. I do believe Michaela led him to his wife. The fact that he met Catherine in those circumstances is too much of a coincidence.

Like Michaela, he was undaunted by other people's opinions. Mattie had no problem telling people he did not believe in sex before marriage. Inevitably, I suppose, friends jabbed him a bit. But he was always well fit to take it. Mattie knew he was more likely to meet the kind of girl he wanted if she already knew his beliefs.

Catherine shared his approach to life. During the lead-up to their wedding, they decided to go to Mass and Adoration every day. Football fell by the wayside then because training clashed with the times he wanted to spend in church.

That decision really took Michael by surprise. He sat Mattie down at one stage to try and talk him around.

'What are you at?' he said to him. 'You're 26. You're in the best shape of your life.'

Mattie, for such a young man, was brave enough to follow his heart. And I really admired him. The boys still talk about all the things that families talk about when they get together. But Mattie's prayer life is not for them. So they leave it unspoken. All of them remain deeply passionate about football. Mattie has coached lots of school teams and is still a dedicated Tyrone follower.

Faith is now the most important aspect of his life. And I think he has wisdom beyond his years. Grief, sometimes, makes you realise what is really going on in your life.

When Michaela died, we all had to confront difficult emotions. Mattie's reading of the Bible led him to the realisation that Jesus actually has some things to say about our lives. He calls you to love your enemies and pray for those who persecute you. He said to me: 'If this is for real then I have to pray for and forgive the men who murdered Michaela. What's the alternative? To wish for hell for them. That's not from God.'

Throughout life, I have tried my best to give everybody a fair chance. I look for value in everyone, almost instinctively. Sure, I have strong convictions, but I like to take people as I find them.

Like Mattie, I discovered a place of peace through my faith. Both of us gave our hurt over to God. Life can feel like a train journey and, if your emotions are powering the train, then you can come off the tracks. Let your will do the driving and emotions follow. Everybody has their cross. It just so happened that ours was public.

You know, Michaela possessed an instinctive belief about her faith. If Tyrone lost a big game, she would always say: 'This is part of God's greater plan.'

We were beaten by Down in 2008, Quarter-Final of the Ulster Championship, and she said those words with total conviction. Michaela embodied her faith. Prayer was a central part of her world, an essential element of daily life. Together with Mattie, she prayed during games. Every half time, they said a decade of the Rosary on red and white beads.

Over the course of my lifetime, society has turned away from the sacred. But a life without faith does not truly lead to fulfilment. Get to know God. You miss out on so much when you neglect your relationship with Him.

I look on my faith like a friendship. If you only see your friends at Christmas then those connections have no chance to develop, to deepen. The more time that you invest, the stronger those relationships become. We can be reluctant to move towards those things that do give us contentment.

I often pray the Rosary travelling home in the car. The power of that prayer is another thing that took me years to realise. Our Lady is our mother. She loves us like her own. So we have a mother in heaven, the Queen of Heaven. And the devil is terrified of her. She has power from God to help us and gives us access to that in her rosary. We would do well to listen to her.

When I pray, I meditate on each mystery and summon the intentions of each decade. I keep a list in my head of all the people who have asked me to pray for them. The first decade is dedicated to those who have died. For the second decade, I think of those who are sick or have troubles in their lives. Then the third decade brings Paul McGirr and Cormac McAnallen to mind. Ashlene, Cormac's fiancée, is always in my thoughts. I felt so much for her at the time of his death.

Gratitude dominates the fourth decade. I thank God

for all the gifts that He has given our family. I pray for Marian and our relationship. The last decade, I pray for those suffering from addiction. I think of someone like Cathal McCarron, who went through a terrible time with gambling during his Tyrone career.

I often say a prayer for a local man from Ballygawley. He has had troubles in life, but Peter is a real wit, one of life's characters. The story goes that the local priest met him on the street one day. He said to him: 'Drunk again, Peter?'

'Aye, me too,' he replied.

Where else but home? I love meeting him. I like spending time with people like Peter – my mother's influence, I think. She would look out for the person who had challenges in life. Peter lost his twin brother when he was young and now lives alone. He never fails to mention Michaela and the prayers that he says for her. I can see the goodness in him. He lives in the town and I call from time to time. Any spare Tyrone jackets or coats, I leave for him in a bag at the door, a small gesture that he really appreciates.

I often wonder: How do we know that Christ is still alive today? I find him in the people that I meet.

One line from Luke's Gospel, 22:42, stands out for me: 'Yet not my will but yours be done.'

God's love is limitless. This place I find myself can get better. And these wonderful feelings will continue to flourish as long as I nourish them. I really do feel that the best is still to come.

Our time on this Earth is mysterious. The magic of life lies in its mystique.

DUSK

December 31, 2018: December is always a difficult month. The days grow shorter and night seems to come more quickly. Christmas approaches and the atmosphere grows heavy around the house. Our sense of loss intensifies. Then January breaks, a new year turning, but we remain inside our own globe while the world surges again.

There are so many significant dates around that time of year: Michaela got married on December 30; she turned 27 the following day; January 1 was the last time we saw her alive.

Each winter that passes, these weeks are less of a burden. In the early years, we all went to Michaela's anniversary Mass. Now we tend to do our own thing. We can cope without having to be together. If Marian stays home, I like to be around for her. But she might spend time with her friends as well, which is a good sign in its own way.

I go to the chapel first thing. My day runs much like

any other. Marian prefers not to dig up the past, though she finds it easier to look at pictures of Michaela. Recently I found the Christmas cards that Michaela gave us in 2010.

Mine reads: 'Daddy dear; Wishing you a very happy Christmas. Thank you so much for everything you do for me + just for being you. Love always, Caela xxx.'

To Marian, she wrote: 'Mummy, Wishing you a happy Christmas, you are one in a million, and don't you forget that; looking forward to the end of Dec + 2011. Lots of love, Caela xxx.'

Those messages make me smile.

Ballymacilroy has Mass on Saturday night so Michaela's anniversary is celebrated on the Saturday closest to her date. We no longer hold an individual Mass for Michaela. Whoever comes, comes. Marian slips out before the end.

The period leading up to this Christmas was more hectic than usual. Marian's father, Pat, had been ill for some time and the family were taking turns to visit him in hospital. At 91, he was hale and hearty for his age but the signs of decline were ominous. He did not have the same zest for life.

'Sure I won't be around to see it,' he would say during idle moments of conversation, the kind of remark I never heard from him.

Whatever life was left in him, Pat's mind was on the wane. His loss of independence had a detrimental effect. He was no longer fit to drive and his mood went down. And he sounded like a defeated man. At that age, the body is vulnerable.

One thing led to another. A chest infection, then a problem with his blood pressure. Next thing, he took a fall and was hospitalised. He could hardly walk at that stage but after a while you start to wonder if he had lost the ability or the will. The flame within the man was burning low.

From September onwards, we saw him every Sunday in the hospital. Pat's hearing was always bad and, because his aids were not always in when we visited, the simple act of conversation proved difficult. The chat quickly turned into a shouting match.

He had to get accustomed to a very different world in a relatively short space of time. He was 88 when he had his second hip replacement and breezed through the recovery. Before, he could quip about his age.

But the humour went from his voice. His decline was hard to watch. Changes in his circumstances had taken their toll. We could see the contrast with the life he used to lead, the difference between autonomy and dependency. That journey is not easy for people who have been independent for a long time.

Michaela's death made it harder for Marian to be as close with her father. Her mother died in August 2010 and within six months, Michaela was gone as well. I think visiting home became too much for her to handle. I feel she might not have wanted her dad to see her get upset, which was understandable. Maybe it seemed easier to visit him in hospital.

The week before Christmas, Pat died. His funeral was on December 23. At least Mattie and Catherine were back from America at that stage, which gave Marian some comfort. Mattie had moved to the Franciscan University of Steubenville in Ohio the previous September to begin a Master's in Theology.

Meanwhile, I was debating whether to travel with Tyrone for the team holiday to Thailand. We were due to fly out on St Stephen's Day, a reward for our run to the All Ireland Final. For Marian, that kind of trip is too much to contemplate.

With Mattie home, and the rest of the family close by, there was no shortage of people for Marian to call on. So I felt a bit easier about heading away.

At this stage of our lives, we are comfortable doing our own thing anyway. Both of us are very much our own people; always were. To me, that kind of independence is healthy in a marriage.

I roomed on my own in Thailand. Each time I went back to the room, I found myself checking for signs of disturbance, running my hand across the wardrobe rail, peeking into the bathroom. Instinct, I guess. The trip obviously put me in mind of Mauritius.

The memory of Michaela's death never goes away but it is not so raw for me now. I comfort myself with a simple thought: 'I've lived in that place and I've survived.'

March 2018, we gathered in Garvaghey to watch a *Laochra Gael* episode TG4 had made about my career. Friends and family were there, lots of football people too. Paul McGirr's parents were sitting in front of me. I really felt for them when the '97 Minors featured. A sadness came over me again when Cormac McAnallen appeared. He looked so vibrant, a young man entering his prime.

Then Michaela's face filled the screen and I could hear this collective intake of breath. Suddenly I was conscious of how shocking it seemed to everyone else, as if they were witnessing those scenes for the first time again. Those images I live with every day.

But when I reflect on Michaela's life, I return to the same conclusion: 'I'm glad that we had Michaela for as long as we did.' She was unique, the best daughter any father could ever wish to have.

Football is something that has always grounded me. It gives me a sense of order however chaotic the rest of life might be.

The landscape changed for me with Tyrone after our three All Ireland wins. My position came under increasing scrutiny because I was being judged on the standards that were set in the noughties. But the football world had moved on. And our greatest ever team was breaking up.

That period was probably more difficult for me than I realised at the time. These great players, warriors for Tyrone, were reaching the end and I had to make a lot of hard calls. I made mistakes. Sometimes, you assume that a player knows the time has come to call it quits. But then the end point is not the same for everyone. While some are finished at 25 because of injury, others can keep going until 35. Each person's contribution is ever changing too. Players can adapt to different roles. Part of the problem for me was that certain boys struggled with their changing status: they found it difficult to accept being 20-minute men.

As manager, you must do right by the team, which can make you seem cold. So many players were with me since their Minor days and the bond was intense. I felt for them; I knew how much they had given to the cause. I hated having to leave them off the team, boys who gave me everything.

Rebuilding was a gradual process.

We won lots of big games in the years after 2008 but it became easier to dismiss those achievements as long as Sam Maguire eluded us. A lot of people look at the past through tinted glasses, anyway. I mean, we lost just as much as we won in those first six years. Plenty of games, we were flat, and no sign of that manic intensity we brought on our best days. The same group of players who pummelled Kerry in 2003 were nearly beaten by Down in that year's Ulster Final. We got away with a mediocre start in 2005. The following year, we went out to Laois in the Qualifiers. 2007, we lost an All Ireland Quarter-Final to Meath. How many people mention those games?

Yet, we have been hammered for losing Championship games in the last decade. Usually, the margins were slim. Same time, we got precious little credit for any success. Our competitive status was dismissed. Ulster titles lost value. Perceptions changed.

For various reasons, the Donegal defeat in 2011 is the

one that bugs me. Their rise happened on our watch and we had so many opportunities to stop it that day in Clones. 2011 tilted the balance for Donegal, though I still think we could have gone all the way that year.

Even now, I wonder what might have been. They only beat us with an injury-time goal but that result (2-6 to 0-9) marked an end of sorts. Our team was tired yet still good enough to win that kind of game. Some defeats age players very quickly. The best of a generation in Tyrone, some of our greatest ever, looked beaten. Their time had come and suddenly it was gone.

Ultimately, I think that game was more significant for Donegal. They grew from it, gained a lot of confidence. Say they lost, which could easily have happened. Do they come back the following year?

Jim McGuinness brought something very different to Donegal but he needed the break too. How else could he go back to those boys in 2012 and convince them it was worth all their effort and energy? They needed serious progress to continue down that road. Ulster success and an All Ireland Semi-Final in 2011 inspired them to keep going.

The regret for me is knowing their All Ireland could have been ours. If we held them back for a year, they might never have broken through. And they hardly battered us in any of those games between 2011 and 2016. We never got a shot at them in Healy Park either.

The type of players we lost from 2009 onwards were irreplaceable really. We had game changers in those All Ireland teams, boys like Conor Gormley and Kevin

Hughes and Brian Dooher; Stephen O'Neill and Brian McGuigan and Owen Mulligan. Canavan, of course. Each one of them was a potential match winner. At the same time, our pedigree waned: we were less of a force at underage level.

Our rivalry with Donegal got really heated when McGuinness took over. We were top dogs in Ulster at that stage; they wanted to take over. Those games, 2015 especially, became pitched battles. To get where they wanted to go, Donegal had to come through us. We were the champions. We were hardly going to lie down.

2016, there they were again, standing between us and an Ulster title. By then, roles had reversed: they were the power. That day, Donegal blinked.

Even though we wiped them out the following year, they were a force again in 2018. Only this time, they were blocking our path to an All Ireland Semi-Final. We needed a result from that final round game of the Super 8s. And no team better than Donegal to make life awkward for you. Put it this way, you could never be sure what time your bus would get into the ground.

I left nothing to chance for that trip to Ballybofey. During the build up, a lot was made of their unbeaten home record. That sort of stuff means nothing to me. The players are different: all that talk can seep into their psyche. So I set a small task for them: each man was to pick a tuft of grass from his club pitch. Beforehand, in the dressing room, I collected all the clippings and put them into a clear plastic bag. Then I mixed them together.

'Go and take a bit out of that bag,' I said to the boys.

'Put it into your sock. Doesn't matter where you're playing, you're on Tyrone grass today.'

The grass idea just dropped into my head that week. I was thinking about the power of the team and what it meant. Then I wondered how to symbolise what we had. Spirit needs some type of symbol, something you can grasp, something you can feel.

We were trailing, though, with 20 minutes left. So we needed something even more tangible then. Our subs made the difference: Harry Loughran got the first goal, which turned the game, and Declan McClure scored the second. We finished on a high. And our supporters loved every minute.

One fella came up to me after the game: 'This is better than winning an All Ireland.' Close to the border, in places like Aghyaran, beating the neighbours is all that matters.

'You must be mad,' I said to him.

Nobody thinks that way around my part of the world. And, as much as we savoured that win, it was only a stepping stone. We were back in against Monaghan seven days later, playing for an All Ireland Final place.

I felt we were poised to make a serious move at the start of that season. But we needed a big player to break through.

Every man has to earn his status within the group. The rare few, a great like Peter Canavan, make their mark straight away. You nearly know the first time you see them. My lads used to kick about with Petey Harte when they were younger. Now Petey is a good bit younger than his cousins and yet there was something about him even then, an edge. You look at him and think: 'Aye, he'll be a right good 'un.

Most lads take time to blossom. Cormac McAnallen was a classic example. From 16 to 18, he transformed himself. And he kept improving from there. Everyone respected Cormac, the players looked up to him. So he was an obvious choice for captain, even at 23.

Cathal McShane had to prove himself when he came in from the Under-21s. You can tell what other players think when you put a new man in the team. Do they look for him? Do they trust him with a pass? Do they want to take the ball off him?

I tried Cathal at full forward, initially, without success. He needed to fill out a bit more but his potential was obvious.

Training matches are the first big test. If a lad starts to impress, put him on your best marker. So McShane gets Cathal McCarron for company. Now what can he do? If he keeps performing, you know then. And, more importantly, the rest of the boys know. Some fellas struggle to produce their best stuff in a match, for all kinds of reasons, but everyone has to pass that training ground test first.

Your position in the group ultimately boils down to what you do in a match. Deliver a big moment and you have it made. And Cathal produced his moment in 2018 against Meath, first round of the Qualifiers.

He saved our season in Navan. We were on the brink, one behind, five minutes into injury time, when he came up with the crucial point. That score was massive. Cathal had the courage to take on the shot – no gimme – with everything on the line. Those passages of play, when the pressure is at its greatest, reveal the true quality of any team. I knew then we had something valuable, a real desire.

Whatever about us being in such a tight spot, we got through: park it, then, and move on. We came away from that game with something to build on. Even better, we emerged with a new leader. McShane kicking the equaliser became our new screen saver for team meetings.

With Meath out of the road, things started to open up. We were well on track after our trips to Carlow (3-14 to 1-10) and Cavan (0-18 to 1-12). I thought Cavan showed a lack of ambition when they turned down the chance to play in Croke Park. They opted to play the game at Brewster Park because their Under-21s had a good record against Tyrone at that venue. I would play every match in Croker if I could. To get there, to gain a place in the Super 8s, we had one more hurdle to clear.

The final round of the Qualifiers took us to Portlaoise, a straightforward trip. Cork folded early and we won easing up, 3-20 to 0-13. But the result masked a nagging problem, the kind of thing you need to address before you meet a team good enough to exploit it. Yet it can be hard to pick faults when you win well.

We missed one glorious goal chance, blasting a point with only the keeper to beat. It disappoints me to see the ball going over the bar in those situations. If the goal is on, you have to get it, whatever way the scoreboard reads. The next day, you will need that score. So you must be ruthless all the time: make it habit.

With any player, I try not to be brutal when we review games. Language is key to getting your message across. I often say: 'You may be the fall guy but you'll be helping others by having us pointing this out. Another day, it'll be somebody else in that position. Don't take it too personally.'

Some footballers overestimate their skill levels. You need to keep practising the basics, though that message is hard to get across. I might ask a player to repeat something, kick a point from a tricky angle, to make my case. You can never be too good with your hands and feet.

The current generation is more sensitive, no doubt. I see it all the time and especially in dressing rooms. And, in that respect, there has been a big change since I first started managing teams. Maybe those boys were reared in a tougher environment. Whatever it is, some modern players struggle to accept criticism.

While I am always conscious about framing negative comments to take the sting out of them, you definitely have to be gentler nowadays. Some players have no problem holding their hand up. Others never accept blame, even when you point out something obvious. Silence is all you get.

Frank Burns is good to take it, to be fair. He can be lax in the way that he goes about things, which irritates me at times. But I try to disguise my frustration with a little dig every now and again. Frank, typically, is the last man onto the bus.

'There must not be anyone left to come if you're here,'

I say with him. I can smile and deliver a message to him at the same time.

The thing about playing in the Qualifiers, it puts a team on edge, however you come through. But going from knockout football into a round robin, like we did with the Super 8s in 2018, was tricky. A player's mindset might change without him even being aware. You can be fooled into thinking that the pressure is off. The players must think knockout and play knockout. Your attitude has to stay the same: win every game.

Part of the problem with modern football is that the game is weighted too heavily in favour of the forward. A defender could be merciless in my era, mowing down his man as many times as he liked and rarely conceding a free, never mind having to worry about cards. But the game has gone the other way: far too easy give away a foul. Football is now not fair for defenders, so we have to sit deeper, give ourselves enough cover, while pressurising teams into turnovers.

To get the best out of any player, you have to know what makes him tick. The majority are focused on themselves: Who am I? How am I doing? What am I getting? And you do need a single-minded approach to succeed at a high level in sport. But my picture is much broader: I have to think about everyone.

Some players are all about the collective; others like to be noticed. But you need all types to make a team. The Cavanagh brothers are a good example: we needed Colm's graft as much as Sean's guile. 15 players like Colm would not work, the same way 15 Seans could never succeed.

Sean was incredible for us over the years: an unbeliev-able trainer, immensely dedicated, hardly ever missed a game. With that powerful drive, he was unstoppable. I made him captain in 2014 and he was a huge influence for us when we won back Ulster in 2016.

Every successful team has its unsung heroes. Colin Holmes knew his strengths and limitations. I had him at 16 on the Minors: nothing glamorous, nothing fancy, always steady. And, when the end came, he knew his race was run. Even now, few people would pick out Ryan Mellon. Ryan scored three points for Tyrone in an All Ireland Final but never got the credit he deserved. For his height, he had a great leap and his direct style of play made him really productive.

I always take the same line with players: the more you contribute, the better your chances of winning individual accolades. Poor sides rarely pick up All Stars.

Managing football teams is not always going to gain you friends. Most decisions are mine to make. Canvassing the dressing room is not realistic – imagine asking everyone for their opinion on who should play full forward! You lead from the front.

By all means, we can debate selection, discuss it among the management team. But I must make the final call. And I have to ask myself: 'Can I live with it?'

The buck stops with me, so I may as well be responsible for the buck.

I feel confident before every game. I think confidence stems from self-belief and then you add to it by having faith in the way that you play, in the training that you do, in the skills that you possess.

My message to the players is straightforward: 'Boys, I believe in what we're about. I know we're the best at playing this way. I've seen it. You've seen it. I'm not making this up. Look at what we've done. There's all the substance you need.'

But you also try to get inside your opponent. I put myself in their shoes: how would they approach the game? Take Monaghan in 2018 and our All Ireland Semi-Final. They had already beaten us twice that season, League and Championship, so they were hardly going to fear us. And nothing about our run to the Semis suggested we were going to change tack.

Football management eventually becomes a game of poker: make the bet and play your hand. Then see where the breaks fall.

Monaghan's ball carriers, in previous games against us, had far too much time on their hands. We needed to get in their faces, rush them. I knew that approach would take Monaghan by surprise, unsettle them.

Then there was the psychological battle. An All Ireland Final is a major step. We went to the penultimate round in 2018 with three Semi-Final defeats against our name. A losing record can be a burden but I felt we could channel the hurt from those big games, use it as a driving force to get across the line.

Making the Semis was a breakthrough for Monaghan that year, so the prospect of an All Ireland loomed larger for them, weighed heavier.

The day before, on our way down, we stopped for food in Monaghan Town. Their fans were bouncing around the place, chirping away. Along the bypass, beyond 'Blayney and Carrickmacross, we saw flags and banners everywhere. There was precious little colour in Tyrone. Expectations change with success.

We went to Croke Park with another job to do.

June 10, 2019: I look at my watch and the face shows 04:10. My mind is still spinning from the Donegal defeat. I give up on sleep at that point but I have to do something productive. By 5am, I am sheltered in the chapel at Ballymacilroy. There, I feel at peace.

Maybe football means too much to me. Yet, to feel so strongly about football is a return to some kind of normality. Everything has changed for me. Same time, these heightened feelings suggest some form of healing: my emotions are on the mend.

Our loss to Donegal was the worst kind because we failed to play our own game. We fell into a trap. Our direct approach, which had served us so well in the latter rounds of the League, faltered. Instinctively, I felt we needed more caution. League football can mislead: opponents allow you to play with more freedom. Different rules apply in the Championship.

After winning the League title in 2003, we faced a similar dilemma. On that occasion, Derry nearly beat us in our first game of the Championship. We snatched a draw (0-12 to 1-9) and beat them well (0-17 to 1-5) in the replay.

Defeats often serve a greater purpose, though. Winning over hearts and minds in the dressing room was still a challenge for me in 2019. My gut told me to play on the counter against Donegal, utilising the running game that had become our forte. But management is not as simple as telling people what to do. You walk a tightrope imposing authority and empowering players. Most of the time, you have to step lightly.

With every team, there comes a point when the manager has to cede some ground. Otherwise I am pulling people when I would rather have them walk with me. These situations are difficult. The cost, sometimes, is painful. But to plough on regardless of the prevailing mood would have been more detrimental. Energy is precious and dragging people with you is an unnecessary drain. Hard enough to figure out opposing teams without losing the support of your own players.

Open, adventurous football – however loud the public clamour – does not work. Start out playing that way and Plan B becomes redundant if you fall behind. Five points down is not the time to throw off the shackles. Stay in the game for as long as possible. Then you can afford to go for broke.

For all that I know, sometimes I have to let the team experiment.

More powerful than any theory is actual playing experience. Against Donegal, our players found out the hard way: man-to-man football leaves us far too exposed. We should have known better. Of all teams, Donegal had the capacity to stymie that approach.

During the League, Donegal were praised for playing a more positive brand of football. Not that I saw much to justify that view.

Against us, they reverted to type. At the back, they flooded their defence and blocked off our supply channels. They fooled us. We paid too much heed to what they had been doing earlier in the year. Division 2 allows more leeway.

Championship is a different beast. Unfortunately, there is so much talk outside the camp decrying defensive football – at least the version we play – that it affects the thinking within the group. Even the language I hear is telling. 'Negative shit' is the latest refrain.

Maybe we have a persecution complex in Tyrone. Whenever something undesirable gets highlighted, the microscope finds us first. Other teams pack their defence – Dublin most obviously – and nobody makes a fuss.

Still, we had to hold our hands up after the game. 'We got it wrong,' I told the players.

Losing has an upside: you get the chance to learn. Naturally, you spend more time reflecting after defeat. The good feeling that comes with a win leaves less room for introspection. You can seem like a spoilsport to the players if you pick too many holes in a winning performance.

Defeats, you internalise. Wins are shared experiences and everybody takes a piece of the joy. But nobody knows the depth of your despair when you lose. Those feelings are self-contained.

Football is all or nothing for me. If the game has any meaning then you have to hurt when you lose. How else can you find the motivation to put things right?

People generally hide after a defeat. I think you have to embrace your hurt: those feelings are fuel for recovery.

Maybe that attitude stems from my childhood, me being the youngest, forever fighting for my place. You hear the phrase 'bouncebackability' a lot in soccer. I feel like it has always been a reflex reaction for me.

Among the current generation, I see a difference. Attitudes have changed since I started out as manager. Nobody spoke on the bus when we were beaten in the Championship. Nowadays, the silence only lingers a short while. Then I hear players chatting, cracking jokes, their laughter gradually filtering up from the back. I find it hard to comprehend. And I wonder: 'How much does it really mean to them?'

Life goes on, I appreciate that much more than anyone. But your sporting career goes by in a flash. One season is nothing. Gavin Devlin is more than a decade out of football, now gone 40. And not every player gets ten years playing inter-county. Some might only play a single Championship game. You have to make the most of your opportunity.

I still believe that we can win an All Ireland playing our way. We beat Dublin with this method in the League. So much currency is made talking down our system, the negativity gets into players' heads. They hear it every-where: at home; in their clubs; on the airwaves. And those bad vibes can overwhelm your senses. How we set up might look unattractive at times but we mix it up. Nobody can deny the quality of our running game. We know how to absorb pressure and force turnovers. Then watch us go. My vision of the game can be both practical and beautiful.

However you want to play, you must be robust. That aspect is forgotten whenever someone takes umbrage. And players grow weary: I see the feet drag. Then my job becomes tricky. My words require much consideration: descriptions affect perceptions.

Sometimes, I feel like a salesman. Only I am trying to convince people who should already know the value of my product. Businesses might consider this process a rebranding exercise. The trick is to find the right vocabulary. Lately, that means no 'defensive' labels on anything that I present.

Meanwhile the pundits are telling us: 'Don't revert back.' We lost! Yet they want us to keep going this way.

After the Donegal game, myself and Gavin Devlin met with the players. Our task, as a management team, was to get them on board. We laid everything on the line.

'What happened yesterday,' I said, 'is not serving us well.'

Many modern players are not good at self-reflection. They look anywhere and everywhere but in the mirror. Winning keeps these issues at bay. Unhappy players tend to keep quiet when the team is successful. Once results go against you, unused players measure themselves against non-starters. Every squad suffers with that problem. Human nature at work.

Apart from the tactical mistakes we made preparing for Donegal, I got my match-ups wrong. I thought Liam Rafferty had the physical attributes to deal with Ryan McHugh but McHugh had too much nous and experience. Rafferty is young and still learning. Perhaps that move would have worked if we had more protection in place at the back.

Tiernan McCann had to come off injured during the second half. After the game, there was a furore because he had put his hand into the face of Stephen McMenamin. Between his injury and my various duties, we did not speak immediately afterwards. If I went to confront Tiernan right away, he might feel like a man condemned. He needed time to process the whole thing plus he had an injury to contend with. We spoke at training instead. By that stage, he had phoned McMenamin and apologised.

'What came over you?' I asked him.

'I don't know,' he said. 'I shouldn't have done it.'

Maybe the poor performance affected him. Obviously something switched inside. I wish he had not reacted that way but normal people can do crazy things on a sporting field. I feel empathy in these situations, not outrage. That said, I would not have the same feeling for a member of the opposition.

Sometimes you have to let things be. I could easily exacerbate the situation by making too much of it. The bottom line for every player is the same: 'Do what's best for the team.'

I tell them to channel that thought because a rash act shows a disregard for everyone else. How you feel is unimportant; what matters is the impact of your actions on the team.

In some ways, not much has changed for me as a manager over the years.

My preparation for next season still begins the night our Championship ends. To this day, I watch back every match before bed. If not in full at least the first half. That exercise helps to clarify things in my own head: it helps me get to sleep.

During games, the pace is frenetic. I might look calm on the sideline but my mind is whirring all the time, trying to take in everything. The days are taxing, even when we win. Afterwards , I rerun each game in my head, replaying key moments. A few days later, I start looking ahead.

Most of my energy is used up thinking about the game, the same for any manager. To play is to have a narrower focus. That single-mindedness essential in the player can be detrimental on the sideline. My field of vision must be wider.

2017, its aftermath, was dominated by our defeat to Dublin. Yet, until that All Ireland Semi-Final, no team could live with us. We racked up a record number of scores (3-60 over three games) in Ulster and our average winning margin was more than nine points. Our Quarter-Final win against Armagh was our most emphatic (3-17 to 0-8). Those performances framed our narrative: we had earned the right to be taken seriously. Once Dublin put us to the sword, all other chapters were erased. Such is the nature of sport. The reaction was over the top because, like most things in life, the true picture takes time to develop.

We were not as far away from Dublin as the scoreline (2-17 to 0-11) suggested. But detail gets glossed in the rush to condemn and consensus, then, is difficult to prize apart. Nobody is immune from the corrosive effect of public opinion, irrespective of what we know to be the real verdict. So we began the 2018 season with additional hurdles to mount, obstacles of doubt.

We needed an improvement, not a strategic overhaul. However strong my conviction, I had to reassure the players. They get harangued from all sides: clubs, supporters, pundits, Tyrone players of the past. Around every corner, the same chorus: the 'negative shite' is holding us back. This slant, repeated often enough, affects players. They start to consider it might be true.

Criticism is more pronounced nowadays because there are so many platforms. Managers face the hard questions all the time but the pundits are rarely scrutinised. We hear so many extreme points of view because ratings matter most. *The Sunday Game* delights in controversy because they know the papers will pick up the story the next day. Then the whole thing turns into soap opera.

I knew most, if not all, journalists in 2003. Most of the time, I only had to deal with the written press. These days, I look out on a sea of iPhones. Print, radio and television each have their own demands. Then you have social media; people making podcasts. Imagine a young player in that position: they can feel daunted. Some, naturally, shy away. Then journalists might get frustrated because they get speaking to the same players repeatedly.

My first duty is to the team, so we have to manage media demands. A headline story might be good for the journalist but can have an adverse effect on the player.

Certain commentators bemoan how little the players reveal. But a player has to be on his guard. If he speaks openly, his comments are often blown out of the water. Dealing with the media can be a double-edged sword: more coverage is good for the game but we cannot please everyone all the time.

I tell players to be careful: 'Be mindful not to say anything that might stir the opposition or make us sound cocky.'

The last thing we need is unnecessary controversy, not that the players are working from a script. I want them to speak with conviction while being cautious, which is a good approach in every walk of life. Respect your opposition and play them up where they deserve to be played up. We can keep a lid on our plans without shying away from the fact that we feel confident. Picking holes in the opposition is a job done behind closed doors.

Internally, I like to pick a theme for the year. For 2018, we settled on 'Bringing Difference'. If we wanted more than an Ulster title then we needed to bring something new.

At the start of the year, I asked the players to rank Tyrone: 'Where are we now in the pecking order?'

Four was the consensus. Before winning Ulster in 2016, we were top eight and no better. 2017 was another progressive year but how could we finish higher?

I was convinced we would clear a path to the top by continuing to build on our counter-attacking game. The building blocks were in place. We needed to fine-tune, find some new attacking elements. Copying Dublin was not going to get Dublin out of the road.

First, I needed to get everyone else on board. And, in order to do so, I had to concede some ground.

Stephen O'Neill joined the management team for 2018. Stevie was one of the finest forwards to ever wear a Tyrone jersey. But talented players, when they start coaching, can struggle with the transition. How do you teach what felt natural? Certain skills are not instinctive in all players. My career was frustrated by my own limitations and the limitations of the game as we played it. I spent more time figuring things out, which stood to me when I became a manager. I could identify with players, empathise more easily.

Stevie, naturally, tends to look at the game through the eyes of a forward. And his influence was quickly borne out in our movement patterns. He wanted players running into space, their body pointed in a different direction to where they wanted the pass, always trying to fool the defender.

I love learning from people like Stevie. He comes out with things that never occurred to me.

'Don't turn in front of the defender where he can see you,' he told the forwards. 'Turn on the blindside so the defender has to look behind his back to see where you've gone.'

Such a simple concept – making your run behind the defender – and yet it was something I never fully appreciated. That move came naturally to Stevie, which is why he was so hard to mark.

Just because you make those runs does not mean that you will get the ball. So we have to preach patience too. Nothing drains a defender more than persistence. Some forwards get disheartened: they give up after the first or second run. But you have to believe that the ball will eventually get through; a door will open. And the best players, especially finishers like Stevie, are always ready to pull the trigger when that moment arrives.

At times, he grew restless with the players, which is something every coach goes through. For Stevie, it was going to take time to realise that some boys would never reach his level. Not everyone can see what he sees.

'Settle down,' I used say to him. 'Keep telling them your story. Keep telling them what you need to see.'

Stevie never really watched games during his playing days. For the first time, he was looking at football with a discerning eye. 'As a player, it's dead easy,' he said to me. 'You just play.'

Initially, Stevie was focused on attack almost to the exclusion of everything else, but he soon recognised the comprehensive approach a modern-day coach needs to embrace. Gavin Devlin played as a defender but he could see the bigger picture, how everything fitted together. As a player, he had eyes on the back of his head. He was the smartest player I ever coached. To this day, I am convinced if Gavin had been blessed with pace he would have been the best defender that ever played the game. Playing a sweeper was a revolutionary idea in 2003 and Gavin was brilliant in that role. Mentally, he calculated quicker: he read the game better than anyone else. Gavin played so much of the game in his mind that he always thinks ahead. He was destined for coaching.

I feel that the public at large fails to appreciate how much thought goes into the preparation. There are so many elements to consider. Think of it this way: the manager is responsible for the whole group; the player is only responsible for himself. And we both need enough space to do our jobs properly.

Management is not about being liked. Respect is key. Try to be popular and you will fail. The same principles applied in my previous life as a teacher. Players, no more than students, need parameters. They like them, in fact, although they may not realise. Standards benefit us all and, whether I am working with a class or a team, my aim is to do things for the betterment of everyone. I want Tyrone to be the best, so I must set a high bar to fulfil that ambition.

I can be friendly with the players but the relationship can never be so close that I become one of them. A distinct distance is necessary for the team to function effectively and losing sight of that gap is detrimental.

You need to be at a certain remove to be the man in charge. I cannot be anybody's buddy. At the same time, I am always available to the players. My assistant can filter things through to me. So, too, the physios and the medical team: they pick up a lot of valuable information. They can mark my card, let me know when an injury might be more than what it appears.

Management is often a political game. We had to experiment at the start of the 2018 season, otherwise people start labelling you pig headed. Players, as much as supporters, needed a taste of the 'traditional' style of football that everybody seemed to think would set us free. Any team coming at you with pace would have a field day.

I went with that approach at the outset of the League. That way, everybody could judge for themselves. But we were well beaten by Galway in the first round. Then we went down to Dublin at home, lost to Donegal in the Dr McKenna Cup Final, and lost again on the road against Monaghan. Often the best way to convince people about your method is to show them the alternative. I never intended changing but had to adjust things in the short term. To succeed, I had to play the long game.

The Dublin game held a lot of significance, if only because it was our first time meeting them since the 2017 All Ireland Semi-Final. But our defeat the week before against Galway in Tuam was a downer, a miserable day. We gave up a goal inside the first minute, purely through lack of concentration, and had to play most of the game with 14 men. We showed plenty of fight in the second half but there was a sense of inevitably about the result.

Round two of the League, your season is only getting started. Still, you have to guard against a bad atmosphere within the camp because people can become negative very quickly. Doubt gets into players' heads.

Players outside the 26 can present problems in a way you might not expect. They tend to compare themselves with the men just ahead of them. Those players need to measure themselves. Then he has a chance of moving up the pecking order. I want him thinking about what he needs to do to get into that bracket. Certain players perform all the time but many boys are up and down: their form fluctuates. Team selection is always fluid.

I pick the panel after Thursday night training and send a WhatsApp to the players. With only six substitutions available, at least five players will not get any time on the pitch. Form is not the only reason a player might not make the team. Other factors come into play: how others are performing; our next opposition; the conditions that prevail.

I sit down and chat with every player during the season. Whatever thoughts I have about their progress, my primary concern is how they see things. If a player thinks his form is good, I ask: 'How would I know that? Can you give me an example?'

Emotionally and psychologically, football at the highest level is relentless. As a player, once you go up the ranks, there are always others ahead of you. You need the right attitude: be patient; know your own limitations; give the best of yourself. That mindset will take you a long way. Progress can be slow for a year or two but then a spurt comes. Some players, when they get on a roll, climb to new heights.

Momentum is key in sport. Could we generate any against Dublin?

I was encouraged by the mood among the players before the game. You can just sense when everyone is keyed in: you feel this nervous energy in the room, nobody is casual about things. Sometimes, you need to experience a bad atmosphere to realise what a good one feels like. And yet, at the time, you think everything is right.

My own routine for matches has changed. I used to make my big speech after our pre-match meal, before we left for the ground. But I started to rethink that approach: 'What was the point in giving the players my best stuff when it wasn't needed?' I decided to change tack, tone it down at the team hotel. For the Dublin game, I spoke about the need for 'continuous focus'. I told the boys: 'You don't focus for a little while on this team and then take a time out. You focus and then you refocus. Play the 30 seconds in front of your face and reset for the next 30.'

Then I say to them: 'I don't just want you to hear what I'm saying, I want you to feel what I'm saying. But set it down. When we come to the game, get that feeling back again.'

Finding new ways to motivate players is an ongoing challenge. Delivery matters just as much as the message. As I start to speak, I feel myself getting into the zone. I try to embody what I say, bring all my passion to bear. That way, I can really connect with the players, move them. The day before each match, I make some brief notes. Then I focus on the key words, always trying to create a story.

Motivation is just one part of the mix. The tactical battle in Gaelic football has never been as exacting. The sweeper has become a regular position on the field, part of everyone's armoury. You need a player with power and pace to perform that role, someone your opposition want to avoid. Your opposition need to know that it will take a seriously good piece of play to beat the sweeper.

At times, we can push up three forwards and, depending on the formation we go for with those three players, life becomes far more challenging for the sweeper. Part of me would like to go for broke against teams but we have to keep a balance. I know we need a certain amount of protection at the back.

Every system has its drawbacks. Defending in numbers is not as simple as it sounds because players can develop bad habits when they think they have lots of cover. You see a lot of lads coming back without any purpose. They take up a position and almost switch off, as if occupying the space marks the end of their job.

Your initial task is to get back as quickly as possible. I tell the boys: 'Don't even look at the play.'

Then you scan the field, watch where the threat is coming from. The opposition are constantly trying to pull your players out of position or create mismatches. You need to be switched on all the time, keep your shape, hold the line.

Dublin, under Jim Gavin, perfected the wide man and the late runner. Niall Scully is always a danger, ghosting in from different positions. Scully waits and waits, delaying his move until the moment is ripe. Once he decides to get involved, he can go full throttle. Done well, these moves are difficult to combat because the defender is always reacting. And the Dubs are brilliant at working their chances until the shooter gets into an optimal position. People might like to think that Dublin play freewheeling football but much of the time they are simply better rehearsed.

Things were getting to me midway through the 2018 League, though.

We had only one victory: a last-gasp winner from

Mattie Donnelly against Kildare. Keeping more men in attack was clearly not working for us. And I was fed up experimenting just to keep others happy.

So round five against Donegal (March 10) became another significant game. I decided to go back to basics: structured defence and fast breaks. No more trying to play pretty football for the sake of it. We needed to get serious about winning matches again.

I set out my stall to the players: 'Delay the opposition when they have the ball. Force them into nests. Then cut through them when we get possession. I want five players inside the opposition 45 within eight seconds whenever we win a turnover.'

I started talking about preordained football because the language was important. The players had become allergic to any mention of defensive football. They knew what I wanted to see. At our meetings, I stressed the same things over and over: 'If you want the ball, get ahead of the ball. Run at different angles to the ball carrier. Take a pass moving forward.'

Even talking about those things gave me renewed energy. I get excited watching that kind of play.

Our defence had to work as a unit, moving back and forth across the field like a soccer team. A Gaelic pitch is wider, though. So you can only ever cover two-thirds. You must delay the opposition as much as possible when they gain possession to stop them exploiting the space.

Speed is everything when you play on the counter. The quicker you can get forward on a break, the more likely you are to create good chances. But, if the move slows down, you must recycle. Then you try to stretch the opposition, playing laterally. How else can you break down a packed defence? Players are naturally attracted to the ball. So, when you work down one wing, space naturally develops on the far side. How fast you transfer the ball across becomes key to unlocking the defence.

Goalkeepers have become major assets because they now direct attacks. From the kickout, they can bypass midfield, taking out most players. One good kick, then, can beat any system.

The middle third is still the major battleground. You could have 14 or more players covering that area at any one time. For that League game against Donegal, we went with a maximum of two players up front and used Frank Burns as a second sweeper. Our seven remaining outfield players worked between the 45s in a 2-3-2 formation. Our three most valuable men are needed across the middle. That line is the most demanding, pushing you to the limit in every sense. Nobody survives too long in that zone without serious strength and stamina. But you also need explosive speed to get forward on those fast breaks and the same determination to get back when an attack breaks down. Only the brightest players can handle all those competing demands. Think of Mattie Donnelly and Peter Harte, complete footballers.

Crucially, we got the result, 2-13 to 1-10. But the win was worth a lot more than two points. More doubts would have surfaced if we had lost playing my way. Securing hearts and minds inside your dressing room is every bit as important as the final score.

By the time Kerry came to Healy Park for the final round of the League, we were safe from relegation. Another win and we could finish third in the table, a minor consideration in the overall scheme of things, but these things count at the time. You have to grasp every opportunity, keep moving forward.

On paper, the game was a dead rubber but every contest has its own context. And Kerry were starting to earn a reputation as the coming team of Gaelic football. At that time, there was talk of a top three and maybe Tyrone next best. So I used that notion to motivate the players. Proving people wrong has never been a big driving force for me. Still, it can be a useful trigger from time to time.

'Today is our last game before the Championship,' I said to the players. 'We want to make Omagh a fortress. For too long now other teams have considered Healy Park a place where you can come and win. That has to change and we're the only ones who can change that. These things have to start somewhere. If not now, when?'

Every group eventually has to start coming up with their own solutions. Before our previous game against Mayo, the players had their own get-together. They discussed specific situations: red cards, injuries, how the team might react. We were better able to cope against Mayo when Padraig McNulty got a straight red card. And there was a long stoppage after Hugh Pat McGeary got a bad cut on his leg. But the boys were unfazed. They were mentally prepared. In those moments, other players knew to step up. And they had confidence in our system. So it was easier for them to deal with those setbacks. The whole point of how we play is to make the whole greater than the sum of its parts. One missing piece should never scotch the team.

Any kind of win against Kerry is valuable. And they are past masters at playing the game beyond the game. Before the throw in, I noticed their management suddenly becoming very warm towards the referee, Maurice Deegan. Kerry's *maor foirne* went to Deegan first. Then their manager, Éamonn Fitzmaurice, had a word. I copped while we were going through our warm-up. I thought to myself: 'We'll not have that imbalance in proceedings.'

I drifted out to midfield for a chat: 'Despite what you may have heard, you're welcome to Omagh.'

Deegan laughed. My comment lightened the mood. You have to watch out for those things. Who knows when someone might be trying to steal a yard.

With the preliminaries out of the way, our boys got down to business. We were comfortable enough in the end, winning by five, 1-16 to 0-14. Neither of us were at full strength but they had plenty of new lads in the side. I wanted their youngsters to feel uncomfortable playing Senior football against us.

Every team should leave Healy Park with the same impression: 'Those Tyrone bastards are hard to beat.'

Maybe the trickiest thing about League football is how it ends. You find a rhythm playing regular matches but then the lag before the Championship feels like a lull. Anything more than four weeks is definitely too long of a break, so I like to break up the run-in. Some time back with their clubs is good for players: everyone keeps active while getting a breather from the county scene. You could pick up a knock just as easily on the training field.

A month out from our Ulster Championship clash with Monaghan, we had our weekend away. Going abroad has never appealed to me. You need at least five days to get value from it because of the travel. Wasted time is too costly plus I would find it hard to justify the expense. Why train in warm weather when we play precious little football in those conditions?

Anyway, can you train any more than once a day? Is it even sensible in a condensed period of time? Injuries are inevitable. And then the camp can feel like a burden.

I prefer to go to places like Carton House in Kildare or Dunboyne Castle in Meath or Johnstown House in Enfield. The journey is not taxing and the facilities are just as good. Typically, we travel down on a Saturday morning. Monday afternoon, we head home. Any longer than that would sit uneasy with me. We all have families and careers.

These camps are about more than football: being together in a different environment helps to cement relationships. So we give the players plenty of free time. The games room sees plenty of action but the most important thing is that the boys are hanging around with each other. The current generation have far less time to socialise because rest and recovery have become an extension of their training. They go from one session to the next and hardly a break in between.

2015 was the starting point for a new Tyrone team and every side has a life cycle. First, you have to create a strong nucleus, establish leaders within the group. After that run to the All Ireland Semis, we won Ulster for the first time in six years. We defended our title in 2017 and got back to the Semis. By then, we had the building blocks for a genuine All Ireland bid.

• • •

August 11, 2019: Another trip through the Qualifiers leads back to Croke Park, our third Semi-Final in a row. All week, my mind has been focused on Kerry. Last time we met in the Championship, we were also contesting an All Ireland Semi-Final. That four-point defeat in 2015 still rankles even if our run through the back door that season rejuvenated the team.

Kerry are Donegal mark two: an emerging side with lots of promising youngsters. They seem to be playing an open brand of football but I expect we will face something closer to what we met in Killarney during the League. We went there anticipating an open game and they produced a mass defence. How ironic was that? But it worked for them. They took us by surprise and we found them difficult to break down.

They may close shop on us again and we know what their kicking game is like. Yet, if Kerry play all-out attacking football they can be exposed at the back.

Today, the game is up for grabs. I appreciate Kerry are a quality side with a good mix of players. But our maturity and our conditioning should be ahead of theirs.

Sean O'Shea is central for them. Negating his influence

will curb their inside line. Conor Meyler will stay with him full time. That should reduce the effect of their danger men.

David Moran is important as well. He plays as a sweeper without being labelled as such. He gets on a lot of ball in his own half. We have to throw a spanner in the works. Michael Cassidy will be in his face so that Moran is not an easy out for the Kerry defence. Colm Cavanagh will take Moran for the kickouts and Cassidy will be free when we get the ball. That leaves Moran with a decision to make on whether to track Cassidy or to let him go.

Mattie Donnelly and Cathal McShane will stay up the field whenever possible but if Kerry put 15 men behind the ball then we may switch Mattie out. He can attack from the middle then.

Kerry are not as well structured as they need to be. Sometimes they defend too deep and allow gaps to develop. The lateral space between defenders is just as important as the distance separating your defensive lines. If a player switches off, the opposition can exploit that gap.

Playing a sweeper provides an extra layer of security. This year, we have been instructing our inside forwards to position themselves close to goal. That way they can make their runs behind the sweeper's back.

The way we play, your ball-handling skills have to be silky smooth. Economy in possession is essential: the less touches you need to find that space the more chances you will create.

Three players will have man-marking assignments today: Ronan McNamee takes David Clifford; Rory

Brennan picks up Killian Spillane; and Paudie Hampsey goes on Paul Geaney. Our defenders need to be so close to their men that Kerry will find it hard to give the forwards ball. They need to be intense and aggressive but within the rules. Play with a snarl. They cannot be nasty though: nastiness draws fouls. And an early card makes your job precarious.

Clifford is class. Often, he makes to go for the ball and then checks to run in behind the defender. He wants to get behind his man all the time. The biggest problem marking Clifford is that your job is never finished. He stays in the play until the ball is cleared. Usually, he turns back on to this left when he shapes to shoot off his right. If his first option is a right-footed kick from the right, he will lay off the ball. His unselfishness adds to the difficulty.

We have to get that ball in fast when Kerry are short at the back. People talk about the great forward lines of other teams without recognising the quality we have. At this point in time, I rate Cathal McShane in the same category as Con O'Callaghan.

If we can get ahead of Kerry, we can play the game on our terms. They are less likely to plant men behind the ball. I think we can put pressure on their goalkeeper, Shane Ryan. On kickouts, we will push up to a degree, almost like a false press, because we want him to go long. Normally he targets David Moran. Then we can swarm.

August 12, 2019: Ultan Blee rang this morning. He calls regularly during the season. Ultan lives in Canada now but hails from the Clann na nGael club in North Tyrone.

I first met him in 2003. He had his van painted red and white for the All Ireland that year. We have been friendly ever since. Even after defeats like yesterday's, he remains a staunch supporter. I always make time for him. We spoke for half an hour. He gets exercised by stuff on social media. At this stage, I pay it no need. Ultan wades into those debates, defending my corner. I admire his passion. He is a genuine lad.

At the shop in Ballygawley, one woman said to me: 'I'm proud of the way the team played.'

I was heartened by what she said. A text from Fr Gerard McAleer, my long-time friend and sideline partner, also resonated: 'Keep your head up. Enjoy the grandchildren. May you continue to inspire.'

Those messages are comforting; they give me a lift.

We had Kerry snookered in the first half yesterday. They were struggling with our defensive shape and we had built up a 9-5 lead at half time. Even allowing for their second-half blitz, and a few decisions that went against us, we had enough chances to win the game.

Kerry's goal proved decisive. We were attacking inside the 45 when we turned the ball over: a handpass from Kieran McGeary went straight to Stephen O'Brien. From there, O'Brien launched a Kerry counter and covered 100 yards to finish the move. There were so many opportunities for us to prevent that goal. We made it easy for Kerry. Too many men converged on Paul Geaney when he picked up possession and nobody covered the central channel. Our defenders switched off when O'Brien came steaming through.

Conceding big scores through your own errors is far worse than giving up a goal to some piece of individual brilliance. Once Kerry went ahead, they could keep us at arm's length.

The most disappointing thing is that we will not be back in the Final. To gain the experience of playing for an All Ireland is great so long as you get the chance to use it again quickly.

I watched *The Sunday Game* last night and Malachy O'Rourke was on the panel. Malachy had stepped down as Monaghan manager during the summer and the fact that he lives in Ballygawley made him a candidate for the Tyrone job in some eyes. The panel suggested that O'Rourke was preparing his CV before the show even though I had one more year to run.

Naturally, Kerry got all the credit for winning the game (1-18 to 0-18) but we mesmerised them in the first half. We should have been more than four points clear.

While Cathal McShane and Mattie Donnelly were thriving in the full-forward line from our kicking game, Peter Harte was pulled and dragged the whole time. And plenty of it went on where the referee could clearly see it. Petey was left totally frustrated. No doubt Kerry were aware of Petey's precarious position given the three black cards he had already picked up during the Championship. One had been rescinded but another black would have put him out of the Final. Still, our players should have been wiser. The way to counteract those manoeuvres is to get your man on the ball as often as possible.

At half time, I told the players we needed to find a

balance between our kicking and running game. Yet we continued to play in the same fashion at the start of the second half. We needed more men behind the ball to make Kerry come at us. Then we could have hurt them on the counter. You become predictable repeating the same ploys.

Early in the second half, we had possession on their 45 when the referee, Maurice Deegan, stopped the game because Paul Geaney had pulled down Niall Sludden. Deegan decided to give both players a yellow card. In my opinion, Sludden did nothing wrong. From the resultant throw ball, Kerry won possession and scored a point from that attack, potentially a two-point swing. These moments often shift the momentum in a big game.

My frustration deepens when I think about those things. We should have beaten Kerry. I know how close we came. Three weeks and 365 days, at least, until we might reach the top.

Perspective is everything when you lose. 2018, Sam Maguire was not for Tyrone either. But however hurt you feel, the season cannot lose all value. And any campaign that ends in a Final holds significance. We contested the biggest game of the year, the one that every footballer wants to play. That season brought the team to a new place.

The players experienced an All Ireland Final and all that goes with it. We had three weeks to prepare and I set out my stall on our first night back after beating Monaghan in the Semis: 'This is the beginning of the last three weeks of the season. The team won't be picked on the Thursday night at the last session. It'll be picked across the three weeks. Every piece of action will be important.'

The way that I prepare for big games has changed over the years. Traditionally, we played an in-house game the Sunday before the final, starting at 3.30pm to mimic the day itself. But your best players tend to pace themselves. Everyone else is busting to break into the team.

Playing A versus B is less than ideal: players think the team is already decided then. If you play a full game, 70 minutes, the tempo wanes in the last 20 because the boys are full on from the start. So I started mixing the teams, a few regulars in each side to give everyone a reasonable chance. And the second goalkeeper gets a proper opportunity that way. Every player feels like he is being watched, which is key.

Set plays are crucial when you reach a final. Your opponents will have covered every eventuality: any slip at this stage could be catastrophic.

A lot of time is spent on kickouts, perfecting our best options. We try to get the ball away quick, before the opposition are ready. The keeper, ideally, wants to hit a player on the run, moving into a good position. Whether the ball goes short or long is immaterial if the receiver is heading for the opposition goal with the ball landing ahead of him.

Then we go through various scenarios. We put the forwards to work in small zones where defenders are crowding them. They have to figure out ways to protect the ball or break free. Games like backs and forwards are less useful. Instead, we recreate game scenarios: one versus one, two versus two, two versus three, three versus two. I always say: 'If you can perform in this environment, when the other players know exactly what you're going to do, then it shouldn't be as hard in a match.'

A walk through gives the players a clearer picture. The boys can better appreciate how our setup works when they stand in set positions. This work makes them feel more comfortable when the real action starts. Formations look different from every angle. So you need to see the game from different perspectives.

Video analysis begins with a broad review of the Monaghan game: who played well; the key moments; our general feeling. Details, then. Frank Burns came up for discussion again. I said to him: 'Frank, you could have been man of the match in the first half.'

We replaced him at half time: I felt his performance was draining the team. Too much of what he was involved in ended with no return. And his mistakes stood out: poor decisions, shots missed. Yet I could see, looking back on the game, that he deserved more time. He had done well in defence, made a number of important interceptions. But those things tend not to register as much during the game.

Tactical calls in real time are difficult. What if we ended up substituting him five minutes into the second half? I genuinely agonise over those kinds of decisions. Frank took it well. He was disappointed, naturally. But, in his heart of hearts, he knew he could have been more productive.

Some players move away from goal before they shoot,

shuffling left or right, narrowing their angle. Purely out of habit. So I kept hammering that message: 'Always shoot from the best position.'

Dublin were ahead of us in that regard. You rarely saw them taking on a low percentage shot. Apart from getting our own house in order, we needed to find a way of upsetting their rhythm. They were beginning to look unbeatable. But, in my mind, their approach was becoming prescriptive, predictable even. And that state of affairs was a slight on the rest of us.

Every team is susceptible in some way, every programme corruptible. Parking the bus was not going to trouble Dublin unduly. They would just play around the fringes, bide their time. But what if they went behind and were trying to break us down with five minutes to go?

Psychologically, I put the focus on desire. There was too much talk about our lack of experience. So I said to the players: 'They have their medals. Can they want it more than us?'

Winning an All Ireland is life-changing and our boys were playing to be the next generation of heroes in Tyrone. I told them how I saw things: 'If I match us with them, player for player, I would still want to be with Tyrone. This dressing room is the one I would choose every time.'

Our plan for the Final revolved around the first 15 minutes: I was hoping to ambush them. More than likely, they were expecting to face a Tyrone wall.

'Take them on, boys,' I said. 'Attack them every chance you get.'

At some point, you have to call off an ambush. I knew we could only sustain that tempo for so long. But when do you retreat? What if you can go for the kill?

After 16 minutes, we were 5-1 ahead. At that stage, I thought: 'We've got this.' And we should have been further ahead. They were struggling to cope. We missed a good chance to stretch our lead. Then, bang, a Dublin goal.

The penalty rocked us. At best, it was a 50/50 call. One kick and they were back in the game. We were scrambling, trying to recover our senses, when they hit us for a second goal. Those scores ripped the heart out of us.

By half time, we were facing a mountain. Toe to toe, we had some chance. Seven points down, a comeback was all but impossible against a team of that calibre and experience. If we went 8-1 or 9-1 ahead, the gap would have allowed us to sit back.

Still, I had to be positive for the players. We needed to show heart in the second half, continue to fight. Our future was at stake: the next 35 minutes would shape it.

We stayed with Dublin, troubled them at times, especially when Colm Cavanagh went to full forward. Our goal came too late to really threaten them but by no means were we hammered. We closed the gap to four points and missed two decent chances to make it a one-score game. Unfortunately, we conceded the last two scores. Despite our serious wobble in the second quarter, we could well have stopped the Dublin juggernaut. A lot of teams would have sunk without trace. We could be satisfied with the performance given that ten years had passed since our last appearance in a Final.

September 30, 2019: This past month has been exhausting, the most frustrating period I ever put down in charge of a Tyrone team. No sooner had we exited the Championship, the clouds rumbled. In one sense, a manager's work never ends. But some jobs catch you on the hop.

First up, Stephen O'Neill. We were due to meet because I wanted to discuss his role. But he decided to step down before I got that chance, which was a pity because I always found Stevie a straight-talker, easy to work with. I was at an underage inter-county blitz when he called out of the blue.

He simply said: 'I'm not going to carry on.' His mind was made up.

And I was just about to speak with the Tyrone Under-14 academy squad, so I had no chance to talk with him properly. He has always been single-minded. That temperament probably helped him as a player. You need a different mindset for coaching because not every player sees the game the same way. I think Stevie needed time to appreciate that aspect. A lot of people presumed he was a forwards coach. We brought him in as a coach. That distinction is important; forwards do not play in isolation.

The search for a new coach soon took us to Kevin Madden's door. Through Gavin, I heard that Kevin had finished with Creggan in Antrim. And we knew that he would be in demand. Adding Kevin was a new departure for me as my coaching team had always come from within the county. I was impressed by his confidence, the way he speaks with authority. Players warm to him and I could sense he was well fit to challenge them. Peter Donnelly, our strength and conditioning coach for the last five years, also decided to move on. During the summer, he told us that he would be moving to a new job with Ulster Rugby. Peter said he would still have time to work with us – his new role was a 9 to 5 position. We wanted to keep him in the fold and I told him we were prepared to work around his Ulster schedule.

All appeared fine until finalising Peter's new arrangement, which was beyond my control. Previously, he had been a full-time employee of Tyrone but would now be classed as a service provider. I met with him and Michael Kerr, the county chairman, to resolve the matter at the end of August. We discussed Peter's situation and he told us what he wanted. Michael explained that he would have to talk it over with the county board first, which I felt was fair enough. At that meeting, I made it clear to Peter that the players wanted him to stay and I wanted him to stay.

Soon afterwards, it transpired that Peter had an alternative offer from an inter-county team to be their strength and conditioning coach, which he accepted.

Coupled with Stevie's departure, some people were starting to think the whole show needed to get out of town. But then the snipers always appear at the first sign of trouble.

A small group of players came together in an effort to keep Peter, and I met with them. They felt we needed to keep him, yet these situations are rarely simple. Mattie Donnelly, our captain, was the most important person during that period. Only for him, it would have become a bigger issue. He saw the full picture.

Of course, the players who were bemoaning Peter's departure threw a few more issues into the mix, which is par for the course in these affairs. Some players want to find fault elsewhere when they lose. And problems are magnified when you fall short.

Even with all my experience, I found the situation tricky. There was a lot of disquiet around the place. The players needed reassurance that standards were not slipping. At the same time, I had to deal with the clamour for big names, which is nonsense in my book.

The county board were 100 per cent behind me, so there was never a threat to my position. Still, I needed to bring in good replacements. Mattie introduced me to Jonny Davis, who had been head of strength and conditioning with Ulster Rugby. He was now working for himself and immediately made a big impression. I knew we had the right man when he spoke to the squad for the first time.

'I don't do needy people,' he told them.

I liked the fact that he challenged the players to take more responsibility. Jonny took on the nutrition side of things as well, which solved another problem for me. He decided to change the whole system. The players would now get a precooked meal to take home instead of being fed after training. They get protein shakes immediately afterwards and then they have the option of heating their meal at home that night or the following day.

I have never known such a busy period from the end of one season to the start of the next. Ultimately, it was unnecessary stress. All the energy we used up during those weeks had nothing to do with our performance on the field.

Important as it is, strength and conditioning is still just one piece of the jigsaw. Quality of coaching and quality of player are equally important. Football matches are still largely decided by basic skills and teamwork.

After everything settled down, I thought about my situation. Maybe I needed to make the most of 2020, the fact that it was the last year of my term. And 30 years managing Tyrone teams seems like a nice number to finish on.

February 1, 2020: February, start of spring, brings back the light. The year opens up again.

People are conscious of the anniversary when they meet you in and around Christmas. You know the Irish way: 'Is it ten years now? My God, my God. How's everybody?'

February comes and the sense of relief is palpable. Nobody really thinks to ask those questions anymore. Life goes on, which is a good thing. Within the family, we let each other be. Each of us has our own supports, our own coping mechanisms.

I cannot put a price on family. The boys are lucky in that they have grown up surrounded by their cousins. They lean on each other. Most of the wider family are still in regular contact. Support from club and community is constant. Not every society has that backup.

But the story of Michaela's death never ends. And soon the next generation of our family will find out what happened. For Michael, that day is fast approaching. Liam, his eldest boy, is 10 in January 2022. So the questions will come sooner rather than later. Hopefully, Michael gets to tell him before he finds out elsewhere, but nothing is guaranteed in life.

Whatever lies ahead, I feel that we will be okay. You hear people say 'Oh my God' all the time. But the most unbelievable thing in life has already happened to us. What else can shock us at this stage?

Michaela could pop into my head at any time. July 13, 2019, we were staying at the Sheraton in Athlone before the first round of the Super 8s against Roscommon.

I was looking through my phone, reading back over a message from Ciara Quinlivan. Ciara's father, Peter, has always been part of my backroom team with Tyrone. Pete is quiet and unassuming by nature, low key, qualities which became invaluable at the time of Michaela's death. Without being asked, he became a link man for me, tending to various jobs and things that required a delicate touch. His presence is a rare gift. The Quinlivans are near neighbours in Glencull and Ciara had been married the day before. She went to primary school with Michaela; they were close friends.

The two of them were in our kitchen one time when Tony Donnelly came to grief doing his Garth Brooks impression. The girls were just back from a night out;

Tony had come over for a few drinks. I think it was gone 2am when Tony started strumming an imaginary guitar. Next thing, he shuffled backwards, lost to whatever song was in his head. Only he backed into a chair and landed in a heap. We nearly fell down with laughter.

Always good to recall those moments.

Ciara chose the Michaela Foundation for her wedding favours, a gesture that meant a lot to me. And she sent me a lovely text during the week: 'I hope you are keeping well. I am missing Michaela more than ever in the run-up to my wedding. She's smiling down on us, I know.'

Those messages bring back Michaela for a short while.

Other times, a stranger might come to me with a random story. One woman told me that Michaela had appeared to her, like a vision, and sent a message for me: 'You will always be my daddy.'

I found that one surreal because it was bang on. Michaela often said those words to me: no matter what I became in life, I would always be her daddy.

If I could stop the clock at a point in time, Michaela's wedding would be it. I can still hear 'Caledonia' starting up as she turned to walk back down the chapel, the congregation leaning in to look at the bride. Michaela was ready to begin the rest of her life and I thought to myself: 'It doesn't get much better than this.'

Michaela could have died without ever living through that day. And we would be without all these wonderful memories.

So I return to that scene because the alternative vision is bleak. Michaela's wedding has become my template for dealing with her death. Our future on this earth was shattered but we shared a brilliant, brilliant past. We gained far more than we lost.

I know not everyone would think the same way. But why detract from something wonderful just because it belongs in the past? That day happened and the feelings are locked inside. My heart holds it like hidden treasure. Life, to me, is about creating those moments that live forever.

Only the grace of God allows me to feel this way. I consider it a blessing. The memory of Michaela's wedding day is an antidote for all the hurt that has come my way. Every minute that I spend in Adoration at the chapel brings me back into His grace, this sense of being in His wonderful presence.

I miss Michaela before matches. Sometimes I dream about her coming to meet me before the game. I see her walking across the hotel lobby, decked out in red and white, the children in tow, pure excitement.

One more match with Michaela would be magic. I can picture her with the Rosary beads, praying like mad while the game is going on.

Several times a day, I say to myself: 'God bless you, Michaela.' I salute her picture in the house whenever I walk past, a quick thumbs-up. A statue of Padre Pio sits on our landing window and I ask him to bless us all. Praying, to me, is like breathing: you can do it automatically. Prayer is a constant reminder of the presence of God in my life. I think of Him when I wake and before I go to sleep, always grateful. God gave me so much in my life that I can only think to be thankful.

Maybe I should be full of rage but I never felt angry about losing Michaela. My reaction surprises me, even now. I would not have believed it possible if someone had predicted what lay ahead. Never did I consider myself a particularly courageous person. My brothers always seemed much stronger to me, far better equipped to deal with adversity.

Yet when the news came, I found this new strength, something that must have come from a higher plane. Divine intervention is my only explanation. And, in the end, nothing can separate me from the love of Michaela. Not even death.

March 31, 2020: Life without football in this time of coronavirus would be far worse for us if our last game had been the loss to Galway (February 23). The restrictions came into effect before we got to play Donegal in the penultimate round of the League on St Patrick's weekend. Who knows how things will pan out from here; at this stage, even the Championship is doubtful.

The Galway game (2-25 to 0-12) was the worst defeat in my time managing Tyrone, at all levels. Our performances were somewhat Jekyll and Hyde before that match: sluggish win at home against Meath, bad defeat away to Monaghan, gallant victory against Kerry in Edendork.

We produced a real gritty performance against Kerry. The game was scheduled for Omagh but stormy weather left Healy Park unplayable. Edendork was our alternative venue. We gave Kerry the option of a postponement but they were keen to play because they had travelled. Afterwards, there was talk about the size of the pitch but Healy Park is actually smaller. The conditions made it a dogfight. And it suited us.

All the talk after the game revolved around David Clifford's red card. Everyone thought his second yellow was outrageous because he had been grappled to the ground. Nobody mentioned that the same thing had happened to Peter Harte earlier in the game. He suffered the same fate when one of their players dragged him down and Petey picked up a second yellow. We had to play the last 20 minutes with 14 men. I thought: 'There's saints and sinners in every team.'

The Galway result came from nowhere. Really, it was an accumulation of events that went against us. You get games like that; they happen. Kieran McGeary's sending off, which I thought harsh, was a big thing. They were already in a good enough position. We were seven down and pulled it back to three. While we were dealing with all that, Cathal McShane went down with a terrible injury and had to be stretchered off.

January time, I spent a lot of hours working behind the scenes to keep Cathal in Tyrone. The Adelaide Crows were interested in taking him to Australia, so they flew him out for a trial. He came back with an offer but I felt it would be the wrong move for him, personally and professionally. I hate to see our own players going to Aussie Rules anyway. For Cathal, I thought it was more of a risk. At 17 or 18, you still have options if you come back. Cathal, at 24, was coming off his best year, an All

Star with not many of them walking around Ulster. Two years in Australia can make you anonymous, as plenty have discovered. What if he returned to Gaelic football unable to reproduce the form that made him a star before he left?

Career wise, I thought Cathal could develop something for himself at home. That time away might have hurt him in the long run. Through our contacts in Club Tyrone, we were able to get him a good position with the promise of a solid career path. Sean Coyle, owner of Keystone Lintles, and Jackie Duffy were the key men in putting it all together. Although Adelaide were putting Cathal under pressure to sign, we were able to convince him to stay. It was a lift for the whole county when the news came through.

Two months later, here he was doubled over on a heavy pitch in Tuam, his ankle dislocated. The game seemed immaterial at that point. Still, our collapse was hard to watch. Reviewing the game the following Tuesday was nearly worse. We were so lethargic.

Some players gave out about our warm up, which I found hard to credit.

After a beating like that, Dublin are probably the last team you want to face. But, in hindsight, it was a good thing. We had to move on quickly. You want to put things right after a bad performance and our next game was only six days away.

By right, the Dublin game should have been cancelled. The weather was atrocious, the pitch no better. If another match was available for broadcast, ours would have fallen by the wayside. For once, I was glad it was the only game being shown live.

There was a lot going on away from the cameras: Dublin wanted the game called off; I was desperate for it to go ahead. Before we left Kelly's for Healy Park, I let fly.

'I've been doing this for over 30 years at every level and I've never taken a beating like that,' I began, referring to the Galway game. 'I don't like it. I'm not happy with it. It's time we took responsibility. This crowd from Dublin are not going to come up and walk all over us. It cannot happen. It must not happen. It should not happen. I'm fed up.'

I went ballistic. I had to. A lot of my frustration stemmed from the players' response to the Galway game. I felt there was a lack of honesty from a number of them.

'Be honest,' I told the players. 'The job that we have to do is redemption for ourselves and the people of Tyrone. Galway was embarrassing and humiliating. What have you got inside? Have you got a fire in your belly? Are you going out there thinking Dublin are some super-team? They're just ordinary players like us.'

I finished with a final thought: 'Hold this feeling you have at the minute. You need this feeling when we hit the pitch. Keep this angst with you. Don't let it consume you.'

Throw in was still more than an hour away. Ramping it up that far out is risky: you might lose all that good energy before the start. Sometimes, you waste fuel on the bus. Equally, if I left my strongest words for the dressing room, they might land too late.

Once the players are in the right frame of mind, they need to manage their emotions. I can shape their mindset, help them reach a state of readiness. But then you have to leave down those strong feelings, set them aside until the game starts.

We had two options against Dublin: fold or front up. With the game under threat from the weather, there was a fight just to get the go ahead. After my impassioned address in Kelly's, no match would have been a major downer, a lost opportunity. You cannot recreate an atmosphere: repeating the same speech is futile.

Even when we got the okay, another heavy defeat remained a real possibility. Would the players respond? The conditions were horrible but we still had to perform.

The first half was pure hardship, no let-up. We played through a storm, toiling against Dublin, toiling against the elements. I wanted to play against the breeze to give us a chance to consolidate at the back. Dublin, when they tried to cut inside, were unable to find space. Nobody let the side down.

We went in level, 0-5 to 1-2, just where I wanted us. Then we took over.

Some moments were magical: any one of Niall Morgan's five frees, Petey Harte's ball handling, Rory Brennan's match-winning goal. Petey actually left his sister's wedding to play. We landed into the reception after midnight, beaming.

I said to Petey: 'If you're not pumped after a display like that then you'd never be happy.' My face probably conveyed as much.

Six days after our nightmare in Galway, the boys had unlocked something powerful.

May 17, 2020: Conor Mallaghan, my nephew, sent a screenshot of his calendar on WhatsApp earlier.

'Time to Leave,' the display read, 'Donegal v Tyrone. Today at 14:00.'

My reply was succinct: 'It just keeps Donegal a while longer in this year's Championship!!'

Doubt never enters my head. Today was supposed to be the start of our Ulster Championship campaign but the original fixtures were wiped out by the pandemic. Covid-19 has altered the course of our season and nobody knows when football will come back.

Lately, the talk is all negative: 'Should we have a Championship? What's the point in playing if there's no supporters?'

Even the players are beginning to wonder. But a year without football is a year you never get back. Ask anyone out injured. Me? A game on top of a mountain would do me.

We might yet end up playing provincial games outside Ulster. Tyrone and Donegal would easily attract 30,000 people to Croke Park. A knockout Championship, if it comes to pass, makes home advantage even more valuable. Neutral venues seem the fairest approach to me.

Part of the challenge at this level is to be able to handle the crowd and the occasion. Football is not just about the players on the pitch. The whole county comes together.

At the moment, the players are maintaining their fitness. Jonny Davis keeps them right with training programmes. I talk to the boys individually from time to time. If, at some point, we can get together in small groups without contact, Gavin and I can devise some drills for them. Formal sessions are futile when the Championship is months away.

Stories about other teams training are rife. According to some, Tyrone are at it too. I know the truth, so what do you believe?

Lately, my days begin and end in the garden. There is enough work around the place to keep one man more than occupied. Rarely has the place been so well organised. Even my office space looks tidy, which is definitely a first.

Regular runs keep me reasonably fit. Three days a week, I take refuge in the garage, sweating out a few kilometres on our old treadmill.

The strangest thing about this period is the way life has simply taken over. Days fill easily. The break made me realise just how much of my time was consumed by the game. At the start of lockdown, I looked at bits of video but that work soon stopped because it seemed pointless. Then the cleaning and the decluttering took over. You develop new habits. Mostly, we took things easy. We were blessed that the weather was so good: Marian and I got out for walks and picnics. Drive-by visits became part of our routine. Tony Donnelly lives about five miles away from us, across country. On good days, we could sit outside.

Marian and her friends take turns having garden get-togethers. They bring tea and some snacks with them.

The grandchildren are another great outlet, something to get excited about. Becoming grandparents gave us a new lease of life, Marian especially. We love our time with them. Liam, Michael's eldest, came first. He was born in January 2012. Then came Michael Junior, in March 2014, and Aidan, in October 2016.

We love being able to help out. I knock great fun out of them. Michael moved into his new house recently, which is just down the road from us. So we can do a drive-by visit there as well. Michael's boys regularly come to our house for a kickabout. Aidan sticks with me; Liam and Michael are fit to do their own thing together.

Aidan has a whale of a left foot on him. I roll the ball to him and he meets it on the fly. He tries with the right now as well. Liam is a big lefty. So I have him practising with the right too. Young Michael spends a lot of time watching the Tyrone boys taking frees, mimicking their routines. His accuracy with the right is really impressive. I just need to get him doing a bit more work on his weak foot.

Mary, Mattie's first child, was born just before Aidan, September 2016. She has her mother's musical ear. You can hear her singing on the baby monitor when she goes down for a sleep. Her younger brother, Pio, arrived in May 2018. Their third child, John-Gabriel, was born in October 2020. Joseph, their youngest, arrived in August 2021. The same month, Michael and Josephine had their fourth child, Luke.

July 2019, we welcomed Jason and Grace into the family. Mark and Sinéad decided to go through the adoption process. We were thrilled when we heard the news.

Jason is six now and playing lots of Gaelic. I spend time teaching him how to kick the ball out of his hands when he comes over to our house. He calls me 'Granda Mickey'. September, last year, he started school at St Malachy's, which is just across the road from our home in Glencull.

Grace is three this December, already a real bright spark. Herself and Jason are part of the fabric now and they love coming to our house. Marian is always busy doing some little project or other with her. I still find it amazing how easily they have adjusted to their new world. The rest of the grandchildren are delighted with their new cousins. Liam was intrigued when they first arrived.

'I don't really understand this,' he used to say. 'I've never heard of this before.'

And yet they adapted straightaway. I love their innocence at that age. For all of us, adoption was new territory.

Best of all, then, came the news that Sinéad was expecting. They got word within weeks of Jason and Grace. We were over the moon for them.

We got our first glimpse of baby Ailagh on April 1, 2020, a wee dote. Not being able to hold her was difficult at first. After she came out from the hospital, we went down every day to see her, looking in through the patio doors.

Mark and Sinéad took her to visit Michaela's grave when she came out of the hospital. I know how he felt about the whole thing. Michaela, I know, is still up there working her magic.

Even now, Mark has to pinch himself. He says to me: 'Is this real?'

I have to marvel at things. Just 18 months ago, the house was so quiet in comparison. Now their home is a buzz every time you walk in. Ailagh came into our lives because of Jason and Grace. I do believe these things happen when the time is right. As Michaela would have said: 'It was all part of God's bigger plan.'

And, for me, Ailagh is like Michaela revisited. Mattie was living in Galway when Catherine had Mary, so Ailagh is the first girl to be around us a lot as a baby. I feel like Michaela is looking back at me.

Michaela is always in my mind. Every day that passes is a day nearer to meeting her again. I feel connected to her. And I sense her presence in the lives of all the wee ones.

July 23, 2020: Stories about Michaela in the press still upset Marian, though she is better able to deal with them. I try to warn her beforehand.

This week, Liverpool announced a sponsorship deal with the tourism board of Mauritius.

This sort of news used to hit her very hard: her thoughts would be dominated by it for a few days, going through everything from deep anger to extreme sadness. Now, at least, she can get over it quicker. Her level of anxiety is more manageable. Plus, she has lots more to be happy about these days.

At times, she would prefer if it was all over, the whole thing forgotten about. If only life was that simple. We were let down by the Mauritian authorities. They promised to do much more for us. Mauritius cannot masquerade as this idyllic country when her killers are still free. Michaela did not get justice.

John spoke out about the deal. He said: 'Seeing this makes me feel sick.'

I was glad that John highlighted the issue. It says a lot about him that he continues to pursue the case. He could leave it all behind him. He could say: 'I just can't handle this anymore.'

Mention of Michaela's murder is not a dagger through my heart. And I know that something else will dominate tomorrow's headlines. The story of the two monks comes to mind, which I read in an Anthony DeMello book. The monks meet a woman in distress, who wants to cross a river. One monk reckons they cannot be seen talking to a woman. The other carries her across. He comes back and the other man is still going out of his mind.

'What do you think you're doing?' he says to him.

The other monk says: 'I left that woman down at the other side. Why are you still carrying her?'

• • •

September 15, 2020: This period without football is not the same as a life without football. I have no sense of being finished with the game. I can find other things to do. Retirement casts some people adrift, not knowing what to do. But I enjoy my own company.

The future is not something that worries me unduly. I see myself as an adaptable person: I know something will occupy me.

The body still needs minding, of course. Keeping cancer at bay is always at the back of my mind. The hospital has been in touch about a checkup this Friday but we only just resumed training. I feel conflicted. At the moment, I cannot afford to self-isolate for seven days. Anyway, my health is good. Plus the risk of picking up Covid is much higher if I do go in for the procedure. So I decide to put it off for a couple of months.

Last night, we trained together on the pitch for the first time since the season was shut down in March.

I wanted to stick to the date given for the simple reason that we had no need to meet before then. You can spend too much time in preparation. The players got enough football with their clubs and they were able to keep on top of their fitness. Inter-county is a lifestyle choice. The modern player has a different mindset: he lives like an athlete, keeps himself right all year round.

First week back, our minds are already focused on Donegal. We cannot afford to hold back. If Mayo beat Galway, they move on to five points and then we might have to go to Castlebar facing a relegation battle. Victory in Ballybofey keeps us safe and may leave Donegal needing a result against Kerry.

I was happy enough with our first session. The players were sharp, probably 6/10 in terms of their skill levels. We work on the skills every night and play small-sided games. We will build up to 15 versus 15 when everyone is back after the County Final this weekend.

Everything hinges on the first round of the

Championship. The way we played against Donegal last year made us look like cannon fodder. We have to take them out and win the Ulster title. Only two games left then.

The GAA needs us at this stage because the top order has to change.

What Jim Gavin achieved with Dublin was incredible. I cannot imagine his record of six All Irelands in seven years will be surpassed. Dublin controlled the vast majority of their games. Confidence grew because so many of their games were one sided. So they rarely faced dilemmas. And Dublin always had really good players hungry to come in.

Gavin keeps his guard up, especially with the media: head tilted to the side, that wee smile. Whatever the question, he tells the same story. I doubt we have learned much about what goes on inside his head.

But Dublin had lots of talented players in the past and failed to win All Irelands. Gavin was the missing ingredient. I regard him as a serious coordinator of talent: he brought everything together in the right way at the right time.

For all the talk about Dublin's various advantages – finance, playing numbers, access to Croke Park – I take little heed: I want to beat them all the more. They may have more support available than any other team but I know what we have to work with is sufficient.

As counties go, Tyrone are one of the most economic. Our main competitors are well ahead of us in terms of cost. Accountancy is not my brief. The county board and

Club Tyrone work hard to raise funds and the officers who manage the money know what we need to run a team. Peter Donnelly was made a full-time employee in 2014, as head of strength and conditioning, but no one else is on the payroll. My expenses are minimal: the journey from home to Garvaghey, where we train, takes less than five minutes.

Resources are important, up to a point, but beyond a certain level, football is about the added value that each individual brings to the group.

All teams can train to a high standard now. They can all get fit enough and strong enough. Once players have the support systems they need to play inter-county football, money becomes less of an issue. Dublin are ahead right now but we have nothing to fear. Focus on raising the stakes in your own department.

Quality players are the number one requirement. Football, in that regard, has not changed. You can have the best advice and backup in the world but once the players step out on the pitch, the game is still 15 against 15. Produce highly skilled players with the requisite mental strength and your team is on a level playing field.

Money helps. Equipment, facilities, coaching: they all come at a cost. But team ethos is paramount. You must have pride in yourself and in your county. Each individual represents something bigger than himself whether he thinks that way or not. Your why is everything and the right why is priceless.

The notion that you have to buy success cuts no ice with me. Traditionally, Tyrone were not a big power.

Those teams of the noughties gave people a sense of belief; winning All Irelands showed that we could dine at the top table.

And success demands respect. Other counties know the challenge that awaits them when they play Tyrone.

We have closed the gap with Dublin since 2017. The current team have beaten them two years running in the League, home and away. We know how to hurt them. I firmly believe that a team from Tyrone will be capable of achieving the ultimate again.

Finding the right balance between defence and attack is an ongoing challenge for us. We condensed the pitch too much in recent seasons, compressing the space within our own 45. Now the boys will spread out as far as the 65 to squeeze the middle. At least two forwards will stay in attack, which means they can defend on the blindside. If all your men stay behind the ball then the opposition get the luxury of playing at their leisure.

Precise breaks are key when we force turnovers. I want players making specific runs: one man down each wing and two through the middle. Whichever man is in the best position goes forward. Anybody could be called upon to make a key pass or to take a score. We want a diamond shape in attack. So we have four outlets. Empty and fill is the name of the game: if one man moves, somebody else takes his position.

The big advantage when you turn the ball over is that the opposition are chasing back. Plus, by pushing forward quickly, we can take men out of their defensive blockade. That extra space gives us the option of running the ball.

But we have to work out how this looks in practice. What happens when an attack breaks down? I need to see how the opposition might counteract this style of attack.

The goal never changes: I want Sam for Christmas.

October 28, 2020: Covid is causing havoc at the moment but I have been lucky enough to avoid it. A few boys in the squad had to step down from training recently because of close contacts. I was nearly a close contact myself. The school in Glencull closed for two days because of a positive case, so the grandchildren are staying away from us at the moment, just to be on the safe side.

At training, I make sure to stay outside as much as possible. I wear a snood whenever I have to go into the dressing room. On the whole, I feel fairly relaxed about the situation. We make the best of things. Maybe my involvement in football stands to me: I know how to cope with straitened circumstances. We play sport to make the most of our time, to find a way.

Something always crops up in management. Colm Cavanagh called time last month, though his decision was not entirely unexpected. A bit-part role held no appeal for Colm and, at this stage of his career, he has more than football to think about. A young family and a new business are rarely compatible with inter-county life.

On the plus side, Conor McKenna has settled in well. He came back from Australia this month after six seasons in the AFL. I kept in contact with him over the years. Watching clips of him playing Aussie Rules was a reminder of the talent we lost when he went over. And I like having him around the place. Conor is a good influence: he gets on with it, no fuss.

His performances against Donegal (October 18) and Mayo (October 25) were something else. We had to win in Castlebar to stay up after losing the week before. McKenna was awesome, two more goals to his name as well as supplying Darragh Canavan for our third. Avoiding relegation was critical: even one year in Division 2 will stunt progress.

Now we face another short turnaround. Donegal had the luxury of resting players in Kerry for their final League outing but I think the Mayo game was really good preparation for us ahead of the Championship game in Ballybofey this Sunday (November 1).

Beating the same team twice is never easy. Donegal are feeling comfortable: they think they have us. We were far too passive in the League game; too many boys switched off. But things will be different this time around. We can surprise Donegal, present them with a new equation.

Circumstances often dictate your hand. Paudie Hampsey is injured and has not been injury free for a year and more. Rory Brennan is suspended. With Ronan McNamee taking Paddy McBrearty, that left us with a decision to make about Michael Murphy. I like Mattie Donnelly on Murphy. Mattie is strong enough for Murphy and mobile enough to give him plenty to think about. If Murphy has to watch both ways then he has less opportunity to shape the game. Ronan McNamee can take over if Murphy goes to full forward.

Cathal McShane is back doing some training but not fit for grass yet. We might get to see him on the field, depending how far we go. Even with Conor McKenna leading the attack, we will miss Cathal's influence. Rory Brennan is a big loss. He was sent off against Donegal for putting his hands on the referee, an innocuous offence. A 12-week suspension is crazy: it puts him out for the whole Championship.

I think we are due a couple of breaks. And we may need them.

November 2, 2020: These heavy Mondays are nothing new. Our weirdest season yet is over after one game, which makes it harder to take.

We played some fabulous football yesterday despite the conditions. At 20 minutes in, we were 0-5 to 0-1 up, Donegal on the ropes. Our plan worked a treat: we blitzed them with our energy, forcing turnovers all over the pitch.

Shaun Patton's bombed kickout was big on our agenda beforehand. And we had all their main players earmarked for attention. But then Patton launched one while we were tuned out and they got Michael Langan on the end of a move: a classic case of watching the cat and the mouse bites you.

That goal was easily avoidable. And it brought them right back into the game. By half time, we were trailing, 0-6 to 1-5.

Darragh Canavan nicked a goal to put us back in front but we stalled too many times in good positions.

We were desperately unlucky too. Conor McKenna had one effort cleared off the line; another time he was hauled down in the square. We went hunting for goals late on when there was still enough time to kick two points. At the very least, we should have taken them to extra time.

Afterwards, the media asked about my future. That discussion is for another day. This season has been so disrupted, it feels unfinished. One more year, a proper campaign, is not much to ask given the circumstances. I would be happy to go then.

Deep down, I wonder is it worth the effort. I think of all the turmoil at the end of last year and the energy wasted trying to sort out what were minor issues, really. Maybe managing Tyrone has become too complicated, too much like hard work. I need to speak with Mattie Donnelly first, see what way he sees things.

As ever, there is some clamour for change. RTÉ led the charge last night and I know the media will stir it again over the next few days. I can see the situation coming to a head but the whole setup has to be replaced if I go. And next season has never been so near.

Legacy is not something that I think about. I know plenty of people far smarter than me and Gavin Devlin is the smartest coach I ever worked with. Each year, I do my best for Tyrone, always trying to move things on. The season comes and then it goes: football is always about today.

November 10, 2020: I knew the end was close. I just never imagined my time with Tyrone would finish on a winter's night in the car above Garvaghey, waiting on a call.

Mattie Donnelly was with me. I spoke to him the week before to check the mood among the players. Mattie carries a lot of sway and not just because he is captain. By nature, he has a strong personality: players listen when he talks. If he told me the squad were set on change then I would have said goodnight. No point banging my head against the wall. Without the backing of your senior players, the game is up: the manager is in the wrong room.

Had the season run as normal, there would have been no need for that conversation with Mattie. 30 years of unbroken service seemed a good time for me to bow out but the disruption caused by Covid-19 turned 2020 upside down. For six months, from mid-March to mid-September, we were idle. We lost the best part of the year and any chance of a proper Championship. We never got started, really. All I wanted was a genuine shot at my final year, an opportunity denied by the corona-virus.

At this stage, I know my opponents. Among the county board sits a vocal minority intent on change. Some officers have been set against me for a long time – background noise, mostly. Michael Kerr, the chairman, always had my back but others were moving against me behind the scenes. Playing politics never interested me and I had no inclination to start now, in the winter of 2020.

Michael Kerr said he would put my request to the management committee and bring me into the meeting when I was needed. So myself and Mattie landed into the Tyrone GAA Centre at Garvaghey for 9.30pm as planned.

How many nights have I spent here since it opened in 2013? Training sessions, meetings, various launches: some weeks took me there every day. Rarely does any day pass without me driving by.

Soon after we arrived, myself and Mattie noticed one committee member leaving the meeting early. For 90 minutes, I sat in my car. No message came from Michael. My fate was in the committee's hands and, unknown to me, they were taking a vote. The split (6-5) went in my favour but I needed 60 per cent, one more ballot, to get my wish.

Finally, just after 11pm, some movement. Lights went low inside the building as the officers started filing out. One by one, they slipped away, headlamps leading them to the gate.

I headed off. Destinations never defined me; it was always about the journey.

But home was the only place for me then.

DAYBREAK

July 23, 2021: Life moves in unexpected ways.

This morning was spent on the golf course in Omagh, a rare outing but a rewarding one, the first hole yielding a surprise birdie when I chipped in from the back of the green. I played with Gavin Devlin and his nephew Oran Mulgrew. It was good fun, a welcome release after yesterday's game in Navan.

A year ago, Gavin and I were still plotting success with Tyrone. Today we had time to reflect on our first Championship campaign with Louth and how close we came to beating Offaly in the first round of Leinster. We missed a great chance in normal time and then gave up two soft goals: extra time put the game beyond us. Another season, we might have taken them to a replay or at least had a shot in the Qualifiers. The world is still trying to cope with Covid-19. So knockout was the chosen option again this year.

With the League divided into two groups of four, we had precious little time to find our feet with Louth. And

Division 4 was new territory for me. Losing to Antrim in our first league game put us under pressure, but I know the value of those challenges. Against Sligo, we found a way back from six points down. We needed that win to make the Semi-Finals. For the players, it was important to realise that they could overcome that situation. You progress in football by learning how to live in difficult places.

Victory over Carlow secured promotion, our first target. Raising the bar was part of the attraction for me coming here: I felt Louth were better than where they found themselves in 2020. They were at the bottom rung and I could see that we had the chance to bring them to a higher level. It felt like the county just needed a spark, a new energy.

Their county chairman, Peter Fitzpatrick, came to me with an ambitious plan. They were already developing a stadium and he wanted a team to match. Building teams has always been the best part of being a manager.

I had a family connection to the county as well through my late brother Pete, who moved to Knockbridge when he married Eithne. His two sons, Peter Bernard and Fergal, are proud Louth men as well as being big Tyrone supporters.

After finishing with Tyrone, I had no plans to get back into management so quickly. But then things just fell into place. The spin down from Ballygawley is just over an hour and the fact that the move was taking me to another province helped as well. And I had Gavin on board. The switch made sense.

I think, on reflection, it would have been hard for me to sit out this year. Being idle is not in my nature. After 30 seasons with Tyrone, I probably needed a clean break.

Sport has always been about far more than All Ireland titles for me. My love of Gaelic football is what drives me. With Louth, we have an opportunity to break new ground. Already, I can see signs in the way that the players have responded, how receptive they are. I suppose they are hearing certain things for the first time, how to link certain passages of play, how to work as a unit. I feel re-energised from working with them. There is serious talent in Louth, players with real ability. Self-belief was probably the missing ingredient in recent years and then players tend to undervalue themselves. But they have plenty going for them: high skill levels, a good age profile.

Louth is a county that loves Gaelic games; they have a history worth talking about. Whenever we met them during the noughties, they tested us. I set out to make teams better, so the challenge for me with Louth is no different than it was in Tyrone. My aim is to turn players into better footballers and better athletes with the character to match. By raising standards, we can develop the kind of culture inherent in all successful sides. The whole county should feel pride in the team.

Ultimately, I want Louth playing at the highest possible level, which is why I took on a three-year term - to give the players belief in my vision.

The shame is that we have to wait until next season now. Another few weeks and only four counties will be left. This Championship has wrecked so many teams. I started out with the County Minors in 1991, when knockout was all we had. This summer has been like going back to the future. But we will stay in touch with the players over the next few months, keeping them on track with training programmes and some coaching sessions. I used to say: 'You don't come training to get fit, you get fit to come training.' That much is still true. I want these boys ready when we come back next year.

Tyrone is in the past at this stage, but I was never one to spend much time looking back. Everything comes to an end. I had a great run, enjoyed some of my greatest days, and always did the best that I could. Of course, I still want Tyrone to succeed; I always will. How it finished was not the way I would have chosen. But I am old enough and wise enough to know that bitterness serves you no good. Life goes on.

I said in an interview after finishing with Tyrone that nobody is put on this world for no purpose. Each one of us is here for our own single purpose. I still think of all the people who had an impact on our lives during that time. Arthur Mallon was on the minor panel in 1993 and sadly lost his life in a car crash. 1997 was the year of Paul McGirr's tragedy. Kevin Hughes lost his brother the same year and his sister a few years later. The sudden death of Cormac McAnallen in 2004 was a terrible blow. Too many others have passed on since: Jim Curran, Jonny Curran, Frank Campbell, Fergal McCann.

Michaela never leaves my mind. But we still face, beyond grief, a fight to get justice. At least there has been some positive news lately. Arlene Foster, on her last day as Northern Ireland First Minister, announced two weeks ago that the Mauritian government have agreed to look into the case again. Seeing the case taken up at a high level politically gives us great hope. We need to keep the pressure on. Michaela's life was worth more than the way it finished on that island.

Thankfully, I live each day without being eaten up by the whole thing. I can only explain it as a grace from God.

A lot of the time, we chase the future. Life has taught me the value of living in the present. I think of myself as being mad about life, savouring every minute.

I love what life has given to me. And the longer I live, the more that I appreciate how much life has to offer.

Acknowledgments

Mickey Harte

To my family – my wife Marian, Mark and Sinead, Michael and Josephine, Matthew and Catherine – thank you for all the hours of my life you have permitted me to indulge in Gaelic games. To John, thank you for being such an important part of Michaela's life. The grandchildren have given Marian and me a new lease of life in recent years: Jason, Grace and Ailagh; Liam, Michael, Aidan and Luke; Mary, Pio, John Gabriel and Joseph.

To my six brothers and three sisters for their kindness and consideration towards the 'baby' in the house. A special word of appreciation for my sister Mary and the Mallaghan family for opening their doors (and food cupboards) to an ever-increasing Tyrone fanbase over a generation of All Irelands dating back to the early '70s.

To the Kelly family, Patsy and Ann Marie and all their staff, who have facilitated myself and various Tyrone teams since I first took charge in 1991. Their service and welcome was always deeply appreciated. During the course of this book, they sustained myself and Brendan with many an early morning breakfast.

To the Tyrone County Board, who afforded me the privilege of working with the best talents in the county at various age levels for 30 consecutive seasons, from 1991 to 2020. To Club Tyrone and all the other sponsors for their contribution to the development of our games over the years. I will always be grateful for the support that the people within my community, Tyrone and beyond, showed towards my family during our most difficult days.

To all the players and people who have worked alongside me with Tyrone and my club, Errigal Ciarán, helping to make the journey such an enriching experience. That journey continues in Louth, an exciting new adventure.

Thanks to INPHO and Sportsfile for permission to use their photos. To all at HarperCollins Ireland, and Conor Nagle in particular, for helping us to complete this piece of work on schedule.

To Brendan I say thank you for the immense time and effort you put into this work when, like myself, you didn't know when or whether there would be an end product. You shared the last four and a half years of my life's journey and with insightful interviewing brought me back through the experiences that formed me into the person that I am today. Your crafting of the information you garnered is a testament to your excellent writing skills. I always admired your calm presence and most of all your hearty laugh. A journey from acquaintance to real friendship is always a treasure.

ACKNOWLEDGMENTS

Brendan Coffey

This odyssey began with a conversation over a cup of tea, appropriately enough. And it would not have been possible without Conor Mallaghan, who has been a vital link throughout.

February 2017, when I first met Mickey Harte, we never got around to discussing a book. Time since has taught me that discussions with Mickey often lead into unexpected places. A large part of his gift stems from this rare ability to put others at ease. He can talk with the best of them, and often does, but being in his company makes you realise that here is one of life's great listeners.

We recognise Mickey Harte for his stunning successes in Gaelic football. My admiration stems from his power of endurance, how he continues to lead such a rich and meaningful life. He has known the bleakest of days and found a way to live beyond them. People, naturally, are drawn to him, particularly in times of grief. Always, he brings this sense of possibility, and his presence often means something more than words can express.

Mickey revisited his darkest moments during the writing of this book and kept going, even when emotions took their toll. For your courage and commitment, Mickey, I will be forever grateful.

To tell this story in full required the help and support of the Harte family. Marian, Mark, Michael and Mattie: thank you for sharing so honestly and so generously.

Without John McAreavey, this work would have been

incomplete. John, your strength of character is extraordinary. Thank you for giving so much of yourself.

Tony Donnelly and Gavin Devlin also played a valuable part, enriching major moments in Mickey's life with their insights.

Many others have guided me along the way. John Scally, the most generous spirit I know, provided the best of advice. Christy O'Connor gave me a great steer when I was getting started. Dermot Gilleece, ever wise and perceptive, helped to clear my view at an important stage. Patrick O'Sullivan is a true scholar, patient and rigorous in equal measure. He has been a brilliant friend and mentor for many years. I am blessed to have learnt from you, Patrick.

I owe special dues to Daragh Ó Conchúir, Ronan Early and Robert Mulhern, former colleagues who remain great friends.

The late John Roddy is never far from my thoughts. I still think of you, John, and all you did for me starting out in this game.

Publishers, finally, make a book real. Conor Nagle was the one to bring it all together, ensuring that the best version made it into print. Thank you, Conor, and all the team at HarperCollins.

Mam and Dad, this work and all that I do has been inspired by your belief in me. I owe you everything.